FACING THE GODS

James Hillman	ANANKE & ATHENE
Karl Kerényi	ARTEMIS
René Malamud	AMAZONS
Murray Stein	HEPHAISTOS
David L. Miller	RHEA
Barbara Kirksey	HESTIA
William Doty	HERMES
Chris Downing	ARIADNE
James Hillman	DIONYSOS

Edited by JAMES HILLMAN

SPRING PUBLICATIONS, INC.
DALLAS, TEXAS

Sixth printing 1994
Published by Spring Publications, Inc., P.O. Box 222069, Dallas, Texas 75222. Printed in the United States of America
Text printed on acidfree paper
Cover photograph by Agnes Szokolszky
Cover designed and produced by Margot McLean

Distributed in the United States by the Continuum Publishing Company; in Canada by Maxwell Macmillan; and in the United Kingdom, Eire, and Europe by Airlift Book Co.

Library of Congress Cataloging-in-Publication Data
Facing the gods / edited by James Hillman . . . [et al.].
p. cm.
Bibliography: p.
Includes index.
Contents: On the necessity of abnormal psychology, Ananke and Athene / James Hillman—A mythological image of girlhood, Artemis / Karl Kerényi—The Amazon problem / René Malamud—Hephaistos, a pattern of introversion / Murray Stein—Red Riding Hood and Grand Mother Rhea / David L. Miller—Hestia, a background of psychological focusing / Barbara Kirksey—Hermes' heteronymous appellations / William G. Doty—Ariadne, mistress of the labyrinth / Chris Downing—Dionysos in Jung's writings / James Hillman.
ISBN 0-88214-312-3
1. Gods, Greek—Psychology. 2. Psychoanalysis.
3. Psychoanalysis—Greek influences. I. Hillman, James.
BL785.F22 1988
150.19'54—dc19   87-32419
CIP

CONTENTS

Editor's Preface

It seemed time to offer the psychologically-minded reader some individual short studies on particular Gods. For as the individual in search of his or her soul soon discovers, the soul is entangled in myths so that uncovering the figures of myths becomes more and more psychologically pertinent. We are learning what other cultures always knew: to know ourselves we must know the Gods and Goddesses of myth. We must face the Gods.

These studies are not straight mythography, however. Nor are they intended to replace the scholarly works that tell the tales of the Gods and Goddesses in all their facets and variations and in relation to social history, textual and linguistic criticism. These nine papers, though exhibiting considerable scholarship, are rather written with psychological intent. They present the psychological possibilities of particular myths and the workings of these figures in human lives. Our ignorance of the Gods and Goddesses has kept them faceless, difficult to tell one from another or remember from one reading to the next the fine details of psychological sophistication that myths preserve. So this book serves to restore to us an awareness of the incredible dominants that affect our attitudes, our work, our loves and our sufferings. It serves as well to restore the features of their individual faces after centuries of programmatic iconoclastic disfiguration.

Mary Helen Gray did the initial editing, Gerald Burns and Dana Anderson the final. Jay Livernois compiled the index. Kate Smith made the cover; Mary Robinson did the photocomposition. All deserve respectful, well-earned thanks.

James Hillman

I

ON THE NECESSITY OF ABNORMAL PSYCHOLOGY: ANANKE AND ATHENE

James Hillman

"Not even a God can cope with Necessity,"

Plato, *Laws* (741 a, 818 b.)

I. The "Infirmitas" of the Archetype

Looking back through the prodigious spiritual and cultural work presented in the Eranos Yearbooks, we see the fundamentality of the engagement here. Each year offers another attempt to go to the heart of things through one's particular speciality (*Fach*) in its relation with those basic and difficult questions that transcend our specialities.

Fundamental to depth psychology and to the soul is hurt, affliction, disorder, peculiarity—"abnormal psychology" or "psychopathology." Depth psychology was called into existence as a treatment for abnormal psychology. Depth psychology was, and remains a *logos* for the *pathos* of the *psyche*. By "psychopathology" I mean that category of psychic events publicly and/or privately declared abnormal and which cannot be altogether repressed, transformed, or accepted. These intolerable aspects show themselves paradigmatically in the symptom which Freud said is the starting point of depth psychology.[1] But I would like to extend our concept of psychopathology by introducing the term *pathologizing* by which I mean: the psyche's autonomous ability to create illness, morbidity, disorder, abnormality, and suffering in any aspect of its behavior, and to experience and imagine life through this deformed and afflicted perspective.

In two long essays[2] on psychopathology I have attempted to refute the contemporary denials of it in various branches of therapy. The nominalism of psychiatry considers its terms contingent, without necessary relation to causes or to the souls of those exhibiting that to which the terms point. Political reformers and existentialists find the field itself fundamentally unnecessary, an accident of historical, social, or political institutions. Humanistic, transcendental, and Oriental therapies assume the primacy of spirit, self, and health, so that psychopa-

1

thology has only secondary, illusory reality. Psychopathology is thus contingent, accidental, accessory: all deny the necessity of abnormality.

Medical and religious approaches interpret psychopathology as something wrong (sick or sinful). They either physicalize or metaphysicalize (moralize). They look for the necessity of abnormal psychology outside the psyche, either to a theory of physical disorder in general (disease) or to a religious doctrine concerning suffering. Neither starts with psyche. Pathologizing is still not a necessity of the soul.

In contrast, we have tried to base pathologizing wholly within the psyche and to show its necessity for the psyche. We made this move by grounding pathologizing within the archetype. Then we showed that when we do start with psyche, as in alchemy, the art of memory, and mythology, we find pathologized events inherent to these psychological systems. Both Freud and Jung adhere to this third, psychological line in their thoughts about psychopathology. From the beginning they connected it with fantasy images and viewed it mythologically.

Starting with psyche means to take pathologizing to be a valid form of psychological expression, as an underived metaphorical language, one of the ways the psyche legitimately and spontaneously presents itself. To understand this language, we place it within similar metaphorical contexts. An obscene, bizarre, or afflicted event or image in our psychic life needs to be examined, not in terms of norms derived from physical 'nature' or from metaphysical 'ideals,' but in terms of norms of the imagination where withered arms, blighted crops, monstrous dwarfs, and every sort of 'distortion' belong and have significance in themselves and as they are. To understand what an individual's abnormal psychology is saying, we may not turn to what is 'normal.' Our norms must be like the stuff we wish to understand, norms that are themselves pathologized.

Here we take our cue from Jung's, "The Gods have become diseases."[3] Jung is indicating that the formal cause of our complaints and abnormalities are mythical persons; our psychic illnesses are not *imaginary*, but *imaginal* (Corbin). They are indeed fantasy illnesses, the suffering of fantasies, of mythical realities, the incarnation of archetypal events.

Following Jung along this path is the main work of archetypal therapy. Much of what I have been attempting at Eranos since 1966 has been along these lines. We have looked at the myths and the implications for abnormal psychology—of Eros and Psyche, of Dionysos, of such figures as the puer aeternus, Saturn the senex, the child, and Hades and the Underworld. In these different examples we saw that the pathological is inherent to the mythical, just as it is inherent to alchemy and the art of memory. Our deepest intention has been to move psychopathology, the basis of our field, from a positivistic nineteenth-century system of mind and its disorders to a non-agnostic, mythopoeic psychopathology of the archetypes.

Essential to the move is the recognition of the Gods as themselves pathologized, the "infirmitas of the archetype." Without elaborating what is familiar to you, I think the main point is made if we recognize that Greek myths (and those of the Celts or the Hindus,[4] the Egyptians or the American Indians) require the odd, peculiar, extreme—the Abnormal Psychology of the Gods.[5]

To envision the archetype as primordially pristine, a perfect form without inherent passion that binds and weakens its power or screws it to mad intensities, isolations and stubborn refusals, without its destructive spearpoints and flashes, and its hapless vulnerabilities, is to idealize and falsify the nature of archetypal reality as given in myths.

From this mythical point of view, each archetype has its pathologized themes, and each pathologized event has an archetypal perspective. The norms of myth give place for what cannot find place in academic psychology, medicine, and religion. Moreover: the pathologizing in a myth is *necessary* to the myth and cannot be excised without deforming the myth. For this very heuristic, therapeutic reason, archetypal psychology reverts to mythology.

The figures of myth—quarreling, cheating, sexually obsessed, revenging, vulnerable, killing, torn apart—show that the Gods are not only perfections so that all abnormalities can fall only on humans. The mythemes in which the Gods appear are replete with behavior that, from the secular standpoint, must be classified under criminal pathology, moral monstrosity, or personality disorders.

When we think mythologically about pathologizing, we could say, as some have, that the "world of the Gods" is anthropomorphic, an imitative projection of ours, including our pathologies. But one could start as well from the other end, the *mundus imaginalis* of the archetypes (or Gods), and say that our "secular world" is at the same time mythical, an imitative projection of theirs, including their pathologies. What the Gods show in an imaginal realm of myth is reflected in our imagination as fantasy. Our fantasies reflect theirs, our behavior only mimetic to theirs. We can imagine nothing or perform nothing that is not already formally given by the archetypal imagination of the Gods.

3

If we assume that the necessary is that which occurs among Gods, i.e., that myths describe necessary patterns, then their pathologizings are necessary, and ours are necessary to the mimesis of theirs. Since their *infirmitas* is essential to their complete configuration, it follows that our individual completion requires our pathologizings.

If so, we are as much in harmony with the archetypal realm when afflicted as when in beatific states of transcendence. Man is as much in the image of the Gods and Goddesses when he is ludicrous, enraged, or tortured, as when he smiles. Since the Gods themselves show *infirmitas,* one path of the *imitatio dei* is through infirmity. Furthermore, it is this *infirmitas* of the archetype that can be nurse to our self-division and error, our wounds and extremities, providing a style, a justification, and a sense of significance for ours.

Without this fantasy of archetypal illness, without returning to the Gods every infirmity, including that 'sickness' called 'normalcy,' we can never find adequate contexts for sick phenomena. They must become merely medical and contingent, or sinfully moral and punitive. Nor can we realize that to see with the eyes of sickness, which is the basic mode of psychologizing since Freud, is also a divine perspective and not something morbidly, perversely human. If the Gods are the true background to human life and we are made in their images, then our sickness too has divine origin; not merely sent by the Gods, not merely carried by us for them, but background and foreground, they and we, conform in archetypal infirmity.

What I am asking you to entertain is the idea of the sickness in the archetype[6]—and this is not the same as the archetype of sickness. That latter approach to abnormality is that of a single scapegoat archetype, a morbid principle like thanatos, a sickness demon, a devil or shadow, who carries the evil[7] so that the others may remain supremely ideal. That approach enucleates the core of pathologizing intrinsic to each archetypal figure and necessary to that figure's way of being. Whereas our approach tries to understand pathologizing as an inherent component of every archetypal complexity, which has its own blind, destructive, and morbid possibility. Death is fundamental to each pattern of being, even if the Gods do not die. They are *athnetos* which implies that the *infirmitas* they present is also eternal. Each archetype has a way of leading into death, and thus has its own bottomless depth so causing our sicknesses to be fundamentally unfathomable.

To express this *infirmitas* of the archetype theologically we would say that Original Sin is accounted for by the sin in the Originals. Humans are made in the images of the Gods, and our abnormalities image the original abnormalities of the Gods which come before ours, making possible ours. We can only do in time what Gods do in eternity. Our infirmities will therefore have to have their ground in primordial infirmity, and their infirmities are enacted in our psychopathologies. If those concerned with the plight of religion would restore it to health and bring its God back to life, a first measure in this resuscitation would be to take back from the Devil all the pathologies heaped on his head. If God has died, it was because of his own good health; he had lost touch with the intrinsic *infirmitas* of the archetype.

II. Necessity

I have submitted that pathologized events participate in the archetype itself. They are a *via* to archetypal experience which cannot be experienced fully otherwise. This implies that pathologized events belong to the archetype necessarily. Consequently, they are necessary to our lives.

But what is Necessity? In search of answers to this question we shall be elaborating this main point: *necessity in Greek mythical thought is spoken of and experienced in pathologized modes.* Pathologized experiences are often connected directly with Ananke (Necessity).[8] Let us look in more detail at this connection.

In an exhaustive monograph Heinz Schreckenberg[9] reviews all the proposed etymologies and contexts of *ananke* and comes to the conclusion that the word in Homer is borrowed from a probable semitic root "*chananke*" based on three consonants, hnk. We can lay out Schreckenberg's findings as follows:

Old Egypt.	hnk	narrow
Old Egypt.	hng	throat
Old Egypt.	enek	surround, embrace, strangle
Coptic	chalak	ring
Akkadian	hanaqu	constrict, strangle; to wind tightly around the neck as the neck-band of a slave
Syriac	hnk	chain, suffocation
Hebrew	anāk	chainformed necklace (Song of Songs 4:9; Proverbs 1:9)
Chaldean	hanakin	fetters laid on the necks of prisoners
Arabic	hanaqa	strangle

| Arabic | hannāka | necklace |
| Arabic | iznāk | the cord binding yoked oxen |

His evidence[10] extends far further than this digest and it tallies with more usual etymologies of *ananke,* relating it with the German *eng* (narrow), with angina, *angst,* and anxiety, with *agchein* (Greek), to strangle, and with *agham* (Sanscrit), evil.[11] Even Plato's etymology (*Cratylus* 420 c-d) imagines *ananke* by means of a metaphor of narrowing. "The idea," says Plato, "is taken from walking through a ravine which is impassable, and rugged, and overgrown, and impedes motion—and this is the derivation of the word necessary."

Schreckenberg places particular stress upon the yoke/collar/noose meanings of his etymology, leaving no doubt that, at core, necessity means a physically oppressive tie of servitude to an inescapable power.[12]

The Latin for *ananke* is *necessitas.* Here too we find the notion of a "close tie" or "close bond" such as the bond of kinship, blood relationship. *Necessitudines* are "persons with whom one is closely connected, relatives, connections, friends."[13] A *necessaria* is a female relative or friend. As well, this word refers to natural and moral ties between persons. This suggests that the family relationships and the ties we have in our personal worlds are ways in which we experience the force of necessity. Our attempts to be free of personal binds are attempts at escaping from the tight circle of *ananke.* That patients in therapy complain that they suffocate in the family circle, or that they are strangled by their marriage partner, or fall victim to pathologizings in throat and neck all bespeak necessity. From this perspective the family complex is a manifestation of necessity, and servitude to kinship-ties is a way of observing her demands.

Let us turn now to *ananke* in poetic, mythological, and philosophical contexts.

First we must recognize the central place that this Goddess Ananke held in the imagination of cosmology-makers. For Parmenides (Frgs. 8 and 10) Ananke governs Being; for the Atomists, too, though differently.[14] In so-called Pythagorean and Orphic thought Ananke was mated with a great serpent Chronos, forming a kind of binding coil around the universe (RBO, p. 332). Time and Necessity set limits to all the possibilities of our outward extension, of our worldly reaches. Together they form a syzygy, an archetypal pair, inherently related, so that where one is the other is too. When we are under the compulsion of necessity, we experience it in terms of time, e.g. the chronic complaints, the repeated return of the same enclosing and fettering complexes, the anxiety occasioned by the shortness of our days, our daily duties, our 'deadlines.' To be time-free is to be free of necessity. To have free-time constellates a fantasy of free-from-necessity. As the physical yoke of slavery is the concrete image within the idea of necessity, so the freedom from this yoke expresses itself in fantasies of free-time and leisure as a paradisaical happiness without pathology.

The dependency of all things upon the chaining limits of necessity is expressed in another, milder, image in Orphic cosmology. The idea that Zeus rules the world through close collaboration with Ananke (Eur. *Alcestis*, 978f.) is turned by Orphism into the image of Zeus and his wet-nurse Adrasteia, another name for Ananke.[15] She is his wet-nurse and, by suckling at the breast of necessity, he draws his power and wisdom with that milk. In some contexts his nurse Adrasteia is his daughter, so that the bind is expressed in the close tie of kinship, of family obligation, even of incestuous love. This Orphic image reveals the possibility of a loving and nourishing connection with necessity. Here the relation with her power is imagined less as oppressive servitude than as dependency upon the milk of the daughter-mother soul.[16]

The image of Zeus and Adrasteia-Ananke presents the idea of *amor fati,* a paradoxical conjunction of what many philosophers conceived to be opposites (Empedocles, Frg. 115: Charis and Ananke;[17] Agathon in *Symposium* 195 c). Macrobius (*Sat.* I, 19, 17) says that two of the four powers present at birth are Eros and Ananke, and they are paired. Eros is the kiss, and Ananke, the knot or tie. Later, and in some detail, we shall see the pair again opposed as Peitho and Bia (persuasion and force).[18]

The tragedians, however, had recourse to *ananke* when things were at their worst. Aeschylus' Prometheus says:

> Oh woe is me!
> I groan for the present sorrow,
> I groan for the sorrow to come, I groan
> questioning when there shall come a time
> when He shall ordain a limit to my sufferings.
> What am I saying? *I have known all before,*
> *all that shall be, and clearly known;* to me,
> *nothing that hurts shall come with a new face.*
> So must I bear, as lightly as I can,

the destiny that fate has given me;
for I know well against necessity,
against its strength, no one can fight and win.[19]

Note the repetitiveness of this suffering: "nothing that hurts shall
come with a new face." This is a quality of *ananke*-caused affliction. It
is not shock and surprise at the unexpected, but the chronic, repeti-
tious complaint.

Prometheus Bound opens with Prometheus being tied and nailed at
the limits of the world under the constraint of Necessity. It is as if at
the very edges of existence, gone as far outward as possible, he meets
the greater might and violence (Bia) of Necessity and there he is
nailed. Only Necessity can limit the Promethean fantasy, and necessity is experienced by that fantasy as an anguish.

Again in Aeschylus (*The Persians*) when the Queen has been
"struck down by disasters exceeding speech and question" (l. 290) the
word "necessity" comes to her lips. The idea that it is useless *to speak*
against necessity appears also in Euripides (*Phoenician Maidens*). At
the very end Oedipus says: (ll. 1762f.) "Yet what boots it thus to
wail? What profits vainly to lament? Whoso is but mortal must bear
the necessity of heaven." Again this opposition between persuasive
speech and implacable force.

Euripides (*Bacchae*, l. 89) uses the term (*anagkaisi*) for physical
anguish. To be in pain, torment, suffering is to be in anguish, in
straits (*Einengung*), in need or necessity. The archetypal sufferer, Sophocles' Philoctetes, whose wound cannot heal, cries out in pain, and
the word the Chorus uses for this pain is *anangas, anangan* (ll. 206 and
215). Being caught or forced by necessity is expressed concretely as
being in the hands of another power (HS, p. 45); e.g., when Apollo
seizes baby Hermes, or Hercules grabs the snakes in his cradle, the
physical pressure, the squeeze, is *ananke*.

But perhaps the most telling description of *ananke* is given by
Euripides in his *Alcestis* (ll. 962ff.) when the Chorus says:

I myself, in the transports
of mystic verses, as in study
of history and science, have found
nothing so strong as Compulsion [*Anagkas*],
nor any means to combat her,
not in the Thracian books set down
in verse by the school of Orpheus,
not in all the remedies Phoebus has given the heirs
of Asclepius to fight the many afflictions of man.

> She alone is a goddess
> without altar or image to pray
> before. She heeds no sacrifice.[20]

Here Ananke is the Great Lady (*potnia*) of the Underworld, the invisible psychic principle that irreversibly draws all things to her, thereby pathologizing life. Only Hades is similarly spoken of as "without altar or image to pray before."[20a] Orphic thought did make this straight-out identity of Ananke with the Underworld Queen, Persephone (HS, p. 70n).[21] Her name has been translated to mean "bringer of destruction," so that the process of pathologizing can be understood as a mode of moving the psyche (in this particular drama the soul-image is presented in the figure, Alcestis) toward the underworld. That this movement from life to death is heroically stopped by Hercules also belongs to the theme explored in detail in *The Dream and the Underworld.*

May I draw your attention to the fact that in the *Alcestis* passage the language for dealing with *ananke* is that of therapy: remedies of Asclepius—and there are none. Nor are mysticism, orphicism, history, science, a match for her force. Is this because she has no image, no altar to pray before? Here it is suggested that not only is Necessity beyond the reach of speech, but further, that necessity is experienced when one is compelled and there is no image of what is occurring. It is as if there were a relation—even an inverse proportion—between images and drivenness: the more the image and altar, the less the blind necessity. The more the compulsion, the less we are able to sacrifice, to connect our personal compulsion with something divine.

This inverse proportion is a signal idea in Jung's notion of the archetype. There is a red compulsive end and a blue imaginative one. As the red is the body of the blue, the blue is the image of the red. Without images, we are more blind for we have not been able to imagine the force that drives us. With images, the *necessity appears inherent to the image itself.* This shifts the compulsion from the red to the blue. We recognize that compulsion is essential to the very nature of the image and that what drives us are images.

The relationship between necessity and images can also be put this way: Necessity seizes us through images. An image has its own inherent necessity, so that the form an image takes "cannot be otherwise"—whether when we paint, move a line of verse, or when we dream. An image exists in its specific epiphany and course of behavior (the compulsion of necessity which Jung calls "instinct").

9

Because the force of the image is inseparable from the image, it is spoken of as unimaged. Necessity has no image because it works in each and every image. We must not take this unimaged force literally and metaphysically, as if archetypes were in themselves unimaged, unknowable, and transcendent to their appearances. The unimaged power of the image is right in the image itself: the archetype is wholly immanent in its image. This unimaged power gives an image its compelling effect and the implacable law of its precise forming. This *inexorability of the image* is none other than Necessity who, as the *Alcestis* passage says, is herself "without image."

Thus fantasy is no carefree daydream, but the implacable carrier of the necessities that drive us. Psychic reality is enslaved to imagination. Imagination does not free us but captures us and yokes us to its myths; we are workers for its Kings and Queens. We are tied in blood with what Jung calls our "instinctual images." To insist, as Jung does, that human reality is primarily psychic and that the image is the primordial and immediate presentation of this reality requires a further recognition. Reality is only so if it is necessary. To use the word "reality" implies an ontological condition that cannot be otherwise. Therefore there must be something unalterably necessary about images so that psychic reality, which first of all consists in images, cannot be mere after-images of sense impressions. Images are primordial, archetypal, in themselves ultimate reals, the only direct reality that the psyche experiences. As such they are the shaped presences of necessity.

Personally, experientially, this implies that when we search for what is implacably determining our lives and holding them in servitude, we must turn to the images of our fantasies within which necessity lies concealed. Furthermore, this implies that we must beware of being too 'active' with our images, moving them around to redeem our problems. For then active imagination would become an attempt to dodge the necessity of the image and its claim upon the soul.

Even if Necessity is said to be unimaged, there does belong to this great Goddess, who is at the same time a metaphysical principle, a cluster of particular metaphors which tell us how she works her ways. Since she refers to the binding, encircling limits,[22] we find that bonds and ties, the ring,[23] cord, noose, collar, knot, spindle, wreath, harness, and yoke[24] are ways of speaking of the rule of *ananke*. So too is the nail. The nail driven into a figure (like Prometheus, like Christ) or into the head of a figure—Etruscan, Norse, Latin—indicates the ineluctable claim of necessity.[25] No way out.[26] It must be.

We may pause to reflect here upon the wreath: for instance, the crown of laurels of the poet laureate, or the garland given the victor in a competition. This acknowledgement also implies a binding obligation, a necessity to be that for which one has been crowned.[27] The wreath is the yoke and collar of the brow. The singer must go on singing, once the laurel has been placed around his head. The acknowledgement, moreover, sets limits to the range and possibility of one's powers. Recognition binds one's soul to a specific destiny.

We have been concerned mainly with the *person* and *images* of Necessity. The *idea* of necessity receives further elaboration from philosophers. Philosophy has generally considered necessity in two different ways. Sometimes philosophers speak of it as lawless chance (like the Greek *tyche*), as a principle of randomness, blind, mechanical, statistical, pointless. Other times they take the converse position, relating necessity with the regular, predictable, and *gesetzmässig*. Arguments about necessity often lead into pitched philosophical battles between determinism versus free-will, or between physis, nature, and matter versus spirit.

Philosophers define necessity succinctly: "nicht-anders-sein-können" or in the words of Thomas Aquinas: "quod non potest non esse" (that which cannot not be). In Aristotle, necessity is brought into relation with "compulsion," just as at the opening of *Prometheus Bound* Necessity appears together with Bia (Force or Compulsion). This same pairing was observed at Corinth according to Pausanias (II, 4, 6), for in that city Ananke and Bia were honored together in a temple, access to which was forbidden. Again: no access to necessity.

Closed rigidity, inaccessibility, is precisely the feeling of Parmenides' idea of Ananke.[28] She holds his universe fast in permanence, immobility, and absoluteness, allowing no change. His immovable necessity repeats in a philosophical description the implacable ananke of the *Alcestis*.

When we read Parmenides psychologically, then the real events in our souls, those having true reality, are those that do not move. It is just in immobility, in the changeless fixations of our psychic cosmos, where we are bound and stuck, that necessity is operating.

Aristotle gives a few clear statements about necessity in his *Metaphysics* (1015a)[29] which have determined our thinking about it ever since. Aristotle says: "And necessity is held to be something that cannot be persuaded—and rightly, for it is contrary to the movement which accords with purpose and with reasoning." Further: "that which impedes and tends to hinder, contrary to purpose." Note here:

"contrary to purpose," which colors by definition our experience of necessary events as useless and against our purposes. We usually experience our pathologizings as purposeless. We feel them to be hindrances, impediments without reason. Here, we can see how well Aristotle's notion of necessity services the medical position that regards pathologizing as having no purpose, an irksome hindrance to be removed. The necessity is painful, says Aristotle, "for every necessary thing is ever irksome." [30]

We may read Aristotle, too, from an archetypal viewpoint. To us he is saying that the Gods themselves, because they are necessary, are forever plaguing us. Their irksomeness is inherent to their very necessity. They must be a bother. We must be in their service and feel their yoke. There is a Greek answer to Job: not a devil's trick or satanic force makes the divine plague our mortal life; pathologizing is given with the nature of the divine itself.

Another of Aristotle's formulations is also of special value. This is the idea that necessity works as an inexorable internal cause, as a virtue or inherent property of an event itself. "Necessity is that because of which a thing cannot be otherwise"; it is that "without which" a thing cannot exist. He notes that necessity can operate as the function of the nature of a thing, rather than being only an external mechanical cause. Necessity belongs to the state or condition itself, to the very nature of an image, as we said above. An event is not only forced from without, but forced from within by its own image. As Guthrie puts this difference:

> To us, problems of causation in science are concerned with the explanation of sequences, chains of cause and effect linking together x and y and z. The Greek on the other hand investigated what he called 'the nature of things,' and asked himself 'what is it *in* x that causes it to behave as it does?' [31]

Here Jung's archetypal theory and therapy is traditional and Greek. It asks: "what is it in the very nature of my disturbance and my affliction that is necessary, self-caused (caused by self)"? Other therapies look outside to external necessity—society, family, or other kinds of conditioning—searching to unravel necessity in the linkages between x and y and z. They ask the more technical question "how"; archetypal therapy asks the more philosophical "what"—and eventually, the religious question "who," which God or Goddess, which daimon, is internally at work in what is going on. Jungian therapy is therefore theophanic, in Corbin's sense. It asks the God in the disease to come to light.

It is, however, in Plato where we can find the most illuminating and explicit ideas concerning the relations between necessity and the troubles of the soul. In the *Timaeus*, Plato's cosmology or system of the universe, there are two main principles at work. The first is *nous*, the logos, or intellectual principle, reason, order, intelligibility, mind—or however else we wish to translate *nous*. The second principle is *ananke*, Necessity. The famous passage in the *Timaeus* (47e–48a) puts their relation as follows:

> Now our foregoing discourse . . . has set forth the works wrought by the craftsmanship of Reason [*nous*]; but we must now set beside them the things that come about of Necessity [*ananke*]. For the generation of this universe was a mixed result of the combination of Necessity and Reason. Reason overruled Necessity by *persuading* [italics added] her to guide the greatest part of the things that become towards what is best; in that way and on that principle this universe was fashioned in the beginning by the victory of reasonable persuasion over Necessity. If, then, we are really to tell how it came into being on this principle, we must bring in also the Errant Cause . . .[32]

In this discussion the term *archai*, first principles or starting points, occurs in various senses. Plato says that it is not fire or water or the four elements that are the true *archai*. There are two: Nous and Ananke, Reason and Necessity.

Here necessity is characterized as the Errant Cause. Jowett translates *planoumene aitia* "variable cause," Thomas Taylor "erratic cause," and Plato's commentators use, for the operations of this principle, such words as: rambling, digressing, straying, irrational, irresponsible, deviating, misleading, deceiving, irregular, random. *Planos* can refer to the wanderings of the mind in madness and to the fits of a disease. Such is the way Plato speaks of *ananke*.

Necessity operates through deviations. We recognize it in the irrational, irresponsible, indirect. Or to turn it again: necessity appears in those aspects of the universe (and let us recall that the Platonic universe is wholly ensouled, always a psychic universe) that are errant. Moreover, necessity is particularly associated with that area of experience that is unable to be persuaded by or subjected to the rule of mind.

13

Grote called this Errant Cause: "The indeterminate, the inconstant, the anomalous, that which can be neither understood nor predicted. It is Force, Movement, or Change, with the negative attribute of not being regular, or intelligible. . . ."[33] And Cornford explains: "The body of the universe . . . contains motions and active powers which are not instituted by the divine Reason and are perpetually producing undesirable results . . . these bodily motions and powers can only be attributed to an irrational element in the World-Soul."[34] Necessity resides as an internal cause in the soul and perpetually produces irksome results. These resulting irrationalities we call the deviations of abnormal psychology, and this creating activity I have called pathologizing. As Freud's "starting point," the symptom, is conceived to be different from and foreign to the rational ego, so this "starting point" (*arche*) of Plato, the errant operation of *ananke*, is equally alien from the realm of reason.

You may have noticed that I continue to call pathologizing a *creating* activity. Plato presents *ananke* in a similar manner. He assumes it to be an *arche*, a first principle not derivative of anything else. It is also a creating principle entering into the formation of the universe. And it is necessarily always there, not gradually overcome through the extension of the rule of reason. As the demiurge never wholly reduces chaos to order, so reason never wholly persuades necessity. Both are present as creating principles, always. "In the whole and in every part, *Nous* and *Ananke* cooperate; the world is a mixture resulting from this combination."[35] Or in our terms, the abnormal is mixed throughout every act of existence, for psychic life is based in the complex, and pathologizing never comes to an end.

Let me put my thesis still one more time, now through the voice of the greatest contemporary classicist, E. R. Dodds:

The inferior soul [in Plato's *Laws*] seems to stand to the good one in the same relation as Necessity to Mind in the Timaeus myth: it is a sort of untrustworthy junior partner, liable to fits of unreasonable behavior, in which it produces 'crazy and disorderly movements' (*Laws* 897d)—a phrase that recalls both the 'scared and crazy movement' attributed to the souls of human infants elsewhere in the *Laws* (791a) and the 'discordant and disorderly movement' of the mythical chaos . . . in the *Timaeus* (30a). All these movements I take to be symbols, not of deliberate evil, but of irrationality, the element both in man and in the *cosmos* which is incompletely mastered by the rational will.[36]

14

This abnormal, scared, and crazy movement of the soul is not only necessary. It is Necessity itself.

When my eminent colleagues here at this Eranos Tagung, Professors Sambursky, Hadot, and Rowe, each of whose field is Greek thought, work over these same texts, they will read them in the light of their interests and persuasions. Plato is indeed speaking of their fields—cosmology, cosmogony, metaphysics, physics, philosophy in the widest sense. But Plato is also speaking of Soul[37] and therefore of psychology; so I beg their indulgence to allow us to read these same passages with a psychological eye, attempting to draw insights for depth psychology and therapy of soul from what Plato says about errancy, chaos, and the necessity that is never brought fully into order. The psychological viewpoint sees Necessity and Chaos not only as *explanatory principles* only in the realm of metaphysics; they are also *mythic events* taking place also and always in the soul, and thus they are fundamental *archai* of the human condition. To these root principles the *pathe* (or motions) of the soul can be linked.[38]

Psychology has already recognized the faceless, nameless Chaos, this "scared and crazy movement" in the soul, as *anxiety*, and by naming it such, psychology has directly evoked the Goddess, Ananke, from whom the word anxiety derives. If anxiety truly belongs to Ananke, of course, it cannot be "mastered by the rational will." When anxiety floods us or attacks us, we can but receive it as a gap (*chaos*) in rational continuity. Hence, anxiety does not submit to analysis; it works its ways inescapably until its necessity is admitted. Why not, then, view experiences of anxiety as reflections in the depths of human being of the operations of Ananke? Psychology has tried to reduce her necessary movements to specific necessities: the drives of sexuality (Freud), the dread of death and non-being (Heidegger), original sin (Kierkegaard), or to physiological mechanisms. But no rational theory of it is possible. There is no reason for it but the necessity in it. The grounds of anxiety reside in necessity itself, as it is at this moment constellated, the necessity of this constellated image, the present *pathe* of the soul where the soul is now scared by the necessity yoking it to its destiny.

The relation between Necessity and the human condition can be made yet more explicit if we turn to the very end of the *Republic*; Plato describes the Moirae (Fates).[39] Each soul receives its specific lot from Lachesis. Clotho then ratifies it, and by the spinning of Atropos, "the web of destiny is made irreversible." No way out. It cannot be

15

otherwise. "And then," Plato goes on to say, "without a backward look it [the soul] passed beneath the throne of Necessity." Thus do souls enter the world. Each soul is born by passing under the chair of Ananke.[40] Despite the fact that Plato insists all through his works upon the affinity of the soul with *nous*, in the myth of Er he presents Ananke as she who determines psychic life from the beginning.

As Ananke is located mythically in the middle of the universe and formally in the middle section of the *Timaeus* dialogue, so following Friedländer's suggestion, we may conceive of her locus in the human being not in the head, place of the noetic psyche, but lower down in the middle, a region of the "absolutely indefinite. Called by various names, the indefinite represents the power of unreason, chaos, and the anti-divine."[41] These central depths in Platonic physiology refer particularly to the liver.

One way of reading the wayward movements of the errant cause would be by studying livers (*Timaeus* 71a–72b) and entrails. The diviner, as Cornford points out, is the one who reads, not the rational, but the irrational and appetitive soul for insight into fate.[42] The practice of divining *literalizes* a 'depth' psychology of 'internal' necessity into actual liver and entrails by the art of hepatoscopy and haruspicy. Today seers similar to those of the *Timaeus*—analysts of the psyche— often fall into a similar magical literalism when trying to read the motions of the irrational and appetitive soul in a divinatory way, calling signals from dreams in regard to the future movements of fate.

Hellenistic magical methods that attempted to harness the power of Necessity were directed to this inner depth, especially the *phrenes*, air region or air soul.[43] The magic formula (derived from *ananke*) *hepanagkos* meant to put into a spell, to fix or bind, to compel the inner essence through magic power.[44] One tried to rule a person's fate and make a person one's slave by forcing a necessity upon the *phrenes*. It was believed that one of the ways necessity bound the soul was through the soul's being fettered to the body, and the place of this attachment was the *phrenes*. Therefore by gaining control over the *phrenes* or air-soul of a person, one could govern the motions of his physical actions (behavior). Here again we see the notion of necessity as an Aristotelian internal cause, i.e., working internally within a thing and necessary to that thing, but now literalized into the physical interior of a person. Necessity is reduced to the literal flesh (cf. HS, pp. 61–64).

This literalism about the body supports philosophies of transcendence (Gnostic, Neoplatonist, and other redemptive religions of late antiquity: HS, pp. 157–64). A similar literalism affects today's redemptive religion—psychotherapy. Differences between *nous* and *ananke* become an opposition between mind and body. Freedom from necessity then becomes freedom from the physical body (or freedom of the physical body) where the soul is 'bound' (cf. *Phaedo* 82e[45]—or Wilhelm Reich). The locus of this deep place can be the lungs (*phrenes*), liver, the "inmost marrow" (*Timaeus* 73b–d)—or the deep musculature of Rolfian therapy. The fantasy at work here is that necessity rules from 'deep inside,' and the deeper one goes the more one discovers how rigidly determined, how enslaved one is inside the armor of the body.

As the redemptive ancient religions offered release from necessity through physical death, modern redemptive therapies use physical methods aiming at the same freedom. In both, ancient and modern, thinking in terms of physical positions is countered by thinking of metaphysical oppositions. This is the style of thought that operates within the transcendental denial of pathologizing (*RP*, pp. 64–67). To be free of 'hang-ups,' and especially from the symptoms the flesh is heir to, is another way of hoping for freedom from Ananke who reaches us precisely through the enslaving servitudes of the irrational and appetitive soul and its errant ways. But not only—.

Not only the literal flesh, which is neither irrational nor errant but an ancient animal full of grace, binds us; but rather the soul in which that flesh has its life. The image by which the flesh lives is the ultimate ruling necessity. We are in service to the body of imagination, the bodies of our images. And what fills our souls out and gives body to our images and experiences is the sense of necessity that is always, in all systems of psychic and religious discipline, associated with 'body.' Whenever necessity holds sway, it is blamed on body. So, if we hear these systems psychologically, they are also saying: when you flee necessity you suffer in flesh, and worse, you lose the body of your imagination, literalizing the body of its imagery into clinical diseases and medical treatments.

When we think *psychologically* about the fantasy of the locus of necessity in the deep body, then neither bodily death nor body-therapy are the issue, for both have taken 'body' literally as flesh. Rather: the deeper we go, the more we come upon what "cannot be otherwise." The further we interiorize, the more our psychic necessities take on body. Then such aims as release, freedom, and transformation fade as we become drawn into an attentive caring for (therapy) and imaginative understanding of the necessities that rule the soul through its psychic body, its images deep inside, the mythic depths inside its fantasies.

*

The difference between Nous and Ananke is presented as a tearing conflict in the soul of Orestes at the end of the Oresteia trilogy in the tragedy called the *Eumenides*. Orestes has sinned, but sinned at the command of a God, Apollo, who in turn represents Zeus. Orestes has committed an act of criminal psychopathology: matricide. In the language of the Empedocles fragment (115), he has "polluted his hands with blood," and is thus hounded by the Eumenides, another way of speaking of Ananke. They demand revenge, fulfillment of necessary laws. And they are the unknown causes of our hurts (*plegai*),[46] for

> All that concerneth mankind they dispense.
> Yet whenever a man falls foul of their wrath,
> He knoweth not whence his afflictions approach. . . .[47]

They bring the collaring noose, which, as we have seen, is one of the specific attributes of Ananke. Orestes says (1.749): "This is the end for me. The noose (*agchones*) or else the light." Eumenides or Apollo, Ananke or Nous (Zeus).

The balloting over Orestes' fate is equal. Then Athene intervenes. There is a climactic argument back and forth between her and the Eumenides. But finally Athene *persuades* them and wins Orestes his life. The key word in her victory is persuasion, *peitho*, the word translated in our language as rhetoric. *Rhetoric persuades necessity.* The greatest trilogy of all mythical drama ends with the reconciliation of Zeus and Destiny, which as Cornford[48] says is another way of putting Plato's principles of Nous and Ananke, Reason and Compulsion, or what Herodotus calls Peitho (persuasive argument) and Bia (violent force).[49] (We have already seen Bia [child of Styx]—as Ananke's partner in the temple at Corinth and as instrumental in the nailing of Prometheus.)

What has made this reconciliation possible? How has it come about? What does Athene do to heal the division between light and mind and reason on the one hand and the unknown causes of afflictions on the other? First, we know that Athene has an affinity with Necessity, because Athene has also invented *instruments of limitation and containment*, bringing the arts of pottery, of weaving, of measuring, of the bridle, yoke, and harness. In her is combined the very contradictions she must reconcile: the Nous of her father and the binding force of Ananke with whose collaboration (*Alcestis*, l. 978) her father rules.

But the deeper clue to the entire resolution, and to this part of our investigation, is the term *peitho*: the persuasion of Athene, the winning speech, the charm of words. We must recall here that all along the tragedians and philosophers have insisted that Ananke is implacable, unable to be reached by persuasion, beyond the power of words. But Athene finds a way: "Persuasion guided the speech of my mouth," she says (l. 971).

The content of Athene's words is that she offers the Erinys—the torturing furious forces of necessity who oppress Orestes—*a place* within the divine order. She offers a sanctuary, a cave, an altar ("new chambers," l. 1005) where these powers may reside and be honored—and yet *remain alien*: or "resident aliens" as they are called (ll. 1012, 1019).[50] The unimaged nameless ones shall be imaged and named. Sacrifice is possible. Reconciliation occurs.

And—mark you—the reconciliation occurs between the divinities themselves when Orestes and his patron Apollo are offstage, having already exited 250 lines before the final triumphal procession.[51] It is not Orestes, the suffering hero in the center, who brings about the healing.

Although the problem from which Orestes suffers involves his father and his mother, their sins and their murders, it is neither Orestes the person, nor the archetypal protagonist of the human ego that is finally the problem. It is a cosmic, universal agony in which he is caught. By returning to Greek myths we can see our personal agonies in this impersonal light.

This conclusion to the *Oresteia* has often been discussed as political and transcendental, as representing change in Athenian society, or in terms of conflicts between patriarchy and matriarchy, between Upperworld and Netherworld Gods, between kinds of legalities—but I wish us to understand these matters psychologically. This tragedy bears upon the suffering of the riven soul, Orestes. It tells of the fundamental conflict between the reason within us and the powers of fate that cannot listen to that reason, that cannot be reached by understanding or moved from their compulsive course. This course is like our psychopathology which I defined earlier as that part of us which cannot be accepted, cannot be repressed, and cannot be transformed. Orestes is a figure of the soul torn between *archai*. He is both normal and abnormal psychology. Like Oedipus, Orestes is psychological man, a mythical case history.[52] But unlike Oedipus, Orestes is relevant to the problem of *general* psychopathology rather than to a specific form of it. The *Oresteia* bears upon "The hurts of life without whence and why" (l. 933), and ties them to necessity itself. Where the affliction of Oedipus refers eventually to a heroic ego, its blindness, mistakes, and repentance, Orestes suffers the cosmic conflict of the soul torn between Gods, the necessary psychopathology of the universe.

There is a great deal to be said, and little time to say it, about the relations between words and force. This relation is at the very root of psychotherapy which is, in short, the discipline of this relation, since much of its work tries to move compulsive actions into words. Freud first called psychotherapy the talking cure, recognizing it to be a work of *peitho*, an art of persuasion or rhetoric. An analysis repeats the struggles in the soul of Orestes between reason and compulsion, and it repeats the speech of Athene, who persuades to reconciliation by finding place and giving image to the driving necessities. In the mouth of Athene speech becomes a curative *hymn*, a word which etymologically means "spun" or "woven" words[53] (see below on Athene and weaving).

The relation between word and force is also reflected in society, suggesting to me that the rule of coercive violence increases when our art of convincing words declines. *Peitho* takes on an overwhelming importance both in the healing of the soul and the healing of society. Our engagement at Eranos—a spoken meeting, a ritual of speech— belongs also to the devotion and cult of *peitho*. For here too we try to find persuasive, convincing words that can touch and move the unun- derstood, unimaged forces of the spirit. The task of formulation can- not be overestimated.

Why are words so important in a culture, and why has the art of persuasion, Athene's *peitho*, so fallen into disuse in ours? The conclu- sion to the *Oresteia* answers the first question: words are able to per- suade the darkest elements to take part and have place. We must speak and let them speak. The answer to the second question again refers to Eranos and a point of view that reoccurs in many speakers. I mean their regard for psychological and spiritual reality.

If ultimate reals are objects, things, material events—dead things out there as Descartes would have it and materialism insists—then speech has no effect. *Flatus voci*—empty words, a waste of breath. Actions speak louder; Bia not Peitho. Then language must become simplified, an operational tool, part of the positivist's and materialist's kit for clear directions in handbooks, words that fit computing instruments to move and shape objects out there.

If, however, reality is psychological and spiritual, by which I mean ideational, religious, imaginal, fantastic—as it is especially in psychotherapy, as it was in the Greek world view, and as it seems to me to be here at Eranos—then affecting reality requires instruments for moving ideas, beliefs, feelings, images, and fantasies. Then rhetoric, persuasion, holds major importance. Through words we can alter reality; we can bring into being and remove from being; we can shape and change the very structure and essence of what is real. The art of speech becomes the primary mode of moving reality.

The relation of words and healing has been beautifully developed by Pedro Laín Entralgo, the Spanish medical historian, in his book *The Therapy of the Word in Classical Antiquity*. There he says: "Words, vigorous and persuasive words: they are the key to interhuman relations. . . ."[4] He paraphrases what Ulysses says in the *Philoctetes* (l. 99) of Sophocles, a phrase that is an epigram for psychotherapy: "In the life of men it is the tongue and not the act that governs all."[5]

My words now are an attempt to remind us of something Professor Izutsu wrote nearly twenty years ago: that language is primarily a magical power which resides "in its very semantic constitution" and determines the organization of grammar, syntax, and meaning; that it is the voice which actualizes the "sacred breath" into words; and that language can heal because it is *eo ipso* and *a priori* sacred.[6] Speech exposes the inmost nature of man, said Sophocles (*Oed. Col.*, 1188). The Goddess Peitho—who can and does alter necessity—"has no other temple than the word," said Euripides.[7] If so, then right speech is also one way of restoring "the Temple." Rhetoric, as I conceive it, is a *devotio*, an attempt to return the word to the Gods and to give appropriate form to the divine magic, the sacred breath in language. Little wonder that speaking at Eranos so often produces that pathologizing phenomenon the French call *le trac* (stage fright).

Free speech, such as we enjoy at Eranos, is therefore a psychological fundament, a requirement of soul that finds freedom within necessity through language. Speech arises from the same inmost depths

21

where necessity holds the soul in bondage creating our pathologizings. Speech expresses the air-soul of the *phrenes*. Human speech, especially in psychotherapy, is never wholly the logos of Nous. It is always also wayward, spontaneous, digressing like the Errant Cause.[58]

Therapy through the word cannot end Ananke's archaic and furious dominion, nor does it intend to, for then we would lose the connection of the archetypes with our physical experience and our mortality. Nor is our aim to foreclose her claims as resident alien in the soul. But we can give her modes of expression, ways to image herself in words, persuading her from her implacable silence[59]—an archetypal therapy, a therapy of the archetype itself.

III. The Fantasy of Normalcy

The movement of our line of thinking leads now to this formulation: if pathologizing is necessary and is the expression and experience of Necessity itself, then this errant, disordering activity must be a 'norm' of the soul, much as Plato imagined it. If the archetypes themselves are internally limited to and by their images, so that they too show pathologies (the *infirmitas* of the archetype), then pathologizing is woven throughout all psychological existence, and whatever we call 'normal' must include it. All structures of consciousness, all conditions of existence as archetypal perspectives, including those called healthy, whole, realized, or normal, are also pathologized.

Let me press this further: rather than trying to understand the necessity of psychopathology and what place pathologizing has in the soul, we now would turn to understanding normalcy and what place normalizing has in the soul. We would turn to normalcy not as it literally presents itself in its own terms as 'normal,' but as a specific archetypal perspective with its own style of pathologizing.

By this I do *not* mean that everyone is sick—the therapeutic fallacy, or that normalcy is sickness—the Laingian variation of that fallacy. Rather I am trying to circumvent the dualistic model of normal-abnormal by suggesting that each archetypal structure imagines a cosmos which includes its pattern of pathologized events. Furthermore in what follows I shall be trying to expose the normalcy fantasy itself as an inherent necessity within one specific archetypal perspective.

"Norm" and "normal" derive from the Latin word *norma* meaning a carpenter's square. *Norma* is a technical, instrumental term for a right angle; it belongs to applied geometry. *Normalis* means "made according to the square"; *normaliter* means "in a straight line, direct-ly." The 16th- and 17th-century meaning of "normal" was: rectangu-lar, perpendicular, standing at a right angle. But the word in our present sense betrays distinctly 19th-century usages: normal as regular (1828); normal school for teacher training (1834); normal as average in physics (1859); normalize (1865); normative (1880); and normal as usual (1890).

This last definition contains two distinct meanings which fuse with each other:

1) Normal in the *statistical* sense, i.e., what is usual, common, frequent, regular, hence predictable or expected. This sense can be demonstrated graphically as that which falls in the middle region of a Gaussian curve, hence mean, middle, average, centered. Abnormal, in this same quantitative approach, refers to that which is unusual, ex-treme, exceptional, deviate, out-of-line, outstanding, rare, odd, anoma-lous. The statistical sense is not meant to imply any values other than quantitative. Unusual means simply infrequent.

2) Normal in the *ideal* sense, i.e., what most or best approximates an ideal standard, a pre-established image or *Vorbild*. This standard can be given by theology (imitatio Christi); by philosophy (Stoic man, Nietzschean man); by law (the citizen); by medicine (environmental adaptation); by culture and society (conformity with canons). For the sake of exposition we can call this second kind of normalcy qualita-tive. It does imply value judgments, since nearness to the ideal is normal in a laudatory sense, and remoteness from it is abnormal in a pejorative sense.

The two usages of normal—statistical and ideal—may be quite distinct. For instance we may suffer from a psychosomatic duodenal ulcer. This is frequent in men of certain sorts doing certain things. As frequent, it is statistically normal, even if ideally it is abnormal. Or, we may have the highest intelligence quotient in a community of likes (age, sex, economic level, ethnic group, etc.) and thus approximate most closely the ideal norm, even if this intelligence be statistically abnormal.

Generally, however, the two kinds of norms merge in our minds. There may be several reasons for this. First, even the bony language of statistics carries metaphorical connotations. When we say *mean, mid-dle, average* or *extreme, exceptional, deviate,* we are denoting statistical frequencies but also connoting qualitative valuations deeply embedded in language. Second, the populist, egalitarian, sociological vision of

the world that dominates our value systems ar of the
two norms, of quantitative and ideal. Under
René Guénon has called our age, *ordinary*
predictable have become ideal norms and ha
soul. 'Abnormal' is both a statistical defini
tion. What is odd becomes wrong; wha
becomes reprehensible. Third, the psyche
norms or ideal types, the *"universali fanta*
Vico. We seem unable to exist without
ideal standards. But today our shrines ar
the vacant niches appear the secular cor
averages ennobled into ideal norms by
We witness the Reign of Quantity in
of common sense, the infiltration of
norms.

The quantitative approach represen
towards psyche, of matter toward soul.
ogy from the science of material natu
meanings of normal is "natural." Th
uses the regularities of nature (phy
"Aristotelian." This method implica
fallacy,[60] i.e., judging psychic events
events in nature. When physical, lit
psyche is being viewed usually fro...
archetype and her hero.[60a]

The Aristotelian approach derives from defining the psyche in
terms of the natural life of the body;[61] whereas we have been working
out a psychology that is more Platonic. Its examination of soul is
related primarily with death, with what is below and deeper than
natural life and its viewpoint. The difference between the Aristotelian
and the Platonic can also be put as one between the medical and the
mythical in regard to pathologizings. Norms for the soul that speak of
adaptation, life-enhancement, balance, or golden mean are "aristotelian" or medical;[62] they remain within the natural perspective and fail to
appreciate the necessity of pathologizing for myth and the necessity of
death-boundedness for soul.

Although Plato praised the middle path, he also encouraged steps
away from it, as in the *Symposium* and the *Phaedrus* where erotic
intensity and various styles of extreme mania are presented as favored
ways of soul. Furthermore, in the *Phaedo* (81–2)Plato speaks of *andras*

metrious, ordinary decent citizens, who in their reincarnation are compared with bees and ants, wholly collective souls happily bound to the lines of nature, predictable, communal, undeviating. The very word *metrios* (the middle class praised in Aristotle's *Politics*) refers to *metron*, the rule, standard, norm, measure.

The Platonic approach is carried further by Marsilio Ficino in his translation and commentary of the *Symposium*.[63] This work was one of the most influential treatises of the Renaissance. It is an esoteric, ecstatic psychology book whose intention is to lead the soul to love. For Ficino (*Comm. Symp.*, VI, 8), the middle path which neither ascends nor descends is the position of practical men of action, whose concern is with morality and whose position is that of observer. Such men "remain in the pleasures only of seeing and social relations." The middle path avoids both the descent into voluptuous touching and ascent into contemplative abstraction.

Some Platonists[64] held this middle path in less regard than the other two, since the voluptuous movement into animal generation was a model for the experiences of the upward exaltation—*les extrèmes se touchent*. Ficino's characterization of the middle path implies a profound critique of the realm of perception, action, and social relations. Only to observe, to ask the moral question of events, to turn the movements of the soul into practical actions, all belong to the horizontal middle way which is a defense against the daemonic power of love that draws one vertically down or up. The middle path of social-moral-practical man is the *defense of normality* against the compelling involvement of the other two ways.

The great passions, truths, and images are not normal middles, not averages. Tongue-tied Moses who kills, has horns and a black desert wife; Christ turning miracles, lacerated on the Cross; ecstatic Mohammed; Hercules and the Heroes, even Ulysses; and the extraordinary awesome Goddesses—all these are unpredictable extremes that bespeak the soul *in extremis*. And these mythical figures show *infirmitas*: possessions, errors, wounds, pathologizings. In Vico's terms, metaphorical truth is more than life, other than life, even while it presents the ideal standards for life. The very ideality is partly expressed through pathologized enormities.

I am not pleading for a baroque Romanticism or Gothic horror, a new cult of the freakish to shock the bourgeois. Such is merely the other side of normalcy. Rather I wish us to remember Plato's *Timaeus*: reason alone does not rule the world or set the rules. Turning to the middle-ground for norms, norms without enormity, refuses the errant cause of Ananke.[65] Such norms are delusions, false beliefs, that do not take into account the full nature of things. Norms without patholo-gizings in their images perform a normalizing upon our psychological vision, acting as repressive idealizations which make us lose touch with our individual abnormalities. The normalcy fantasy becomes it-self a distortion of the way things actually are.

To put it in the language of academic psychology: the nomothetic must include the idiopathic within its formulations as an inherent part of its general statements and laws, else our vision of soul, too, be-comes normalized, indistinguishable from bees and ants: social, practi-cal, natural; *1984*. Then we are defended against the archetypes in our lives and against the powerful images of our culture that can no longer reach us, or only do so through the middle path of perceptual observations, archetypes as allegories of moral practical action or as aesthetic illustrations without persuasiveness. Then we have modeled ourselves upon norms without archetypal dimensions, man the mea-surer of all things, the observer outside, even outside his own suffer-ing, treating it also from outside, observationally, objectively, living a life without any inherent sense of necessity.

IV. Athene

Now this middle position too must be archetypally influenced. To call it a defensive delusion is not enough; it too must reflect a God since there are Gods in our diseases.

Here we return to Athene who performed the great reconciliation between Zeus and the Furies, Nous and Ananke. I have already point-ed out that Athene shares limiting, harnessing attributes with Ananke. Besides, she has a Persephone aspect;[66] a horse[67] aspect like the Erinys; she wears on her breast the Gorgo, that terrifying image of irrationali-ty; her animal, the owl,[68] is her "wisdom," but it is also a bird of doom, a screeching night-creature that can be situated among the Harpies, Sirens, Keres, Moirae—winged images of fateful necessities.

However, and in contrast, Athene is the head-sprung daughter of Zeus, the very epiphany of his Nous, his introjected Metis (Athene's mother). Metis ("wise counsel") stems from the same indogermanic root ME as *metron*, measure, rule, standard.[69] It is particularly in the realm of the city that Athene Polias[70] upholds the norms of the cultur-al canons. One of her later epithets was Pronoia, *providentia*, foresight, for her structure of consciousness can espy predictabilities, prepare for them, and thus normalize the unexpected. Athene, as Hygieia,[71] shows the same foresighted preparedness in the realm of health. Do we not appeal to her still today under the conceptual guise of "mental hygiene" and the community mental health centers organized by the state? Athene's name itself, according to Kerényi, refers to a containing receptacle "'a kind of vessel, a dish, beaker, or pan'";[72] she was the protective divinity of the potter; and the clay bowl was a primary votive offering in the Athene cult.[73] Normalizing occurs also through having a receptive openness and contained inner space for whatever comes.

The Roman Athene, Minerva[74] (whose name derives from *memini, mens,* mind) had under her protection all craft guilds, school teachers ("normal school"!), and the medical profession—groups whose task is exercising governance over the Errant Cause through the wise counsel of practical intellect.[75]

As giver of bridle and yoke and "the science of numbers,"[76] Athene presents the persuasive necessity of reason, the mathematical and logical necessities where, as Aristotle (*Meta.* 1015a–b) says, "a conclusion cannot be otherwise" for it follows necessarily from first premises in the deductive processes. Thinking is yoked and bridled by the logics of reason. Athene brings Zeus and Ananke together because *in her very person reason and necessity are combined.* Athene-Minerva moves Ananke from the violence of Bia to the force of mind of which her convincing speech (*peitho*) is example. Athene is necessity moved from otherworld to thisworld, from blindness to bright-eyes (*glaukopis*), from spinning to weaving, from impenetrable erratic compulsion to the practical intellect's foresighted protective measures in regard to necessity, which measures themselves become another kind of necessity.

This psychological process I would define as normalization and I would consider Athene to be the archetypal person within the fantasy of normality. When psychology speaks in terms of norms, when it attempts to normalize, when it represents the point of view of the cultural canon and gives wise counsel from the practical understanding—protective, hygienic, politic, sensible—then psychology is enacting Athene.

Moreover, we can bring support for our having called the normative perspective "maternal." Unlike Hera and Artemis who were *not* addressed in Greek cult with the term Mother, Athene was called *Meter.* This virgin without offspring was nonetheless a mother—

however, she was never depicted holding a child.[77] Here we have occasion to discriminate with more precision the term "mother" used sweepingly in depth psychology.[78] The mothering of Athenian consciousness is institutional, a mothering of non-religious, secular brotherhoods (*phratriai*). To find Mother Athene we must turn to the conventions of like-minded men, the nomothetic standards of science, business, trades, professions, and government and their unavoidable norms of inclusion and exclusion.[79] When the soul is examined from an institutional standpoint or approached with conventional thinking and feeling, the perspective operating is that of Athene.

In another place I suggested that Plato's dialogues can be examined archetypally in terms of the Gods[80] and the variances within his philosophy can be understood as appropriate to the polytheism of his consciousness. The dialogue that appears to be especially the "child of Athene" is the *Statesman*.

There we find that the particular craft with which statesmanship is compared is the art of combining, and the images for this art are those of Athene: measuring and weaving (*St.* 283–87).[81] Athene's handwork is the paradigm used by Plato for the craft of politics. We have already seen Athene's ability to combine or to weave the revengeful, implacable forces into the structure of the Acropolis by that remarkable combinatory term "resident aliens" which is, after all, a resolution of the "Orestes problem" by means of a political metaphor. Plato says that Athene (together with Hephaistos) governs the crafts for the "daily needs of life" (*Laws* XI, 920e)—as if to say that the maintenance of daily, practical life of the community is her main concern. Inclusion of the excessive and abnormal by weaving it in is the art of political consciousness. Such weaving, as Plato takes great metaphorical pains to establish, is not patching quilts, tacking boards, stitching leather, darning holes. It is not repairing. It is not collage. It is not bricolage, haphazard, without inner necessity. Rather, Athene's art is the systematic plaiting of strands together; and as her own person is a combination of Reason and Necessity, her art of combination produces a whole fabric (*St.* 283b). All strands find place in and contribute to the gestalt—as do the Erinys. The old Furies brought in, nothing left out, no extremities hanging over the edges: integration as ideal norm.

It is in this integrative sense that we can understand the importance of Minerva in Bruno's art of memory.[82] Minerva makes possible the very art itself; her ladder connects all things by means of gradations of images. Or, as we have seen in the *Eumenides*, it is Athene (Minerva) who makes space within. She is the inner space-making function of mind, the Goddess who grants *topos*, judging where each event belongs in relation with all other events. She is mind as a containing receptacle which normalizes through interior organization.

However, this structure of consciousness can turn norms into weapons. We see this in the *Iliad* (21:399ff.). Athene takes up a boundary stone (that which sets limits) and hurls it at Ares, striking him in the neck! (place of necessity). He is flattened by her force, 'subjugated' to her limits.

It becomes more apparent why those Gods who are strongly contrasted with Athene are 'irrational': Ares and Aphrodite (in the *Iliad*); Poseidon (in the *Odyssey*); Dionysos (whose drunkenness can be cured with an owl's egg,[83] and who calls Minyas' daughters away from their weavings); Pan (—no goat was allowed on the Acropolis and its spittle was poison for her olive tree.)[84] The dynamic emotionalities, rages, possessions, moist hysterics, depressions, and wild nature outside the *polis* do not belong within the cosmos of Athene's normalization. They cannot be held in her wide, but shallow, bowl.

These syzygies continue to work in our perspectives. It is difficult to imagine the nature of Athenian consciousness without ourselves falling into one or another of these affect-laden stances with which she is in an opposition.

A second metaphor from the *Statesman* also refers to the weaving in of Ananke within the body politic—and of course the body politic is also an image, a way of speaking about the constitution of the soul. This time the metaphor concerns the social hierarchy from slaves to kings (*St.* 287–91) which are combined by the art of statecraft. From what we have already seen, we know that 'slaves' refer to *ananke*, and that within the soul the slaves are the compelled and the compulsive.

Following a proposal I have made elsewhere ("An Essay on Pan"), that ideas and behaviors (including pathologized behaviors) are always the enactment of mythical fantasies, it would now be appropriate to develop the relations further between the mythical imageries of Athene and the ideas of norms, and then to link these images and ideas with behavioral pathologies. In other words we are obliged to recognize the *pathologizing of Athene*. In the same way that ascension belongs to the puer archetype, constriction to Saturn, will-power to the Hero, growth to Magna Mater and her Child, so normalizing belongs to Athenian consciousness. (This is so the case that we still today call

"Athenian" the normative ideals of "nothing to excess" and the doctrine of the Golden Mean.) And in the same way that these other ideational attitudes—ascension, constriction, will-power, growth—provides background support for a manner of pathologizing, so normalizing too is a manner of pathologizing containing its own archetypal justification.

Athenian justification takes place by means of the appeal to objective norms. To feel that norms are objective and to think that objective norms *are*, independent of structures of consciousness and the archetypal persons governing them, reveal that we are standing in Athene's temple. The interweaving of normative and objective thinking is precisely the blindspot in Athenian consciousness. Here it cannot see through itself and into the archetypal fantasy it is enacting. This consciousness experiences norms as objective and the objective as normal, and from the objective we must derive our norms. Athenian consciousness turns outside to objective 'others' (*polis*) for validating the necessity of its perspective.

This consciousness remains eternally bound to its 'father,' Zeus, giving it a certainty of judgment and a conviction of objectivity; it maintains an impersonal and selfless concern for 'the good of the whole.' This whole, however, by being objectified (rather than individualized) becomes abstracted into an idealized norm. The subtle infusion of the abstract into the practical has the advantage—and disadvantage—of removing actual practical concerns into principled standards and objectives. It becomes hard to distinguish between the virtue and the tyranny of judgment in Athenian consciousness.

That there is abnormalcy in normalizing, that the watchword of integrated normality is the very place of Athene's style of psychopathology, is most vividly imaged in her function of protectress of the "city," where the preparedness of her *pronoia* is also the military defensiveness of paranoia. She is patroness of weapons and is herself "an armed goddess with body almost wholly covered by a shield."[85] The structure of consciousness keeping us rational, practical, and *en garde* for the daily needs of life is the very same structure that keeps us encased in our body armor, the defensive postures that are archetypally necessary to civilized normality.

This protectively practical structure is so close to our habitual ego defenses that it is especially difficult to recognize. Otto reminds us of Athene's closeness to action, her readiness and immediacy. He speaks of her as the intelligence that guides us in the midst of the operations of life, much like Piaget who defines intelligence as an ego activity that solves problems through operational combinations. This is an archetype that does *not* reveal itself in affects. She has neither the savagery of battle nor the distance of contemplation (says Otto); she is therefore not discernible through affective seizures or spiritual highs. She is "ever near,"[86] and because she is so close we do not see her.

To locate Athene psychologically we must go close to what we call the ego (and Athene was counselor of many heroes).[87] Athene acts as self-restraining voice or insight within our reflections. She is the internal Mentor—and it is as mentor-bird that she appears so often in the *Odyssey*.[88] When one takes counsel with oneself, the act is itself Athenian, and so the counsel that emerges reflects her norma. She is the reflection awake in the night, like the owl and the sudden call, like her trumpet, that makes one hear despite one's inner deafness. When we speak of reflection in psychology or call up inner figures of the imagination to reflect our concerns, we need to remember that reflection has many styles. Athene's counsel presents the norms of this world, and its necessities, in close cooperation with the ego's interests. This is not a reflection that is nymphic and fantasyful, pueric and inspirational, Saturnian and abstracted, Apollonic and clarified, not a musing reflection, nor one that is erotic, speculative, or Hermetic.

The upshot of what we have been working out here can be summed up as follows: 1) the normative is only one archetypal perspective toward psychological events as Athene is only one of twelve Olympians—and there are further perspectives, *particularly* of the Underworld, that are not Olympian. 2) Norms having objective validity are "absolute," "normal," and "objective" only for Athenian consciousness for which such fantasies are archetypally necessary. 3) The normative approach to the psyche is inherent to a Weltanschauung that feels its primary obeisance to 'outside' images, or what we today refer to as 'conscious' psychology (statistical, social, practical, preventative, hygienic, communal); or 'outside' as above, the high objective truths of Zeus. 4) The normative approach experiences Necessity as it is translated by Athene, i.e., necessity presses upon us as demands to comply with images that are *représentations collectives*, coming from *res publica*, from normative standards that are rationally demonstrable, rather than from images of the imaginal. Pathologizing is eo ipso abnormal. We conceive ourselves as social, economic, natural, or political man, rather than as imaginative man. We formulate our necessities in terms of 'outside' needs; our actions are guided by what is rational, politic, hygienic, foresighted, precautionary. 5) Imagination itself receives an inspired and prophetic interpretation from Athenian consciousness. Its fallen forms will be either denounced as unprincipled and impractical or ennobled with foreshadowings and implications; but they will not be permitted the independence of their deformity—for each and every event must fit, be fitting, and fit in. 6) To be normal in any society is to enact a particular style of that society's fantasy. The appeal to normality conceals a defense against other archetypal enactments which then must perforce be judged 'abnormal.' 7) From this standpoint there must be abnormality against which this style of consciousness defends itself and integrates by normalizing. Thus we have arrived at "the necessity of abnormal psychology." Also we have exhibited our main concern in this paper: before psychotherapy is in a position to do anything at all in regard to psychological abnormality, it is obliged first to recognize the archetypal dominant in the style that casts a world into norms, normalizing, and normality, i.e., the archetypal person of Athene.

The image of Athene, helmeted in full armor, returns us to our opening reference to Freud. The little symptom so alien to the normative view of the ego is the chink in the structure cracking all normative images of how we should be—all denials of pathologizing made impossible by the persistent backaches, the indigestion, the bad moods and hounding ideas. The fatal flaw is indeed Fate, Necessity, reaching our soul through her daughters, despite all shields of providence that would take arms against it. Through the power of the image, expressing itself as a symptom and presenting the erratic claims of Necessity, we discover a psychological vision of man for whom neither naturalism, nor spiritualism, nor normalism applies. Natural man who is at one with harmonious development, spiritual man at one with transcendent perfection, and normal man at one with practical and social adaptation are transformed by being deformed into psychological man who is at one with soul.

1   S. Freud, *New Introductory Lectures on Psycho-Analysis* (§31), trans. W.J.H. Sprott (London: Hogarth, 1933), p. 78 on the symptom as starting point of psychoanalysis.
2   "On Psychological Language," Chap. 2 in my *The Myth of Analysis* (Evanston: Northwestern Univ. Press, 1972) and "Pathologizing," Chap. 2 in my *Re-Visioning Psychology* (N.Y.: Harper & Row, 1975) hereafter "RP."

3 Jung, *CW* 13, §54.

4 Cf. David Kinsley, "'Through the Looking Glass': Divine Madness in the Hindu Religious Tradition," *Hist. of Rel.* 13/4, 1974, pp. 270–305.

5 In stressing the pathologized aspect of the imaginal, I am aware of diverging here from the view of Henry Corbin who is the founder of the term imaginal and to whom my work is, and will ever remain, profoundly indebted. Corbin considers the imaginary of "the fantastic, the horrible, the monstrous, the macabre, the miserable, and the absurd" to reflect secularization of the imaginal. "In contrast, the art and imagination of Islamic culture in its traditional form are characterized by the hieratic, by seriousness, gravity, stylization, and significance" (H. Corbin, "Mundus Imaginalis, or the Imaginary and the Imaginal," *Spring 1972*, p. 16). Clearly, pathologizings of the image do *not* belong to the *mundus imaginalis* as he has given us this word. But in the soul-making of actual psychotherapy, pathologizings are often the via regia into the imaginal. Here we follow Jung for whom there was no image that could not become the vehicle of active imagination and the movement of consciousness to mythic depths. In fact, the more irksome the image, the more likely it was a symbol mobilizing precisely those mythic depths. Just these perverse thoughts, obscene words, obsessive fears and memories are the materia prima. Each beginning is with "the macabre, the miserable, and the absurd." And we return to the *materia prima* with each new move of the psyche. "It must be remembered that sensations of the ugly and evil impress us more violently than those of what is agreeable . . . sickness makes the rougher mark . . . ," said Plotinus (V, 8,11), an idea confirmed also by the Art of Memory (*RP*, p. 92). The refinement of our imaginal sensibility must begin where sensibility itself begins. From the gross to the subtle is an operation, not an ontology. The ontological priority of Corbin's world is nonetheless arrived at via the operational priority of Jung's method—because we must begin where we have fallen, flat on our backs in personal pain. The difference between Jung and Corbin can be resolved by practising Jung's technique with Corbin's vision; that is, active imagination is not for the sake of the doer and *our* actions in the sensible world of literal realities, but for the sake of the images and to where they can take us, *their* realization. Active imagination begins in *their* Fall and is, in fact, their activity going on in our hearts. The alchemist concentrates upon the fallen spirits imprisoned in nature which symbolize coevally with his fallen spirits in his nature. The focus, however, is always on *them*.

6 By "archetype" I can refer only to the phenomenal archetype, that which manifests itself in images. The noumenal archetype per se cannot by definition be presented so that nothing whatsoever can be posited of it. In fact whatever one does say about the archetype per se is a conjecture already governed by an archetypal image. This means that the archetypal image precedes and determines the metaphysical hypothesis of a noumenal archetype. So, let us apply Occam's razor to Kant's noumenon. By stripping away this unnecessary theoretical encumbrance to Jung's notion of archetype we restore full value to the archetypal image. Cf. my "An Inquiry into Image," *Spring 1977*, p. 70.

7 Our polytheistic psychology has no one Devil to whom all destructive processes belong: "The Greeks have no category of divinities generally recognized as essentially malignant, no real Devil or devils. . . ." (A. D. Nock, "The Cult of Heroes," *Harvard Theol. Rev.* 37, 1944, p. 172). In this view the shadow is not a separated archetype, but is archetypal, i.e., an ontological distinction within the Gods themselves, always with them, never cast down into the human world only. Each God contains shadow and casts it according with how he or she shapes a cosmos. Each God is a way in which we are shadowed.

8 E.g., Empedocles (Fr. 115) where exile, wandering, and being ceaselessly buffeted by elemental forces result from Necessity.

9 H. Schreckenberg, *Ananke—Untersuchungen zur Geschichte des Wortgebrauchs, Zetemata*, Heft 36 (München: Beck, 1964), hereafter "HS."

10 HS, pp. 169–74.

11   Liddell and Scott, *A Greek-English Lexicon* (Oxford: Clarendon, 1964), hereafter "LS"; R. B. Onians, *The Origins of European Thought* (Cambridge: Univ. Press, 1954), p. 332, hereafter "RBO."

12   HS, p. 176, with photographic *Anhang* of prisoners and slaves with cords around their necks. The special emphasis which HS lays upon the yoke and slave's collar in his etymology opens a perspective towards the perplexing question of slavery in the same antique cultures from where he draws his etymology. Following his line of thought joining servitude with necessity, slavery becomes eo ipso justified, even implied, by the word necessity itself. (The jailhouse in Athens and Thebes was called *anankaion*.) Slavery might then even have been experienced as an operation of Ananke, part of the way of all things, a founding principle of universal order. My point here is not to justify slavery, but to suggest that archetypal ideas, persons, and myths, such as Ananke, are determinants in social attitudes and structures.

13   RBO, p. 333n; Lewis and Short, *A Latin Dictionary* (Oxford: Clarendon, 1894).

14   HS, pp. 114ff. For a discussion of *ananke* in Leucippos and Democritus.

15   HS, p. 133; W. H. Roscher, *Lexikon der Griechischen und Römischen Mythologie* (Hildesheim: Olms, 1965), "Necessitas," hereafter "WHR."

16   Cf. "Of Milk" in my "Senex and Puer," *Puer Papers*, Spring Publ., 1979, pp. 38–42.

17   On the relation of Love (Philotes) and Strife (Neikos) in Empedocles, see D. O'Brien, *Empedocles' Cosmic Cycle* (Cambridge: Univ. Press, 1969), pp. 104–127. P. Friedländer, *Plato*, transl. H. Meyerhoff, Bollingen Series (Princeton U.P., 1969), vol. 3, p. 362 and note, makes clear the identity of Love with Aphrodite-Charis and Strife with Ananke. (That necessity works through discord and strife, and that discord and strife are necessary, is also a psychological lesson we learn from these mythological relations.) Ultimately Aphrodite and Ananke become interchangeable: they can both create Eros and can both appear through Nemesis (revenge). We experience this identity particularly in the immovable fixations of love. Parmenides expressed this psychological experience in metaphysical language, Guthrie, vol. 2, p. 62; F. M. Cornford, *From Religion to Philosophy* (N.Y.: Harper Torchbook, 1957), pp. 222–23.

18   Bia and Ananke are interchangeable terms and figures (Pauly-Wissowa, *Real-Encyclopaedie der klassischen Altertumswissenschaft*, Bd. 3, 379–80, hereafter "P-W.") Peitho was another name for Aphrodite who was worshipped in that form (WHR, "Peitho," 1796–1804).

19   Lines 96–104; David Grene transl., *Aeschylus II* (Chicago U.P., 1956), italics mine.

20   Lines 962–975; Richmond Lattimore transl. *Euripides I* (Chicago U.P., 1955). For textual comments on this passage see A. M. Dale, ed., Euripides, *Alcestis* (Oxford: Clarendon, 1954), pp. 119–21.

20a   Cf. my *The Dream and the Underworld* (N.Y.: Harper & Row, 1979), pp. 27ff.

21   WHR, "Necessitas," p. 71, reports that Ananke is associated with Persephone on two graves.

22   The subject of encircling limits in Homer and after has been treated exhaustively in RBO, "peirata," pp. 310–42. It is mainly in that chapter that we find Onians' discussion of *ananke*.

23   Cf. HS, p. 144.

24   Cf. Aeschylus, *Agamemnon*, l. 218.

25   Particularly a *steel* nail (Horace, *Odes* I, 35, 17ff; III, 24, 5ff, where it is Tyche [chance] who drives the nails into the scalp of her victims). Eurip. *Alcestis*, l. 979, for a steel image in connection with necessity.

26   Cf. HS, p. 41, on the relation between necessity and the "ausweglose Situation."

27   "In being crowned as a singer . . . he is bound with a particular fate, obligation as well as power." RBO, p. 407, n. 1; p. 376: "Attention was paid to the head because it contained the *psyche*." Also, pp. 444–51.

28   Guthrie, vol. 2, pp. 35–37, 72–73.

29   I have used both translations: Hugh Tredennick, Loeb Classical Library (London: Heinemann, 1961) and W. D. Ross, *The Works of Aristotle*, 2nd ed. (Oxford: Clarendon, 1940).

30   Lyperon = "irksome" (Ross); "disagreeable" (Tredennick); both compare with Empedocles (Fr. 116) who calls Ananke "intolerable."

31   Guthrie, ibid., p. 417.

32   F. M. Cornford, *Plato's Cosmology: The Timaeus of Plato* (London: Routledge, 1948), p. 160.

33   George Grote, *Plato*, vol. III, Chap. 36, quoted from Cornford, p. 172.

34   Cornford, p. 176.

35   Friedländer, *Plato*, vol. 1, p. 205. Cornford, p. 203, makes the same point.

36   E. R. Dodds, "Plato and the Irrational," in his *The Ancient Concept of Progress* (Oxford: Clarendon, 1973), p. 116.

37   Cf. ibid., "[Plato] has projected into his conception of Nature that stubborn irrationality which he was more and more compelled to admit in man (*Tim.* 90c–d)."

38   In the *Timaeus* (48b, 52d) the four elements are spoken of as *pathe*. *Pathe* basically means a "passive state," and then secondarily, suffering, affliction. The elements are not themselves *archai*. Rather they are modes of happening, ways of being moved, modified, affected. Cornford (pp. 198n, 199) and Friedländer (vol. 3, p. 370–71) call them "qualities" of Chaos. They are the modes through which Necessity works. They are, so to speak, the elementary modes of being affected; they give four styles to the workings of the errant cause in our chaotic conditions. Or, in alchemical language, the four elements are modes of the *prima materia* and are experienced as four modes of our primal suffering. Empedocles' suffering that is ordained by Necessity is described (Fr. 115) as his being buffeted from one element to another; Plato sees the ur-elements in their primordial chaotic conditions as perpetually tossing (52e) and swaying ("perpetually in motion, coming to be in a certain place and again vanishing out of it"—52a). The four elements as *pathe* suggests an "elemental psychopathology" or a logos of the soul's suffering in terms of the elements. (Cf. T. S. Eliot's four modes of "death" in *Four Quartets*, "Little Gidding" II.) Bachelard's work presents the four elements as the fundaments of consciousness; as well they may be considered the basic qualities of pathologizing, enabling us to examine the phenomenology of images and behavior in terms of fire, air, water, and earth. This move is not meant to lead away from the concrete image into just one more fourfold system of abstraction, but rather to explore the therapeutic implications of the image, whether its possibilities belong more appropriately to fire, say, than to earth, air, or water. For the worst suffering is that of Empedocles who is tossed from element to element, belonging to none.

39   For a full and recent discussion of the Moirae (and also the other "fate goddesses"), see B. C. Dietrich, *Death, Fate and the Gods* (London: Athlone Press, 1967). On the one hand, Ananke rules the Erinys according to Orphic Hymn 69 (T. Taylor transl.); on the other, she is a later conceptualization of them (Dietrich, p. 98).

40   For a rich discussion of "The Knees of the Gods" and Ananke's spindle, see RBO, pp. 303–09. The myth of Er has provided a grounding image for Platonist fascination with astrology as a mode of psychology. The same Necessity governs the soul's movements as well as the motions of the stars. As souls pass beneath her seat, so on her lap turns the spindle ruling the planetary motions. What happens to soul and to stars is on the same web. So one tries to puzzle out the compelling necessities of the soul by consulting the motions of the planets. As Paracelsus explained, a physician of pathologies cannot consider himself as such unless he has knowledge of the other half of the soul in the planetary bodies. But astrologers have taken this correspondence literally, rather than imaginally. For it is neither the actual stars nor the astrological planets that are the rulers of personality. Astrology is a *metaphorical* way of recognizing that the rulers of personality are archetypal powers who are beyond our personal reach and yet are involved necessarily in all our vicissitudes. These powers are mythical *persons*, Gods, and their motions are not described in mathematics but in myths.

41   Friedländer, vol. 3, p. 382.

42   Cornford, p. 289. The relation of psyche and internal organs (guts and liver) is a subject

FACING THE GODS

all for itself: cf. Ernst Bargheer, *Eingeweide, Lebens- und Seelenkräfte des Leibesinneren* (Berlin: de Gruyter, 1931); Nikolaus Mani, *Die historischen Grundlagen der Leberforschung*, I (Basel/Stuttgart: Schwabe, 1959); RBO, pp. 84–89; E. Fischer-Homberger, "Zur Geschichte des Zusammenhangs zwischen Seele und Verdauung," *Schweiz. med. Wschr.* 103, 1433–41 (1973).

43 HS, p. 133. The Eumenides (Erinys or Furies, divinities of Necessity, see below on Aeschylus and notes) affect man and drive him mad through the *phrenes* (*Eumenides*, ll. 301, 331, 344) which Lattimore consistently translates "heart," Thomson "bosom." On *"phrenes"* see RBO, pp. 13–15, 23–43. His work shows that the term refers to an *organ of consciousness* and not only a physical place (lungs or diaphragm), hence I have used the term "air soul."

44 HS, pp. 133–164, examines the whole "Fragenkomplex"; cf. M. P. Nilsson, *Opuscula Selecta* (Lund: Gleerup, 1960), pp. 163–64.

45 When Porphyry in his life of Plotinus (Chap. 22) gives answer, in an oracle from Apollo, to the question of where Plotinus' soul had gone after death, we can read: "The bonds of human necessity are now loosed from you." *Nota bene* the role of Apollo in this style of thought (*Phaedo*) and what elsewhere I have called the "Apollonic consciousness" of transcendent approaches to the problems of the psyche.

46 *Plegai* can also mean blows, strokes, hurts, afflictions. It is the source of our word "plague."

47 G. Thomson (with W. G. Headlam), *The Oresteia of Aeschylus* (Cambridge: Univ. Press, 1938), vol. 1, p. 345 (ll. 931–35).

48 Cf. Cornford's brilliant "Epilogue" to *Plato's Cosmology* on the comparison between the *Timaeus* and the *Oresteia*; also Thomson, vol. 2, p. 321.

49 "Peitho und Ananke sind terminologisch Gegensatzkomplemente." HS, p. 102, n. 77. Their opposition is already in Empedocles as one between Ananke and the Charites (WHR, "Peitho" [with Charis], 1796). An attribute which the two Goddess-figures have in common is the *necklace*. Ananke's collar and necklace we saw above in HS's etymological analysis; Peitho decorates Pandora with golden necklaces (Hesiod, *Works and Days*, l. 73) Evidently, what one wears around one's throat has the implications of fate; and the woman (so often a nude) with a necklace in paintings is the woman of fate. Neck-dress—from numbered dogtags to collar-and-ties or golden chains and inset gems—particularizes destiny. The undressed throat is the unarticulated and inarticulate flesh without a specific sense of its own necessity. See further on jewelry and joints, A. J. Ziegler, "Rheumatics and Stoics," *Spring 1979*, pp. 19–28. For a full discussion of the pair Peitho-Ananke (as Bia), see Pedro Laín Entralgo, *The Therapy of the Word in Classical Antiquity*, trans. L. J. Rather and J. M. Sharp (Yale U.P., 1970), pp. 64–90.

50 Cf. Thomson, vol. 1, p. 68 for "resident aliens." Lattimore translates "guests of the land." The psychologically important point is that these figures are not fully integrated. They keep their specific identity. They remain "outsiders," guests, aliens, even if having received a place. *Placing*—neither repressing nor transforming (converting)—equals archetypal healing in this context.

51 Cf. P. Wheelwright, *The Burning Fountain*, Chap. 10, "Thematic Imagery in the *Oresteia*" (Indiana U.P., 1968), p. 238.

52 The place of Orestes in modern consciousness has already been superbly exposed by David L. Miller in his "Orestes: Myth and Dream as Catharsis," in J. Campbell, ed., *Myths, Dreams, and Religion* (New York: Dutton, 1970), pp. 26–47.

53 Ch. Boer, transl. *The Homeric Hymns* (Spring Publ., 1979), pp. 137–8.

54 Laín Entralgo, p. 68.

55 *Ibid.* There is an irony here, however, since in that play Ulysses is shown as a man of action whose words are most deceitful. Moreover he is unable to convince Philoctetes, even more a man of action; only Hercules can.

56 Toshihiko Izutsu, *Language and Magic*, Studies in the Humanities and Social Relations,

36

Vol. I (Keio Institute of Philological Studies: Tokyo, 1956). The pages from which I quote are 103, 26.

57 These two quotations are discussed by Laín Entralgo, pp. 66–7.

58 Izutsu, *op. cit.*, p. 13: "as there can be no magical use of language without at least a minimum of logicality, so in ordinary descriptive use of language—or even in scientific discourse—the actual words employed cannot in the nature of the case be entirely free from illogicality. In natural language there is always something that stubbornly resists a thoroughgoing logical analysis. . . ."

59 It is not only that Ananke and Bia cannot hear (deaf) and carry the usual epithet "blind"; but like death, necessity works in silence, does not speak. Empedocles, according to Plutarch, contrasted musical Persuasion with non-musical and silent Necessity: cf. Laín Entralgo, p. 90.

60 *RP*, pp. 85–87.

60a Cf. my "The Great Mother, Her Son, Her Hero, and the Puer" in *Fathers and Mothers,* (Spring Publ, 1973).

61 Cf. Aristotle, *De anima* 412–13; 415 b 10.

62 See Wm. A. Scott, "Conceptions of Normality," Chap. 19 in E. F. Borgatta and W. W. Lambert (eds.), *Handbook of Personality Theory and Research* (New York: Rand McNally, 1968) for a collection of such norms where normality = mental health, adjustment, happiness, productivity, social integration, minimum of conflict and destruction, etc.

63 M. Ficino's Commentary on Plato's *Symposium*: text, translation, and introduction by S. R. Jaynes, *University of Missouri Studies* XIX (Columbia, Mo., 1944).

64 Cf. Edgar Wind, *Pagan Mysteries in the Renaissance* (Harmondsworth: Penguin, 1967), pp. 50ff., 68f., 273f., for a discussion of Neoplatonism and *voluptas* with references to Plotinus, Ficino, and Lorenzo Valla.

65 It is worth recalling here that Nous uses geometry for ordering the unformed into the four fundamental shapes. As Cornford says (*Plato's Cosmology*, p. 210): "Thus the operation of Reason is carried, so far as may be, into the dark domain of the irrational powers." *Norma*, we remember, is originally a term from geometry. Where mathematics makes order out of the unordered, it is also a move "out of" the unordered, a move away from the dark domain of irrational powers and the necessities of pathologizing. Psychological books which emphasize geometrical descriptions of the psyche (Jung's *Aion*, for instance, or M.-L. von Franz's *Time and Number* [Evanston: Northwestern U.P., 1974]) also belong among the transcendental denials of pathologizing and as such are less psychological than spiritual, less representative of imaginal soul realities which are always pathologized, than of an abstract metaphysical reality which presents itself in 'pure' forms.

66 On Persephone-Athene, see K. Kerényi, *Athene: Virgin and Mother in Greek Religion*, transl. by Murray Stein (Spring Publ., 1978), pp. 31–2, 42–3, and the translator's excellent postscript. Hereafter *Athene.*

67 On the horse (Athene) see *Athene*, pp. 7, 9, 23, 45ff. (Gorgo, Mare); M. Detienne, "Athene and the Mastery of the Horse," *History of Religions* 11/2, 1971, pp. 161–86; on the horse (Erinys), cf. Dietrich, *op. cit.*, pp. 137ff.

68 On the owl (Athene), see *Athene*, pp. 31, 32, 58, p. 99, n. 312; E. A. Armstrong, *The Folklore of Birds* (London: Collins, 1958), pp. 113–124; on Moirae as flying gray night-daemons, Dietrich, p. 71 (also on Keres, pp. 240–48); J. Pollard, *Seers, Shrines and Sirens* (London: Allen & Unwin, 1965), p. 140.

69 W. W. Skeat, *An Etymological Dictionary of the English Language* (Oxford: Clarendon).

70 On the city (Athene), see *Athene*, pp. 8, 29, 32, 39, 74, 79, p. 86 n. 101; R. F. Willetts, *Cretan Cults and Festivals* (London: Routledge, 1962), p. 278, discusses the movement of Athene from earliest Minoan-Mycenaean household and palace protectress to Goddess of the *polis*.

71 "Hygieia," WHR, 1/2, 2772.

72 *Athene*, p. 29.

73 *Ibid.*, p. 32.

74 WHR, II/2, "Minerva," 2986, -89, -91. Like Athene Ergane (Worker), Minerva was the patroness of artisans, among whom numbered physicians, and also school teachers who were paid their annual honorarium on the day of the Minerva festival.

75 "The word *metis* always signifies *practical* understanding. . . ." W. F. Otto, *The Homeric Gods*, transl. M. Hadas (New York: Pantheon, 1954), p. 52; cf. *Athene* on Metis-Athene, pp. 11–13, 21–2.

76 R. Graves, *The Greek Myths*, Vol. 1 (Harmondsworth: Penguin, 1960), p. 96.

77 W.H.D. Rouse, *Greek Votive Offerings* (Cambridge U.P., 1902), p. 257, n. 2; *Athene*, pp. 13–16.

78 It is insufficient to call Great Mother, or the mother archetype, every female image—Luna, Demeter, Hera, Isis, Mary, Artemis, Cybele, Aphrodite, etc.—as does E. Neumann in his work on this subject. He only amalgamates what is beautifully, precisely, and subtly differentiated in the particular persons and images. For one attempt at differentiating mothering from nursing, see my "Abandoning the Child," *Loose Ends* (Spring Publ., 1975), pp. 35–38.

79 On Athene and the *phratria*, see *Athene*, pp. 15, 52; M. P. Nilsson, "Appendix II: The Phratries," in his *Cults, Myths, Oracles, and Politics in Ancient Greece* (New York: Cooper Square, 1972). Nilsson says (p. 170): "The phratries obtained such Gods common to them all, as maintained the social and civic order, Zeus and Athena. The phratries give an example of the diluting and secularising of religion when the State lays its dead hand upon it." Admission was through voting: standards of inclusion and exclusion.

80 This method is indicated in Plato himself (*Phaedrus*, 252–53) who describes styles of loving in terms of "followers" of the different Gods. In the dialogues themselves we see imagery and ideas—and pathologizing—appropriate to Apollo in the *Phaedo*; we see Pan in the *Phaedrus*, Dionysos in the *Symposium*, Hermes in the *Cratylus*, Zeus and Athene in the *Laws*. According to Wind, *op. cit.*, p. 203, "Athena and Eros were worshipped jointly in the grounds of the Academy." It is from these two sides, 'Athenian' and 'Erotic,' that Platonic commentators have attempted to grasp Plato's Socrates—or have been grasped by those Gods through him.

81 Cf. Friedländer, III, p. 289; *WHR*, I/1, "Athene," 681–82.

82 Cf. Yates, *Art of Memory*, p. 290; Yates, *Giordano Bruno and the Hermetic Tradition* (London: Routledge, 1964), p. 312, where Bruno confesses himself a child of Minerva ("Her have I loved and sought from my youth, and desired for my spouse, and have become a lover of her form. . . ."). The relation between Minerva and images of the mind may help us to understand (beyond the evident artisan or handcraft meaning) the fact that it was to Athene that sacrifice was made by burnishers at Olympia before polishing the image (Rouse, *Greek Votive Offerings*, p. 59, n. 20).

83 In another tale the sober owl drives off bees from the entrance to a wine-cellar (Hyginus, *FAB.*, 136).

84 *Athene*, p. 64. The relation between Athene and goat is treated at length by Kerényi, *ibid.*, pp. 60–69.

85 Otto, *Homeric Gods*, p. 43, referring to her earliest epiphany in Mycenaean art.

86 *Ibid.*, p. 60.

87 Most important of all, Ulysses; cf. W. B. Stanford, "The Favourite of Athene" in his *The Ulysses Theme* (Oxford: Blackwell, 1968), pp. 25–42, where the operations of Athenian intelligence are analytically exposed. Other heroes aided by Athene are Achilles, Diomedes, Jason, Cadmus, Bellerophon, Perseus.

88 Willetts, *Cretan Cults*, p. 314.

II

A MYTHOLOGICAL IMAGE OF GIRLHOOD
(To my Nine-Year-old Daughter)

Karl Kerényi

So spoke the child and tried to touch her father's chin. But in vain she stretched up her little hands several times. Then with a smile her father leaned down and caressed her, saying: "When Goddesses bear me children like this, the wrath of jealous Hera troubles me very little. Little daughter, you shall have all you desire."[1]

Any reader at all familiar with Greek mythology will recognize in these words the divine p... Zeus. But who is the little daughter, sitting on her great fat... fails to reach his chin? Greek religion, like no oth... is characterized by maiden Goddesses, indeed ... by the acknowledged lordship of Zeus ov... Greek religion to the great father re... Christian religions of our own cu... became exclusively pa... ity of Hellas, retained... time of an older... Zeus worship... her.

... the knee of Zeus ... the fact that this s... temis." What we want to n... st as well refer to some other ... res of the Olympian household. Fo... ned great daughter of Zeus, whose full ... he Greeks associated the word *pallas*—depen... thought of it as masculine or feminine—with ... gorous youth or a stately young girl, or perhaps of a you... say the figure of a caryatid. But the Athenians also spoke ... eir Goddess as *the* maiden, *Kore*, or—to distinguish her from Demeter's daughter, Persephone, who was worshipped in nearby Eleusis under another aspect of divine maidenhood—as the "Kore here with us." What is there, then, in this tale of a little girl, not yet ripened into a vigorous *pallas*, but still sitting on her father's knee (and asking for gifts beyond her age), that is not equally applicable to Athene or Persephone?

We have a human situation, depicted here with the sly playfulness of the all-proficient Hellenistic literature, in which Artemis appears as a very little girl in a patriarchal Greek family. This particular scene may be an original creation of Callimachus. On the other hand, the poet would hardly have falsified what for the Greeks was the human reality of the situation, the actual 'station' and image of a Greek young girl of the age to which the child aspires. For now we must be very precise: what we are concerned with here is a stage of life and an age class. Under natural conditions, among ancient peoples and also much later, such a stage was represented and realized, not only in poetry but also in religion, by definite rules and ceremonies. There existed—and still do exist, mostly in impoverished forms—maturation ceremonies guiding those in the same age group from one stage to another, from one 'station' to another, and originally these were true mystery initiations, though not always so termed.

To belong to an age group—not here to be thought of as in any way a conscious organization but simply as being of a certain age—is for all those who have not reached it, or are not yet ripe for it, a mystery that no words can communicate. The secretive doings, such as using masks and costumes, which characterize initiation ceremonies, give this mystery an outward shape which is often a caricature and sometimes even a misrepresentation. For the being of such or such an age is truly a secret—indeed, a mystery. Those who are younger never really understand it, and even those of the same age cannot put it into words among themselves; at most, they can hint of it. Puberty rites are impressive intimations designed to make the initiants aware of the stage they have reached. In ancient times the intimation of the new way of being was provided by the image of a divinity.

So let us be definite and inquire concerning the age group imaged by Artemis, whom Callimachus describes, surely not without good reason, in terms of the events of a young girl's life in the Olympian family—and therewith in the family as such. Neither Athene, who, so to speak, guards the boundary of the patriarchal family with shield and lance, nor Persephone, destined to be abducted and carried into another realm, could take the place of Artemis. Human existence, in its becoming and un-becoming, progresses through all the stages of life. The being of the immortal Gods is of a different kind. It may be thought of as periodic, corresponding not only to the orbits of heavenly bodies that sink and rise again, but also to the natural periodicities in human life—in the life of women, for example. In this way it can include opposites, like the dying and reigning of the underworld queen, Persephone, or it can in a mysterious way achieve motherhood and yet remain virginal, like Pallas Athene: thus the being of a God is eternally bound to a single, though contradictory, form. When a knowledgeable poet characterizes Artemis' age as girlhood, this must surely refer to a stage of life corresponding to her form of being, to a life form which the Goddess helped mortal maidens to become aware of, even though as an immortal she is usually represented— except in the hymn of Callimachus—as more adult and yet more ageless than a mere nine-year-old.

Callimachus tells us that Artemis asked her father for sixty daughters of Okeanos to be her playmates, all nine years old. That age cannot be explained except as indicating a definite age group, to which as its protectress the Goddess herself belongs and always will belong. The previous stage of life has also been established exactly by Callimachus. It begins with Leto showing her daughter Artemis, as a three-year-old, to her divine relatives and receiving gifts from them, because they were being allowed for the first time to see the child. Callimachus then describes the visit of Artemis to the master smith, Hephaistos, and his fellow workers, the Kyclopes, who are unable to frighten the little girl. The same procedure must certainly have been followed with human children. In Athens little boys were first shown publicly during their third year and were given presents of small wine flasks and toys.

For girls the next life stage began with their ninth year. It corresponded with the *ephebe* or early manhood stage of boys and probably was called the *parthenia*. Artemis announces this age as the only one really conformable to herself when, according to Callimachus, she asks her father above all for an ever-enduring *parthenia*. This means not merely virginity—by which word *parthenia* can also be translated—but the particular way and fullness of life lived by girls between their ninth year and that time, not much later, when a Greek maiden began to wear the cincture of the bride. To us a nine-year-old seems too young to be a "young girl" and no longer a child. The very strangeness of the concept forces us to focus on what is essential: that the ninth year—which seems to us too early, but was not too early for a Greek girl—was established by Athenian custom as the beginning of the stage preceding marriage.

Before marriage, we are told, Attic maidens were consecrated to the Artemis of Brauron or Munichia.[2] In this way they entered a period of service to the Goddess, a mystery initiation—this, too, is expressly reported—and their age could not be less than five or more than ten. It may have happened sometimes that a girl was a few months older than ten when she took the vows, but the ninth year appears to have been the paradigmatic age. That is why in the hymn it is the right age for the playmates of Artemis. But the prototype, the Goddess herself—how much more archaic she must have appeared in the holy places high on the hills of Brauron and Munichia than in the tender family scene described by Callimachus! The girls who were dressed to take part in the cult of Artemis, the representatives of the age group of which we are speaking, were called *arktoi*, "female bears"; their service, the celebration of their stage of life, was called *arktoia*, "bearhood," and the reason given was: "Because they act like female bears."

Here is expressed a strange, disquieting savagery, which is not entirely lacking even in the classic Homeric figure of the Goddess. But in Homer her wildness is depicted as that of a meridianal beast of prey: Zeus has made Artemis a lioness toward women (in childbirth); she is allowed to kill whichever of them she will. And there is another opportunity for the exercise of her hunting lust; there are wild animals, hinds, that she may also kill. This lust for hunting is ascribed by Callimachus even to the young child on Zeus's knee, and it gives her special character. The only reason that Artemis does not ask her father then for the bow and arrows is that she will fetch them herself from the Kyclopes. But she does ask for a short hunting dress: "So that I can kill wild animals!" She provides the Olympian family with game. This practical side of her daily hunting is important only from the point of view of greedy Herakles at whom the Gods all laugh. The other, lustful, side of killing seems more essential. It is stressed by both Homer and Callimachus, less explicitly, not as ferocity but as an incomprehensible aggressiveness directed, in the chase, against animals—beloved animals, like hinds—and, in the human realm, against members of her own sex, against women. The Artemis of Brauron, to whom because of her multiple and close relations to the feminine sex a shrine on the Acropolis was dedicated, was given the garments of the women who successfully survived childbirth. The priestess inherited the clothes of those who died—dread trophies of the Huntress.

The picture of the daughter of the house, who has ripened to young girlhood, turning out to be a huntress is almost as startling as that of a representative of this age group being called a bear. During the historic period with which we are familiar, hunting was not a usual or suitable pastime for Greek girls, although it may appear so in the legend of the huntress, Atalanta, who is the humanized manifestation of the Goddess herself. When Atalanta is changed into a lion, she is given one of the animal forms of the Goddess. The same is true of another metamorphosed figure of the Artemisian circle, Kallisto, who was changed into a bear. Thus the hunting life of Greek youths had about it something of the aura of an initiation. That initiation really was involved is indicated by the ruling in Xenophon's little book on hunting that the Greek mother tongue must be a prerequisite in the selection of beginning hunters. We have further evidence of this in the initiation scenes decorating the marble sarcophagi of Attic *ephebes*, which show the youthful dead immortalized in hunting clothes. In Greek legends, such an initiation is represented in purest Artemisian form by the figures of young men, Hippolytos or some other young huntsman, of whom only the name may be known to us—or not even that, they are so recognizable as a type.

This brings out, even more clearly than before, another trait in the image of the divine huntress. She has a relation to the opposite sex which is in a way boyish, and at the same time sisterly, indeed almost brotherly; since to the huntress Artemis belongs her brother, the hunter Apollo, and also Hippolytos, bound to her as a younger brother. For Greek girls, before (as young matrons) they reached the stage that the Goddess herself never entered, and before the companions of the hunt were changed into the spoils of hunting, there was similarly a time during their *parthenia* when a male pleasure was taken in the chase. Also Greek women in their rites themselves slaughtered the beasts of sacrifice. At the feasts of Brauron and Munichia, goats were provided for this purpose;³ in a way they were the prey of the female bears. However, these bears did not wear the short, fringed hunting tunic of Artemis, but the *krokoton*, another characteristic crocus-colored garment designed to replace the bear hide of prehistoric times. The worshippers of Bakchos, too, wore this saffron-yellow over-garment in place of fur, and the mantle of Meleager the Hunter was of the same color—the color which symbolized a sphere of life in which hunt and ecstasy, dance and sacrifice, did not pertain to the underworld. (Red pointed to that darker realm.) This was the reddish yellow usually worn in Athens for the feasts and rites of women everywhere that womanhood moved freely.

So the life stage of the *parthenia*, in spite of its boyishness, is a very feminine stage. In the figure of the great huntress the little human bears met a new aspect of their feminine nature. It was a meeting with something wild and vigorous which would enable them, if the unwritten laws of the all too patriarchal cities would permit, to compete as siblings with the *ephebes* in all their boyish tests and exercises—as, to a certain extent, the Spartan girls actually did. Moreover, someday the Artemisian strength and aggressiveness pertaining to such activities—ordinarily tempered by the women's tasks of which Athene took charge—would be turned against them: in the savage pangs of childbirth, they would be required to exercise a greater strength than is demanded in any athletic contest in which men can take a part. But at that time they will no longer be bears, nor saffron-clothed slaughterers of goats; they will be victims of the same Goddess who they began to serve in their ninth year.

Dressed in the *krokoton*, to serve the maiden Goddess, the Athenian young girl was herself like a bright flame. A bow and arrow were not given to her then to hold, but another attribute, the flaming torch, which Callimachus mentions among the gifts that—along with the *parthenia* and the hunting dress—Artemis begged as a child from her father Zeus. Flaming torches were carried in the ritual procession and dance that took place, by night, between sea and sky on the promontories that the Athenians held holy. And in Munichia even the cakes offered to the Goddess were ringed with burning candles. How cold and inhuman the moon-interwoven divinity named Artemis (and Diana)[4] would indeed be without this worship of flaming torches borne by rosy-cheeked young girls! In *The Homeric Gods*,[5] Walter Otto's description of her runs as follows:

> She dwells in the clear ether of the mountain peak, in the golden shimmer of the mountain meadows, in the flashing and flickering of icicles and snowflakes, in the silent amazement of fields and forests, when the moonlight shines down on them and drips from the leaves. All things are transparent and light. Earth itself has lost its heaviness. . . . There is a floating along the ground as of white feet dancing.

And in this purity is sublimity:

> [She is] the dancer and huntress, who takes the bear cub on her lap and runs races with the deer, death-bringing when she bends her bow, strange and unapproachable, like untamed nature, who is yet, like nature, wholly magic, living impulse, and sparkling beauty.

And this has an immediate correspondence to something warm and throbbingly alive in our own house: in our own young daughter.

Translated from the German by Hildegard Nagel

1   Callimachus, "Hymn to Artemis." The passage preceding this tells us that the main gift the child asked of her father was a never-ending *parthenia* (condition of virginity or girlhood). Among the other gifts that she desired were a bow and arrows—though these, she says in the *Hymn,* she prefers to get from the Kyklopes—a saffron hunting dress, sixty nine-year-old ocean nymphs to be her companions, and the function of bringing light. Callimachus makes the child approximately three years old when she formulates these desires, but her fixation even then upon the age of nine presages the attributes of the future virgin huntress. This age is in the middle of what Freud termed the latency period of sexuality; it is also the time of an eager acquisition of mental and physical aptitudes, and of delight in the successful pursuit of what we, in all its sometimes cruel forms, have come to call sport. [Translator's Note]

2   Cf. *Antiche Religion,* p. 292, note 460. The present essay is supported by the material presented by Ludwig Deubner (*Attische Feste,* Berlin, 1932, pp. 204–208). Since writing this essay the site of the Sanctuary of Brauron/Bravona has been uncovered and a museum set up, which I have often visited. At this date [1971] this extremely valuable material has not been published, nor has the site of the "Cloister" of the "Little Bears" been found. It seems evident that only a very few girls of the very best Athenian families could have been sent there.

3   Cf. *Athene* (Spring Publications, 1978), p. 65.

4   Cf. *Dionysos* (Princeton, 1976), p. 155.

5   My translations from *Götter Griechenlands,* Frankfurt a/M.: Schulte-Bulmke.

NOTE: This paper, entitled "Mythologisches Mädchenbildnis," appeared originally in *DU: Schweizerische Monatsschrift* (Zürich), No. 5, May 1949, pp. 11f.; included in *Antike Religion,* Münschen, 1971, pp. 224f.

III

THE AMAZON PROBLEM

Translated from the German by Murray Stein

The old art gallery in Munich holds in its collection a marvelous antique vase of black background, which depicts the famous battle scene between Achilles and Penthesilea, Queen of the Amazons.[1] Dressed in a short chiton, the beautiful Amazon pleadingly lifts her gaze to the attacking hero, inexorably advancing, sword in hand. Her hands ward him off, pressing against his chest and forearm, while he, gazing fixedly over her head into the far unknown, completes his murderous work. Beside them the bloody slaughter rages on: a companion of the dying Queen winds her way into the final battle, while behind the two central figures a berserk fighter charges a new victim.

The Amazon theme fascinated the ancient Greeks. One aspect of its mystery is that, according to legends, the battle-eagerness of the hero transforms itself to love at the sight of his victim. But did she also love Achilles? Antiquity has nothing to say on this point. In the Renaissance, however, Torquato Tasso takes up the motif and affirms the love in his *Jerusalem Delivered*. Heinrich von Kleist adapted the theme once more in his *Penthesilea*. Here the Amazon princess literally tears to pieces her secretly beloved, Achilles, who also loves her in return; afterwards she gives herself to death.

Naturally, the Amazons never actually existed.[2] Yet not only the Greeks but the European Middle Ages never tired of inventing tales about them.[3] That the Amazon theme touches on the archetypal motif, in the Jungian sense, is pointed out by Alexander von Humboldt: "The poem of the Amazons," he writes, "has a specific tone running through it: it belongs to that uniform and narrow circle of dreams and ideas around which the poetic and religious imagination of all races of mankind, in every period, revolves."[4]

From the time of Homer[5] down to the latter days of Athenian culture, the legends of their devastating character traits blossomed throughout Asia Minor, Greece and North Africa. Even Aeschylus and the orators of the enlightened fourth century considered it a great

47

deed, worthy to be compared with the heroic feats of the Persian Wars, that Theseus overcame these bold conquerors and thereby saved Athens from destruction.

As is well-known, these mysterious women placed value neither on marriage in general nor on men and sons in particular. According to the dominant tradition, they inhabited the Doiantic fields through which the Pontic river, Thermodon, runs before it empties into the Black Sea. There in northern Anatolia, two queens stood at the head of their populous state. Men were either excluded entirely from this land or simply tolerated for procreative purposes. If allowed to remain, they were held in a position of social abasement and actual slavery, trusted only with the commonplace household tasks, such as the women would otherwise perform themselves (save child-bearing, of course). Forcibly crippling the arms or legs of boy-children, the women robbed the men of ability to bear arms and thereby rendered them harmless to the feminine ruling caste.

The legends, mainly transmitted by Strabo and Diodorus Siculus,[6] say that the women mutilated themselves as well. In early childhood they burned away the right breast of all their daughters. This allowed them greater ease in using the right arm, particularly for spear-casting and archery. Only women bore military arms, and they not only defended their own country but also raided the lands of their neighbors across the borders. On such occasions they became the founders of famous cities and sacred shrines along the Pontos, in Aiolia and in Ionia. These expeditions also gave them the opportunity to meet certain Greek heroes. Wild, terrifying warriors, they fought partly on foot, partly on horseback. For weapons they used the spear, the bow, the double-ax, and the "Pelta," a shield formed like a half-moon. Their dress, made of wild-animal hides, often shows the style of the Scythian horsemen, resembling (roughly) a modern ski-suit; as head-covering they wore a hat on the Phrygian model (just like the one later worn by the French Marianne!). At home they preferred to busy themselves with breeding horses, hunting and war-games. They trained their daughters from childhood in these activities.

According to Strabo, the Amazons would once a year, for two months in the spring, live with a group of men in the mountains, engaging in frequent sexual intercourse in the dark of night so that the fathers would remain anonymous. These encounters were then followed by a common sacrifice to Ares and to their chief Goddess, Artemis of Tauros, who as divine huntress, pursuing wild boars and

48

Ride the Monorail

The Monorail is one of the most fast, fun, and economical ways to travel in Seattle! Our services include commuter passes, corporate travel, and special event options. For more information visit www.seattlemonorail.com or call us at 206-905-2600.

SEATTLE CENTER MONORAIL

WELCOME ABOARD!

ROUNDTRIP

ADULT $ 4.00

06/21/08   14:22

22085   402   300906

PLEASE SEE REVERSE

446625

deer over Taygetos and Erymanthos, does not deny her own Amazon-like quality.

Ever since Friedrich Creuzer and after him Bachofen, scholars have presumed that this mythologem mirrors a matriarchal culture. In fact several lines of evidence do point to the Amazons as the favored daughters of the Anatolian Great Mother. This accounts for their role as founders of cities, since the city symbolizes the Great Mother motif. The Amazonian double-ax is also a symbol of the Great Mother, and according to Usener it stood over Cretan-Mycenean culture as the cross dominates Christendom. Moreover, the Pelta shield, in the shape of a half-moon, as well as the founding of temples, of which that of Artemis in Ephesus was the most famous, point to a Mother Goddess in the background. And not least important as evidence along this line of thought is the point that sexual intercourse occurred, so say the legends, without choice of male partner.

A close scrutiny of Greek mythology, especially of the later Hellenistic tradition, shows it swarming with Amazon figures. If not always referred to explicitly as Amazons, they can still be recognized as such by their detachment from men and by their enmity towards them. One thinks of the legends of the inhabitants of Lemnos. Led by their Queen, Hypsipyle, who was descended from the Amazon Myrine, they disposed of their husbands and the other men of the island by the expedient of murder and afterward themselves assumed authority over the island. To this category belong also the fleet-footed virgin huntresses: first, Atalante, the *puella pernix* ("swift maiden"); then, the wild Thracian, Harpalyke, of whom Virgil sang and who was named after the predatory wolf; also the *bellatrix* ("woman warrior") Camilla, and the lion-taming Kyrene with whom Apollo fell in love; finally Britomartis, the "sure shooter" as Kallimachos named her, who was followed for nine months throughout Crete by King Minos and finally eluded him through the famous ocean spring. Their names are numerous, but all of them present the image of Artemis, the great divine huntress.[7] These untouched, nymphlike, love-shy girls, who in most instances spell doom for a man, usually can be overcome only through the helpful mediation of a God or Goddess.

Amazons and Maenads

However, there is no mistaking a parallel between the Amazons and the wild Thracian Maenads of Bacchus. Except for Ares, who is their father, Dionysos is the only masculine deity who has a relationship (albeit a conflict-ridden one) with these women. This is not only because Dionysos is a God of women (so is Ares occasionally), nor because Dionysos (at least in his Thracian form) bears affinities to Ares[8] and under the cognomen *Enyalios* ("the warlike") reveals battling traits (Macrob. *Sat.*, I, 19). It is also because both Gods show an ecstatic tendency, Ares in his aggressive fury, Dionysos in the *mania* of a nature-intoxicated spirit. And finally, the similarity between the two groups of women rests upon Artemis, who herself betrays Bacchantic traits. She whom Homer[9] calls "the cheerful archer" storms drunkenly about with her golden bow and deadly arrows, her whole appearance fiercely aglow. The peaks of lofty mountains tremble and gloomy forests crash with frightful sound when the hunt rages; the earth and sea shiver; all about her swarm the fleet-footed nymphs, the howling hounds, and the shrill cries of the chase. Like Artemis, Dionysos was a God of the hunt,[10] and the Maenads were compared to hunting dogs and appear sometimes also as huntresses.[11]

Amazons can be transformed into Maenads, as happened on Samos. A group of them, beaten and chased by Dionysos from Ephesus, fled to Samos and were converted there.[12] Lyaios ("the loosener"), the great savior Dionysos, freed them from the bonds of Ares in order to lock them in his own. His bonds, however, were only temporary, for it belonged to the nature of Dionysos that as soon as he appeared among the human race and stirred it into frenzy, he would disappear.

Another association between Amazons and Maenads inheres in the figure of Dionysos' wet-nurse, Hipta,[13] an ancient Goddess of Asia Minor. According to modern research, she is identical with the warlike Anatolian Hepat, the chief Goddess of the Hurrite pantheon. She has the character of a *potnia hippōn,* "a sovereign of the horses," and according to folk-etymology the names of the Amazons that contain "hippo" are supposed to point back to her "horsey," thus martial, character.[14]

We shall later look at a further parallel between the Amazons and Dionysos: the *androgyny* of the God and of the Amazons, here a God in a fluttering double-girdled garment, there the women astride their horses, a picture of double hermaphroditism.[15]

Amazons and Ares

Regarding the origin of the Amazons, antiquity believed that they were the daughters of Ares, God of war, and the nymph Harmonia,[16] who conceived them in the holy Wood of Akmon, near the river Thermodon. The descent of Harmonia is usually credited to Ares and Aphrodite. As such, she becomes a more youthful version of Aphrodite, who herself took the related name "Harma"[17] in Delphi. So the Goddess of love is also the mother of the Amazons.

The name Harmonia signifies properly structured order and balanced relation of the parts to the whole. The old Greek word for the correctly joined-together parts of a war chariot was *harma,* an expression etymologically related to the name Harmonia.[19] Harmonia, daughter of the Goddess of love and the potent God of war, represents the fruit of the union of opposites. But the name Harmonia also, naturally, points to its latent counter-pole, disharmony, the contribution of her paternity; but not only of her paternity, since the antinomy love/war was originally contained within the Great Goddess herself, whether called Ishtar, Astarte, Anat, Aphrodite or whatever. In this connection Ishtar is best known as one who explicitly binds the poles together within her own nature. But Aphrodite, too, bears the marks of these warlike character traits, so much so that in Sparta there was an armed statue of Aphrodite Areia.

How should we characterize this raging Ares, the God in whom the warlike aspect of the Great Goddess appears as split-off animus? Is he, as appears at first glance, merely the God of massacre, military turmoil, murderous warfare?

There are witnessing etymological associations.[20] The name Ares is connected to the Greek word *arsen* = masculine, and to *arsenoma* = masculine seed. From the Indo-Germanic root *eres* one can trace branches that include meaningful relations among "to flow," "moisture," "dew," words meaning "lively movement," also "to wander about aimlessly," enraged," and "stirred up." Also belonging to this etymological nexus are such items as the Old Norse *ras* = course, race; Anglo-Saxon *roes* = course, race, attack; Middle High German *rasen* = to rage. In addition, the Old Indic word for "bull" belongs to the branch meaning "to wet," "to spill seed." To the variations on the Indo-Germanic root *eres* belong the stems that include words for being angry, wishing evil, conducting oneself aggressively, being envious, and also the Vedic words for poet and seer in the sense of "frenzy."

These etymological associations describe the psychological state of the libido in the Ares configuration: flowing and moving as the active, masculine impregnator on the one hand, and as a disruptive aggressor on the other. The positive side of Ares, the fructifying force, sinks into the background before the negative side. In the

51

Homeric Hymn to Ares,[21] however, he is called "the rampart of Olympus," the father of Nike (Victory), the helper of Themis (Law), and "the leader of the most righteous men." There he is invoked: "Grant me the blessed strength and courage to live without suffering, in peaceful orderliness, far from the cry of enemies and delivered from an overwhelming fate." This very God, who is the classical instigator of lethal strife, grants the "blessed strength and courage" to *avoid* the strife of warfare. In psychological terms, the very affect that drives me into a berserk state of unconsciousness is supposed to form the "Olympian rampart," which holds the quarreling Gods, i.e., the opposites, within the walls or *temenos*.

Athene

When the affect-laden, overpowering urge of aggression is resisted and integrated into consciousness, the dark God shows his fructifying side: destructive psychic energies transform, *Dea concedente* ("with the help of the Goddess"), into constructive energies. For this interiorizing process the heroic battler needs the Goddess, since the anima is the psychological factor that contains and reflects. This point is illustrated by Pallas Athene, "the daughter of the almighty father," in a scene in the *Iliad* (I, 193ff.). The insulting words of Agamemnon, who has already stolen the lovely Briseis, enrage Achilles; he leaps to his feet, his hand slides to sword. Then for a split-second he reflects: should he strike his taunter to the ground, or should he use his power to conquer himself? At this moment he feels a tug *from behind*. He turns his head and meets the blazing eyes of the Goddess. She tells him that if he can retain his composure at this moment his antagonist will later be forced to give him three-fold satisfaction. At this, Achilles thrusts the sword back into its scabbard. He alone has seen the Goddess.[22]

This incident points up the helpful quality of the hero's anima: she helps him detach from the chaotic affect through reflection, which means "bending backwards."[23] As the Amazons 'belong' to their father, Ares, so Athene, generally known as the pugnacious battle maiden of the Mycenaean Greeks, belongs to her father, Zeus. The Parthenos repeatedly declares herself obedient to the father. In the *Eumenides* Aeschylus has her say: "A mother did not bear me, for my heart belongs to the masculine in all things. The marriage bond is not for me; I reserve myself totally for my father."

"Athene is a woman, but as if she were a man," remarks Walter F. Otto.[24] "Athene possesses the spirit of action. It belongs to her essence to associate herself with men, always thinking about them, always near them. She reveals herself to those who are separated from the erotic not through prudery but through the austerity and clarity of active effort."[25]

It strikes me as noteworthy that this archetypal pattern associates mythologically with a feminine deity, and it reminds me of an observation Jung once made. In response to a remark that many so-called anima types (women) have a certain masculinity about them, he said:

> It is the soul-image of the man. The unconscious-feminine of the man does not, after all, lack all semblance of masculinity. Therefore a man projects his anima upon a woman who has something a little masculine about her. She can then be a friend to him, and the relationship is not merely heterosexual; it is also a friendship, and that is essential.[26]

Stages in the Development of Amazons

Returning to our main theme, I wish to propose several hypothetical stages of development that lead to the appearance of the Amazon figures.

1. At a certain stage in the development of collective consciousness, an archetypal picture appears of a hermaphroditic divinity who bears feminine features but also exhibits signs of martial frenzy, a trait that later gets separated out as distinctively masculine. War and love appear united in her. At this stage of consciousness the antinomies are near one another—a primitive, labile condition with rapid and unexpected mood swings.

Evidently, the archetypal image of the feminine by which a man apprehends the being of woman[27] possesses a martial aspect. For whether or not a tribe of woman soldiers actually existed is not the question; the *archetypal* image of these martial beings exists as a psychic reality and refers to the psychological experience of man with woman. It is woman as experienced by man over the course of millennia. At the same time, however, this reality exists a priori, since "Goddess" refers to the archetype prior to all experience, possessing real but unmanifested Being.[28]

"Militat omnis amans" (all lovers are warriors).[29] Is it mere accident that the poems of the Troubadours and love-singers circle around the

53

theme of the love-war? Is this a mere 'poetic' metaphor, or a frightful reality? As Jung remarks,[30] for woman love is not mere sentiment (such a concept of love applies only to man), but a will to live, which is frightfully unsentimental and even capable of calling forth the most chilling forms of self-sacrifice. *On ne badine pas avec L'amour* (Do not trifle with love); this holds true especially for 'Lady Soul.' In this connection one is reminded of the suicidal end of von Kleist, the genius-author of *Penthesilea*.

2. The second phase of development severs the martial spirit from the original Goddess. A separate masculine divinity comes into existence, in our case Ares, who embodies the martial spirit but also retains a double aspect as we have noted.

3. After this division into separate components, the love Goddess Aphrodite-Harmonia unites with the war God. The fruit of this *hieros gamos*, a *conjunctio oppositorum*, is a new hermaphrodite with feminine characteristics. This daughter is also warlike and shy of men.

I say "shy of men" and not "hostile to men" because the Amazons' hostility is a reaction against the Greek heroes, particularly against Theseus and Herakles. Plutarch (*Thes.* 26) in particular emphasizes the friendly reception Theseus found among the Amazons: not only did they not flee from him, they brought him gifts. He, however, invited the profferer of the gifts on board ship, and no sooner had she set foot on deck than he weighed anchor and sailed away with her. Similarly Herakles: his ninth labor was to capture the girdle of the Amazon Queen for Princess Admete. The Queen was said to have received this girdle from her father, Ares. Apollodoros (5, 9, 6) reports that Queen Hippolyta received him cordially and, learning the purpose of his visit, promised him the girdle. But Hera (as usual) interferes. In the form of an Amazon she spreads the rumor that Herakles wants to rob the Queen. A battle follows, Herakles kills the Queen and steals her girdle. The Greek word makes clear that this girdle is a military garment, not the usual woman's girdle. The girdle as military garment appears in folk beliefs[31] as the emblem of power and authority; associated with it also is the idea of tying and loosening. Psychologically, the girdle of Ares symbolizes *the bond between daughter and war-spirit of the father*; it also makes of the daughter a hermaphrodite, a metaphor further reinforced by the circularity of the girdle.

From the fifth century on, vases from southern Italy show a separation between the battle themes and the friendly, conciliatory themes.

Here the Aphroditic side of the Amazons, previously repressed, comes forward again. Because the reappearance of the Aphroditic aspect indicates a development in the realm of the collective unconscious, we may deduce a similar change in collective consciousness. In fact, beginning at this time, an increased interest in the world of the woman shows itself; this development reaches its high point in the Hellenistic period.[32]

From the point of view of masculine psychology, the Amazons represent a compensatory anima figure who is not disposed to throw herself at a man's feet; this anima figure is self-sufficient and independent of him. She violates the fashionable image of the meek, cuddly, helpless, frightened turtle-dove who, without fail, confirms for her man that he is the crown of all creation. In his encounter with the Amazon, the man's customarily unimaginative erotic pattern soon reaches the limits of its resources.

The Artemis Archetype

We may regard the Amazon myth as an 'answer' from the central Mediterranean archetype of the Great Mother to the arrival of the Zeus-religion of the Indo-European invaders. It represents an antithesis to the more patriarchal spirit of these strangers, who overcame the autochthonous population and set themselves up as a nobility class. On the other hand, the mythologem of burning out the right breast plays the role symbolically of a renunciation of the *purely* feminine and the integration of a masculine component. This integration of the masculine is concretely expressed in their learning 'male' crafts and engaging in typically masculine activities. Psychologically, this represents the integration of the animus in its form of directed power, i.e., as will and deed. Emma Jung writes:

> For the primitive woman, or the young woman, or for the primitive in every woman, a man distinguished by physical prowess becomes an animus figure. Typical examples are the heroes of legend, or present-day sports celebrities, cowboys, bull fighters, aviators, and so on. For more exacting women, the animus figure is a man who accomplishes deeds, in the sense that he directs his power toward something of great significance. The transitions here are usually not sharp, because power and deed mutually condition one another.[33]

The figure of Artemis, as she has appeared since the time of Homer, we may consider the product of the confluence of the two religious streams. Her secret androgyny reveals itself not only in her huntress's garb but also in her theriomorphic appearance as a horned bitch.

The anima-quality of the Homeric Artemis has been incomparably formulated by W. F. Otto:

> It is the starry-bright, flaming, dazzling, agile life and being whose very strangeness draws the man; the more coy it shows itself the stronger its attraction. It is the crystal-clear being whose roots are still hidden in animal nature; the childlike-simple, yet unpredictable, one; the one made of sweet lovability and diamond hardness: maidenly, flighty, unclaspable, and showing sudden harsh opposition; playful, dancing, joking, and (before one can see it coming) implacably earnest; lovingly caring and tenderly concerned with the magic smile that makes up for eternal punishment, yet untamed even to the point of committing dreadful and gruesome acts.[34]

This eternal image of the paradoxical feminine corresponds in all its traits to untamed, detached, virgin Nature, whose divine inaccessiblity assumes the traits of the *kallista parthenos* ("beautiful maiden").

Originally Artemis was the great female sovereign of nature. In the time of Homer her archaic traits fell into the background, particularly those of the Great Mother who gives birth to all life, feeds it, and in the end receives it back again into her kingdom. Instead, the sisterly, virginal aspect advances into the foreground. True, she is still maternally and tenderly concerned, but in a more differentiated way than mere brood-protection. In this peculiar aspect she is the guardian of all "becoming," of all future developments: she stands near those who give birth; she instructs children and educates them; she watches over the growing youth. The virginal-sisterly aspect of her character, however, also includes her coyness, hardness and cruelty. What is for mankind so intimate—the relationship between the sexes—remains totally alien to her. She reserves her worst punishment for sexual attackers. She represents the anima "within," whose realization is primarily psychological and not biological. Homer names her "shooter of arrows" and "she who strikes at a distance"; this implies the aiming and striking at the essential center of the self, and includes goal-directedness, goal-consciousness, hitting the bulls-eye, and reaching for far-out possibilities.[35]

The spear of the Goddess is a *tellum passionis* ("spear of passion"), for all passion means fundamentally a search for self.[36] Sexual abstinence, represented by Artemis, warns the man from a natural, but fatal, misunderstanding: all too often his concept of a relationship to a woman is limited to its sexual aspect. But this is the area of Artemis' counterpart, Aphrodite: sexual relations, procreation, birth. For the man, Aphrodite is the anima "without," the one leading him into outer entanglements. From her comes, as Otto says,[37] the almighty desire that forgets the whole world for the sake of the beloved, that can tear the noblest bonds and break the most sacred trust to be united with its object. This anima works by enchantment. Artemis, on the contrary, works by inspiration and enthusiasm. Aphrodite's *raison d'être* is grounded in the presence of a partner; without him she is superfluous. Artemis, however, is a maiden, independent and self-sufficient.

We must understand virginity in two ways. On the one hand, it connotes the characteristic detachment of youth, including uncommittedness and irresponsible wandering. This kind of virginity in a woman constitutes the companion-piece to the masculine *puer aeternus*. The *puella* is a hermaphrodite; she has boyish characteristics. Naturally, she is not conscious of a union of the opposites; rather, she is contaminated, an unconscious mixture. It is well known that this youthful period of transition must be buried at a certain point.

The other form of "being-a-maiden" occurs in the woman who is self-sufficient, whether she be wife, mother, or whatever. She is a person "at one with herself," as Esther Harding puts it.[38] This is the essence of Artemis, symbolically understood. She is precisely not the feminine counterpart to a masculine divinity; *her divinity belongs to herself*. On the level of personal feminine psychology, this form of virginity is that attitude that makes a woman independent of the "one oughts," those conventional beliefs and practices to which her own viewpoint does not accede.[39] The motive force behind such an independent attitude is not personal; it is directed toward a super-personal goal, toward a relationship to the Goddess.[40]

Now we can understand the divine Amazon, Artemis, as a new leading-image (*Leitbild*) in a woman's process of becoming conscious. From the point of view of masculine psychology, the Goddess represents an incarnation of the anima;[41] her daughter-likeness indicates an approach to the *personal conscious,* just as Christ, the son, stands closer to mankind than Yahweh, the father.

I see the next stage in the development of our myth exemplified in the association of the Amazons with Theseus, the famous Greek hero and King of Athens. For the first and only time in Greek mythology one hears of a close relationship between one of these daughters of Ares and a specific man. (Of course, the wife of Herakles, Deianeira, had an Amazon name, though she was not herself descended from the Amazon race. Deianeira means "man-destroyer"; Apollodoros (1.8.1.) says she was a horse-master and also "a friend of military practice," as well as a daughter of Dionysos.)

If the king figure represents the dominants within the prevailing collective attitude,[42] then the marriage of Theseus indicates that a new aspect of the anima has been included in collective consciousness. This implies a new style of relatedness, or eros. In the person of the Amazon Queen a *new leading motif of femininity* manifests itself; I would call it the *Artemistic* motif. I understand by it a greater firmness, self-sufficiency, demureness, and independence in the essence of woman.

This marriage did not last long; Theseus switched his favors to the Cretan Princess, Phaedra. Daughter of Minos and Pasiphaë and sister of Ariadne, Phaedra's origin looks back to the mother-religion that prevailed before the invasion of the Indo-Europeans. This highly unfortunate marriage causes a regression: at the wedding of Theseus and the Cretan Princess, the Amazon was dramatically slaughtered.[43] Nevertheless, this first close association between King and Amazon is not allowed to pass without leaving a sign of its existence. A remarkable son, Hippolytus, remained behind as tangible witness to the Amazon. Through the literary tragedy of that name by Euripides, Hippolytus achieves immortality, although perhaps he could have gained it on his own as a typical *puer aeternus* figure.

Now, instead of a daughter standing in the foreground as was customary with the Amazons, it is a son. This son, however, bears the same character traits as his maternal forebears:[44] a boundless urge toward untamed nature with its mountains, forests and animals; a fateful association with horses, also expressed in his highly significant name; a bachelor's typical brittleness and hostility to Aphrodite, and a weakness for hunting and sports in general. Ovid calls him *vir amazonius*. His chastity, too, which was a byword in antiquity, identifies him with his maternal inheritance. The chastity of Hippolytus should not be confused with the Christian virtue: it is not acquired but inherited, a natural state of virginity, a sort of natural innocence.[45] Hippolytus is therefore maidenly in the same sense as were his Amazon forebears, despite their promiscuity. So too women today may remain identified with maidenhood even after years of marriage and the bearing of children.

Of course this attitude of chastity associates him with *kallista parthenos,* the divine Amazon Artemis, toward whom his whole life is oriented. And she, in turn, loves the youth as her masculine reflection. This fateful tie leads him to disaster. What fascinated him about her was doubtless her mysterious androgynous character, through which she is feminine as well as masculine, mother as well as father, therefore also complete and a bearer of the projection of the self. Psychical completeness is still, for Hippolytus, to be found in a feminine archetype.

We remember that in the country of the Amazons sons were usually murdered, crippled, or given back to their fathers to raise. This treatment does not lend itself to happy prognostications for the sons of Amazons.

The death-aspect of such mothers—Herodotus (4, 110) calls them *androktonoi,* i.e., man-killers—is evident in the collection of sayings about Spartan mothers handed down by Plutarch.[46] These mothers seem to have been nothing but brood-mares of warriors, producing sons only to send them out to a probable death. At a certain stage in the development of masculine consciousness, this type of anima is valuable: she wakes in a man the mood for conquest and struggle and battle. Another of her aspects materializes in the realization of risky and daring enterprises such as colonization and the founding of sanctuaries and cities. Here the creation of objective values has its source of energy in the Amazon archetype. In this connection we may recall that the conquest of South America by the Spaniards and Portuguese was partly stimulated by the hope of discovering there the legendary realm of these militant women. Columbus reported on this matter already after his first voyage, and the name "Amazon" for the longest river on the continent is a vestige of this expectation.

The Amazon and Creativity

If we consider the mutilation of the Amazons' sons from the psychological point of view, the 'mother' represents in the son the feminine unconscious, the primordial opposite to consciousness, whence derives the motive for mutilation. Generally speaking, this mutilation is a curtailment or sacrifice of the active masculine principle; this transforms the man into a hermaphroditic being—that is, it forcibly activates his feminine side. His androgyny is the consequence of the weakening of his masculinity, just as the androgyny of the Amazon is based on a deprivation of a part of her femininity.

The creative principle personifies itself in the hermaphrodite, bringing to pass not merely an association of psychological opposites but a union of the feminine receptive and masculine powers. For masculine psychology the creative process means rapprochement with one's femininity, or anima. We find this illustrated in mythology by the serving position of Herakles vis-à-vis Omphale, the Lydian Queen, another Amazon figure. On vase paintings we see the hero dressed in the flowery tunic of the Queen, while she has put on his lion skin. She forces him to take up spinning and hits him with her sandal when she is dissatisfied with his work.

I believe there is a hint that our myth as a whole hangs together with a creative fantasy in the collective unconscious; this fantasy later presses concretely through into consciousness. Let us explore this creative aspect by returning for a moment to the land of the Amazons' origin.

The *hieros gamos* between Ares and Harmonia occurred in the grove of Akmon. Akmon was one of the Idaic Daktyls, "the Tom Thumb (*Däumling*) who lives in the wood."[47] The Daktyls were the first well-known metallurgists on earth; they learned their art from the Idaic *méter* (Great Mother), whose helpers they were. Akmon is the personification of the anvil. Then there is also a circumstantial association with the river Thermodon, which means "altogether warm."[48] Furthermore, the immediate neighbors of the Amazons, to the West, were the legendary Chalyber, the blacksmith folk *par excellence* of antiquity. They were supposedly named after Chalybs, a son of Ares. Chalybs means "steel" in Greek.

Mythical smiths traditionally have some form of physical defect; they limp, or are one-legged, or have only one eye; sometimes they are dwarfish or unspeakably ugly. These cripplings seem to relate to an initiation ritual into the mystery societies of the smiths.[49] Mircea Eliade remarks in *The Forge and the Crucible* that the divinities who were depicted as invalids (e.g., Hephaistos) were associated with the "strangers," the "mountain folk," the "subterranean dwarfs"—i.e., with mountain populations of unfamiliar character who were surrounded by mystery and often identified as uncanny, mighty smiths.[50] This holds true precisely for the Chalyber: the area around the Pontic Thermodon is not only unusually mountainous and forested but also rich in minerals, and the inhabitants practised the metallurgical craft (according to Valerius Flaccus) in underground caverns. It is noteworthy, also, that modern research[51] places the birthplace of ironworking in the mountainous region of Armenia, between Tauros and Kaukasus, in the region of the mythical Amazonic kingdom. In the annotation to the third canto, verse 189, of the *Iliad* the Amazon Queen Otrere ("the swift") is identified as the daughter of the nymph Armenia and Ares. Finally, one notes that Lysias[52] presents the Amazons as the only nation that armed its troops with iron weapons.

The significance of the invention of iron metallurgy can hardly be over-estimated. For the first time tools became so inexpensive that they could be easily acquired for the improvement of the environment, especially for clearing the land and tilling the soil.[53] The appearance of iron altered the face of the earth. Not only did it provide a new material for military applications, weaponry; it also gave mankind a better weapon with which to wage the fight for survival. The fundamental thought of metallurgy lies in the idea of bringing incomplete nature to completion through an accelerated process.[54] Metallurgy therefore is a kind of proto-alchemy. This cultural advance through iron metallurgy implies that the Amazon archetype plays a role in the expansion of consciousness.[55]

Our examination of the literary tradition of these warrior women brings out those characteristics of temperament that, in our culture, we call masculine. In the eyes of patriarchal Greek society the hunt, horsebreeding, warfare and colonization—the highest masculine values—brought about a higher valuation of the feminine precisely within this scale of values. But from the feminine point of view, this higher valuation takes place by approximating masculine ideals or by largely obliterating the culturally determined, psychic sex differentiation, a process we can follow in our own contemporary society. The real purpose of this obliterating process may be to prove that it is *not* the solution to the problematical relation of the sexes.

As Jung puts it in *Answer to Job,*[56] the masculine ideal implies perfection, which is at the same time a fundamental offense against the feminine principle of incompleteness, or all-inclusiveness. The more the feminine deviates in the direction of the masculine, Jung says, the more woman loses the possibility to compensate for the masculine proclivity toward perfection. The resulting situation is ideal from a masculine point of view, but it is threatened by a complete reversal into its opposite.

61

During the mutual assimilation process, as we are now experiencing it, a host of prejudices about earlier sex-roles will have to be thrown overboard. The standard definition of the difference between masculinity and feminity is the result of a massive collective projection. The projection does not lie where a first glance indicates, i.e., in biological or sociological conditions, but in the psychic polarity between Luna and Sol.

To the most unyielding prejudices of our society belong those concerning the typical relations between the sexes. Within the collective consciousness of the Christian West, it is taken for granted that the man is the dominant partner, the bold, objective, active, aggressive one. The woman, however, is characterized *eo ipso* by subjectivity, passivity, receptivity, and sensitiveness. Thus, certain character traits get accepted collectively and become constitutive for the one sex and bluntly denied to the other; or, should the other show them, such behavior gets labeled abnormal. Even psychology is often quick to apply the term "animus" (as an epithet of contempt) to an aggressive woman.

This sexual dichotomy can just as well be non-existent: man and woman can both have identical traits, which in our culture would get divided into masculine and feminine; or there might be a complete reversal of sex differentiation, as in the myth of the Amazons. Credit for elucidating this point belongs to the ethnological field workers, especially to Margaret Mead.[57]

In the northern part of our culture these prejudices are more or less falling apart. As is usual in such times of declining culture norms, a widespread sense of disorientation has set in. There is confusion as to what is masculine and what feminine. Our helplessness before this problem shows also in the scarcity of possible solutions. Only two are prevalent: either a kind of obliteration of the sex role through a sell-out of the woman to the traditional role of the man, or a complete inversion, as exemplified by the Amazon myth.

Pseudo-solutions—such as those practised in Scandinavia where a so-called division of labor exists, with the husband caring for household and children for half the day and pursuing a career during the other half—are unsatisfactory. Given the stage of our psychological consciousness, they are too concrete. They keep the problem fixed on the level where it appears as a psychic projection and where its solutions are literal. What is called for is the integration of the opposite sexes within. That demands a full-fledged transformation of the whole person through an expansion of consciousness, and not a sexual conversion to an opposite role, an enantiodromia, so typical for purely unconscious conflicts.

One can see a materialization of this problem in the recent change in physical build, especially among young women. It is reinforced by clothing fashions. The approximation to the young-boy phenotype is astonishing. Presumably we are emerging into an age of the hermaphrodite. Does this mean we will see concrete expressions of the preliminary stages of a greater integration in each individual of animus and anima? But is it not a misunderstood psychic reality expressing itself concretely, the bodily manifestation of a process in the soul, a process in which such bodily changes come about through the displacement of psychic energies?

Our time shows itself seemingly favorably disposed to what I earlier described as the Artemis female type. But this type has no ready model at hand, and the Artemis-influenced women of today are in many cases simply animus-possessed. This too may be a transition stage whose purpose is to stimulate consciousness by creating a necessary disharmony within a passive attitude. The persistent, self-affirming prototype in our culture still remains that of the childbearer and mother. Beside this *idée force* all others fade away or show themselves at closer scrutiny to be merely approximations to the patriarchal spirit. For this reason, women for whom motherhood would be second-best become mothers anyway as their first choice, merely because motherhood and femininity are still identified. For such women it would be a great advantage if they grasped the notion that they might in reality be standing under the star of the Goddess of the Hunt; accepting this aspect of the transcendent personality is for them a precondition for the later experience of Aphroditic eros.

Artemis is not a mother in the sense of giving birth but rather of protecting the seedling, the new thing that is only beginning to develop. This holds true both in the concrete and in the spiritual sense. The form of behavior that expresses itself through her includes also an *impetus in the realm of feeling*. I would call it "Artemistic eros." This form of eros is a decisive condition for the development of a man's relationship to the anima. A too unconscious-passive condition of the woman drives him compensatorily into a too greatly extraverted activism, which leaves his soul neglected.

But here we touch on an unexpected, profound difficulty. The two Goddesses, Aphrodite and Artemis, in a metaphorical sense a mother

and a daughter, each an archetypal pattern of femininity, stand hostile
to each other already in antiquity. The hatred they cherish for each
other comes to a drastic head in Euripides' *Hippolytus*. This conflict
between feminine dominants constitutes the religious essence of the
tragedy.[58] Similar to Yahweh in *Job,* the female Goddesses want to
remain unconscious of their shadow sides. Giving a reason for the
catastrophe, Artemis makes the following speech at the end of the
play:

> For it was Aphrodite who, to satisfy her resentment, willed that all this
> should happen; and there is a law among Gods, *that no one of us should
> seek to frustrate another's purpose, but let well alone.*[59]

If one were to ask, for what type of man is the Artemistic eros an
essential condition for development of the anima, I should answer by
referring to Hippolytus: especially for the *puer aeternus,* whose religious background M.-L. von Franz has sketched in such an impressive
way.[60] With Euripides the intra-divine conflicts lacks a resolution and
therefore leaves the *puer aeternus* without a solution to his dilemma.
Therein lies a probable reason why the incarnation of the femine
God-image, and *eo ipso* of the anima, has remained stuck more or less
since antiquity.[61]

What we said about motherhood leads to a further reflection.
Next to the threat of annihilation through atomic and chemical warfare, the population explosion is our most pressing threat. Is it far-
fetched to think that nature itself, which compensates the lack of
instinct in consciousness, will intervene in this fateful process? I am
led to imagine that through the constellation of a femininity represented by the archetype of the Divine Huntress the heretofore stubbornly predominant *leitmotiv* of motherhood may become obsolete.
Perhaps even a lot of what we call in psychotherapy "negative mother-
complex in women" gets misvalued, because our consciousness is still
too prejudiced to see Artemis and the Amazon in the archetypal background.

Translated from the German by Murray Stein

1   Munich, Museum antiker Kleinkunst, Nr. 2688 (circa. 450 B. C.); cf. also, C. Kerényi,
    The Heroes of the Greeks, New York, 1959, Plate 73.
2   Toepffer (in Pauly, *Realencyclopädie d. Class. Altertumswissensch.,* Vol. 1, under "Ama-
    zones") remarks that this is one of the most difficult and most disputed problems in the
    study of Greek mythology.

3 Cf. also R. Henning, "Über die voraussichtlich völkerkundlichen Grundlagen der Amazonensagen und deren Verbreitung," in *Zeitschrift für Ethnologie*, 72 (1940), pp. 362–71; and A. Rosenthal, "The Isle of the Amazons: A Marvel of Travellers," in *Journal of the Warburg and Courtauld Institute*, I, 1937.

4 In *Kritische Untersuchungen*, I, Berlin, 1852, p. 275.

5 Homer, *Iliad*, Bk. 3, 184 ff; Bk. 6, 186.

6 Diodorus Siculus II, 45, 1 ff; Strabo 11, 5, 1; on the founding of the temple in Ephesus: Kall. *hymn in Dian.* 237 ff.

7 Cf. K. Hoenn, *Artemis*, Zürich, 1946, pp. 19, 28, 143.

8 *Der Kleine Pauly, Lexikon der Antike,* Vol. 2, Stuttgart, 1967, cf. article on "Dionysos."

9 Homer, *Hym.* 27.

10 Euripides, *Bacchae,* 1189ff.

11 Cf. W. F. Otto, *Dionysus,* Bloomington, 1956, p. 109.

12 Plutarch, *Quaest. Graec.* 56.

13 *Kleine Pauly.*

14 Lysias (Epitaph. 4), bringing out their valor and bravery, asserts that the Amazons *invented horseback riding* and were the only nation to employ iron weapons.

15 M. Delcourt, *Hermaphrodite,* London, 1961, p. 26.

16 Apollodorus Rhodius II, 990ff.

17 Plutarch, *Amat.* 23.

18 Scholium ad Hom. *Iliad,* III, 189.

19 J. Wiesner, *Olympos,* Darmstadt, 1960, p. 185. Etymologically *harmonia* = unification, juncture, bond, order. The derivative verb *harmonizo* = to bring together, to form, shape. The essential root is the common Indo-Germanic *ar* = to join, to unite. Generally, this syllable indicates the *unification of opposing things or different things into an ordered whole.* Related is the noun *harma* = chariot, esp. war-chariot, team (of horses). Also: Latin *arma* = weapons, armor; *armentum* = herd, flock; arm. *y-arma* = fitting, fitted; old Indic *irma* = front, bow of a ship; Latin *armus* = the upper arm; got. *arms* = arm. Cf. H. Frisk, *Griechisches Etymologisches Wörterbuch,* Heidelberg, 1960, "harmonia."

20 Cf. J. Pokorny, *Indogermanisches Etymologisches Wörterbuch,* Bern, 1959, p. 336f.

21 Homer, *Hym.* 8.

22 Homer, *Iliad*, Bk. 1, 193ff. Cf. also W. F. Otto, *The Homeric Gods,* N.Y., 1954, p. 48.

23 C.G. Jung, *CW* 8, §241.

24 Otto, *Gods* (my translation from the German), p. 24.

25 Ibid.

26 C.G. Jung, *Childrens' Dreams Seminar,* Zürich, 1939–40, private limited printing, p. 65.

27 C.G. Jung, *CW* 7, §298ff.

28 C.G. Jung, *CW* 9/2, §41; cf. also Emma Jung and M.-L. von Franz, *Die Graalslegende in psychologischer Sicht,* Zürich, 1960, pp. 66ff.

29 Ovid, *Amor.,* 1, 9, 1.

30 C.G. Jung, *CW* 10, §261ff.

31 *Handwörterbuch des deutschen Aberglaubens,* Vol. 3, Berlin, 1930/31, cf. article on "Gürtel."

32 The Amazon presents not only the exaggeration of a latent possibility within the feminine psyche but also the absolute reversal of predominating sexual roles in Classical Greece. The Greek woman was more or less enslaved: her relation to her family, her relation to her husband (whom she certainly did not choose), and her position in society at large were all of a piece in this respect. With no chance for education, she lived under virtual house arrest. If it happened that she was superfluous in the family, i.e., unmarriageable, she was sold into slavery by her father or brother. Should such a likelihood be obvious at birth, her father would refuse to recognize her and thrust her out to die. Greek society of the classical period offered no opportunity for independence or self-sufficiency to an adult woman of good family; no middle way existed between either becoming the mother of a brood of children or becoming an old maid, which was a burden to others and a family rarity. This repressive attitude in society implies an equal

unrelatedness to the inner world of the feminine unconscious, which reacts on its part in
a rejecting, aggressive way, thus underlining its autonomy towards consciousness. (cf. U.
E. Paoli, *Die Frau im alten Hellas*, Bern, 1955, pp. 40ff.)

33 Emma Jung, *Animus and Anima*, Spring Publications, 1957, p. 3.
34 Otto, *Gods* (my translation from the German), pp. 89–90.
35 E. Jung and von Franz, p. 87.
36 Cf. C.G. Jung, *CW* 16, §353ff.
37 Otto, *Gods*, p. 96.
38 E. Harding, *Women's Mysteries*, N.Y., 1955, p. 125.
39 Ibid.
40 Ibid., p. 126.
41 M.-L. von Franz, *A Psychological Interpretation of the Golden Ass of Apuleius*, Spring Publications, Chapter V, p. 13.
42 C.G. Jung, *CW* 14, §349ff.
43 Apollodorus, *Epit.* 1. 17.
44 Cf. W. Fauth, *Hippolytos und Phaidra*, Abhandl. d. Akad. d. Wiss. u. d. Lit., Mainz, 1958, p. 574.
45 K. Kerényi, *Apollon*, Düsseldorf, 1953, p. 58.
46 Plutarch, *Mor.* 24c seq.
47 Cf. B. Hemberg, "Die idäischen Daktylen," in *Eranos 50* (1952), pp. 44–59.
48 Cf. R. Malamud, "Zum 'Hippolytos' des Euripides," Diploma Thesis, C.G. Jung Institute, Zürich, 1968.
49 M. Eliade, *The Forge and the Crucible*, London, 1962, p. 105.
50 Ibid.
51 R. J. Forbes, *Studies in Ancient Technology*, Vol. 9, Leiden, 1964, p. 216.
52 Epitaph. 4.
53 Forbes, Vol. 8, p. 30.
54 Eliade.
55 C.G. Jung, *CW* 8, §111.
56 C.G. Jung, *CW* 11, §627.
57 M. Mead, *Sex and Temperament in Three Primitive Societies*, p. 205.
58 Malamud.
59 Euripides, *Hippolytus*, Penguin Books, 1953, p. 66, 1327–30.
60 M.-L. von Franz, "Über religiöse Hintergründe des Puer-Aeternus-Problems," in *The Archetype*, Basel, 1964.
61 M.-L. von Franz, *Aurora Consurgens*, Zürich, 1957, p. 174.

IV

HEPHAISTOS: A PATTERN OF INTROVERSION

The murals on the walls of the Detroit Museum of Art, commissioned by Ford and executed by Diego Rivera, depict scenes in the life of the industrial worker: heavily muscled men wielding wrenches and hammers, massed together around glowing furnaces and along endless assembly lines, some of them wearing gas-masks, others struggling mightily with glowing ingots of red-hot steel. Neatly dressed managers of the industry stand off to one side plotting how further to direct this mighty force of labor to their best advantage. In some of the upper panels, heavy-breasted primitive-looking women are bearing children, the next generation of exploitable workers. The whole of this impressive painting is suffused in a noxious, greenish light that gives the scenes a distinctly underworld tone. Ford, it is rumored, was not pleased when he saw what his money had paid for.

The Marxist image of the proletarian worker-masses may be largely a Hephaistian fantasy: the rejected of the earth, by whose labor and sweat civilization has grown; class-conscious and seething with pyromaniacal resentments and grudges; endlessly creative and the source of most of the world's supply of genius; restless, volcanically explosive and ready to take up arms against tyrannical masters, yet not lovers of war and strife but rather peacemakers and natural humanitarians; simple as fire itself and equally energetic. As the proletarian worker is seen by the Marxist to be the workhorse of industrial society, so is Hephaistos the only Olympian God who works. The workers of the world unite under the banner of Hephaistos. Bearing something of the mark of an inferior child who has to take up a trade, Hephaistos stands on the fringes of the power circles that govern the Olympian world, a servant-artisan figure who builds the palaces of the Gods "with skilful hands"[1] and sometimes plays the court buffoon to the great amusement of his fellow Olympians.[2]

Hephaistos is a quintessential fringe-person on Olympus. Included at the edge, he looks uneasily in, into the wheels within wheels that make up the Olympian social structure. But nervously and uneasily, too, he watches the power conflicts, remembering how Zeus "seized me by the foot and hurled me from the threshold of Heaven. I flew all day, and as the sun sank I fell half-dead on Lemnos."[3] Trying somehow to stay in touch with the center, maybe to be ready for the worst or to know what's coming next, he knows all the while that it's impossible really to belong there—there, where they tolerate the fringe-people as long as the work gets done, but where they can never act and feel quite easy and neighborly with them. Hephaistos-consciousness drifts a bit toward the Frankenstein phenomenon: his brother is the monster Typhon, but that goes beyond the fringe of Olympian society.

The feet of Hephaistos tell volumes: they are turned back to front, and when he walks he goes with a rolling gait that strikes the other Gods as somehow hilarious and breaks them up with mirth—"a fit of helpless laughter seized the happy Gods as they watched him bustling up and down the hall."[4] On this particular occasion his buffoonery has the effect of keeping the Gods from each other's throats.

In one story the feet of Hephaistos are misformed at birth, and Hera, his mother, goes into shock (she had bred and borne him by herself to show Zeus what she could do without his help!), grabbing him up and flinging him with disgust from the portals of heaven. This boy-child was supposed to be something she could hit Zeus over the head with, to show off with, to prove that she was as good as he (he had given birth, through his head, to the mighty and highly respected Athene); instead, to her acute disappointment, this misformed cripple shows up her inferiority and embarrasses her, and this (of course) is intolerable. The crippled child threatens to put her on the fringe, too.

The other version tells that Hephaistos' feet were crippled when he hit the ground on the island of Lemnos, having been hurled from Olympus by Zeus who had a fit because the boy was sticking up for his mother, Hera, in one of the many quarrels between the royal pair. As a rule, Hephaistos remains close to women; he's not much in the company of men, except for the blacksmiths. Zeus sometimes passes for his father, but most stories tell that he had no father, only a mother. And since it is generally the father who shows the boy the ropes of society and leads him out into a 'position,' etc., it begins to make sense why he is so much on the edge of things in the patriarchal, masculine world of the Olympians.

Rejected by his 'father' in a rather no-nonsense, brutal way, Hephaistos lands on Lemnos, where he makes friends with the Sintians. Lemnos becomes his home away from home. In fact, this island may be his original home. There was on Lemnos a tradition of Hephaistos-worship on the part of the native inhabitants, those "foreign-tongued people the Sintians."[5] This island-home of Hephaistos throws much light on his background.

The islands of Rhodes, Samothrace, Delos, Lemnos were much associated with a race of creatures variously called Daktyloi, Telchines, Kouretes, Korybantes, or Kabeiroi; on Lemnos they were called Hephaistoi, in the plural.[6] These names refer to dwarf-like servants of the Great Mother Goddess.[7] Invariably they occupy themselves with metallurgy at subterranean forges, deep in the body of the Mother herself, for the islands were in earliest times identical with the Great Goddess.[8] As the Idaean Daktyloi ("Daktyloi" meaning "fingers," thus as the "fingers" of the Great Goddess), these smith-dwarfs learned their metallurgic arts originally from the Great Mother herself.[9]

The dwarfish smiths are not only the servants of the Great Mother; they are also her sons and lovers, her son-husbands: "It will be remembered how she, the Great Mother, always had with her Daktyloi, Kouretes, Korybantes or Kabeiroi, whom she had bred from within herself and with whom she also bred further. . . ."[10] The name of this Mother-Wife was (sometimes) Kabeiro; she was the mother of the Kabeiroi, and her name was variously transmuted into Rhea, Demeter, Hekate or Aphrodite.[11] When Hephaistos mated with Kabeiro, she bore the boy Kakmilos, who again, in turn, mated with her and bred the three Kabeiroi and three Cabirian Nymphs.[12] Hera, the Olympian mother of Hephaistos, preserves associations from earlier, pre-Olympian times with beings of a Dactylic nature.[13] The importance of this incestuous pattern in the Hephaistian configuration is central.

Invariably the mythical smiths were set apart by some physical defect or oddity.[14] Often, also, these dwarfish, crippled or otherwise mutilated craftsmen were, according to Eliade, associated with "strangers" and "mountain folk"[15]—that is, with primitive populations[16] of "unfamiliar character who were surrounded by mystery."[17] Undoubtedly this cripple-motif, as well as the mysteriousness of these populations, hangs together with their incestuous bond to the Great Mother. Here we can perhaps see what lies behind the outcast charac-

ter of Hephaistos: he is a fringe person and slightly monstrous because of his connections with the historically and psychologically re-
gressive servant-son-lovers of the Great Mother.

This Daktylic background places Hephaistos, also, in proximity to
the magical arts of the underworld. The left-handed Daktyloi, those
who originated from the fingers of the Goddess's left hand, were
magicians.[18] And the cousins of the Kabeiroi of Lemnos, the Rhodian
Telchines, were famed as evil magicians.[19]

Hephaistos cannot be separated from his fires. In fact, his name is
said to mean "fire";[20] sometimes, too, he is called *"ephoros tou puros"*
("ruler of the fire"),[21] or again his "breath" is fire, and his "glance" is
a "blaze."[22] But the fire of Hephaistos is fundamentally not a daytime,
Olympian fire but a subterranean fire,[23] and here he connects with the
Roman God Vulcan, who ruled over and in the volcanic Mount Etna
on Sicily. The Hephaistian fire *per se* sprang from a hole in the earth
on Lemnos, "on the small mountain of Moschylos, where his companions were certain Kabeiroi called the Karkinoi, 'the Crabs,'"[24] alluding
perhaps to their strong fingers and masterful hands.

Another association connects Hephaistos to a pre-Olympian
background: in one story, Hera brings the baby Hephaistos to the
island of Naxos and hands him over to Kedalion, who is supposed to
act as his tutor. The name Kedalion "was as much as to say 'the
phallic one.'"[25] Kedalion belongs to the ancient order of the Cyclops
who, besides the Titans and Giants, were the original children of Gaia
and Ouranos.[26] The race of Cyclops is intimately related to the Great
Goddess of pre-historic Greek religion, both as her sons and lovers.[27]

His association to the Daktyloi and to the Great Mother helps in
explaining the surprising connection between Hephaistos and
women's mysteries. In one set of stories, Hephaistos is the son of
Prometheus, and the two of them are visited by Demeter who brings
them her mysteries, "just as she brought these . . . to the King of
Eleusis."[28] His relation to the feminine mysteries of childbirth and
fertility has its reason in the Daktylic background. The Idaean Daktyloi, those "Idaean Fingers" to whom all the dwarfish smiths are related, came into being in the midst of the childbirth event: Rhea,
worshipped in Asia Minor as *Meter oreia*, "Mountain-Mother," had
fled to Ida to await the birth of Zeus, and there, when the time came
due and labor pains set in, "she supported herself with both hands on
the soil. The mountain at once brought forth as many spirits, or gods,
as the goddess had fingers."[29] These spirits are the Daktyloi and proceed to busy themselves in her service.

70

These numerous connections between Hephaistos and the Daktylic-Great Mother-pre-Olympian background would place the subterranean fire of the smith-God in touch with the dark, internal energies of the Mother's creativity; the Hephaistian fire would take its light and energy from the central fires which are at the heart of nature's creativity. Hephaistos is, then, a split-off animus of the Great Mother who 'mimics' the creative processes in the depths of the Mother and brings to birth through this transforming mimicry his works of art.

Indirectly, Hephaistos has quite a lot to do with the origins of mankind. Out of his relations with the Great Mother Goddess "Lemnos" unravel the first sisters for the primordial brothers, and these form three pairs, the first human couples. Until this possibility of brother-sister incest arises, the sons remain incestuously attached to the Mother in a kind of pre-individual, anonymous, not-yet-human cluster.[30] In another mythic tale, Hephaistos is again responsible for bringing the first woman into being; he formed Pandora. Hephaistos fashioned this first human image of woman at the behest of an angry Zeus, who was contriving to punish mankind for possessing fire.[31] Heretofore the human race had been purely masculine, and to create confusion among them Zeus asked Hephaistos to form the image of a beautiful maiden. The story is well known how Pandora opened the box and released misery, disease, suffering, etc., into the world, snapping shut the lid just before the last content, "hope," could escape. What interests us here about Pandora is not, however, her character or what she may indicate about Greek prejudices on the subject of women. What catches our attention is Pandora's artificiality.

The name Pandora, as Kerényi explains, means "the rich in gifts," "the all-giving," and this is, significantly, a name for the earth itself.[32] "In an old portrayal of her," Kerényi remarks, "the name written beside her is actually Anesidor, 'the sender-forth of gifts,' which is one of the names of the earth-goddess."[33] Pandora is, therefore, a representation of the all-giving Mother herself, which has been scaled down to human size through the arts of Hephaistos.[34] But despite her lifelikeness, and even her links to the Great Mother, Pandora is nevertheless 'made'; she is an artificial product of skill and craft, but an *arti*fact which resonates to the ground of nature in such a profound way that there is a kind of confusion between nature and culture, nature and art. Through Hephaistos, the Great Mother develops a "primordial imitativeness" which is the source of cultural and artistic creative energy. The forge of Hephaistos is therefore the birthplace of spirit. This 'new' creativity, which nevertheless roots in and mimics the creative processes of nature, is what the Hephaistian fire symbolizes.

Some Renaissance fantasy supports this view. Because the Sintians were unknown to Renaissance scholars, they read *Sintiis* variously as *absintiis* ("wormwood"), *nimphis* ("nymphs") or *simiis* ("apes"). To justify the last reading, Boccaccio argued that Greek imagination gave Hephaistos to the apes because apes imitate man as man imitates nature. Man, he argues, imitates nature by practicing the arts and crafts. Hephaistos is the God of *techne*, which means according to Aristotle "acting as nature acts."[35] Thus Hephaistos learns on Lemnos to 'ape' nature and her creative processes.

Boccaccio goes on to imagine how Hephaistos (whom he naturally calls by the Latin name Vulcan), as "fire," forms the foundation of civilization; that is, how the keeping alive of fire "led to the formation of the first social units, to the invention of speech, and to the erection of buildings."[36] Boccaccio's fantasy follows closely the model given in the Homeric hymn to Hephaistos:

. . . he taught men	Hephaistos
work . . .	whose skill is
work that was	so famous
noble	they know
for men to do	how to
on the earth	work
men who	life is
formerly	easy
lived in	the whole
caves	year
in mountains	long
like animals	and they live it
now on the	quietly
other hand	in their
thanks to	houses now. . . .[37]

This hymn praises Hephaistos both as God of work and as God of the civilizing process, leading man from the caves and forests through imaginative, imitative work into his houses and palaces.

The greatness of Hephaistian art lies in its naturalness; his works are praised generally for being so astonishingly life-like. Examples of this abound. Homer heaps praise without end on the famous shield which Hephaistos forges for Achilles, precisely for the vividness with which the several scenes on it imitate real life. The shield is literally jumping with life—maidens and young men dancing; ploughmen

72

driving their teams to and fro; reapers taking the harvest; sun, moon and stars shining brightly—and around the whole of it flows the cosmic river, "the mighty Stream of Ocean."[38] Indeed the shield of Achilles contains the entire cosmos; all of nature is vividly recreated in this archetypal work of art. In miniature we find the same phenomenon in the wreath that Hephaistos weaves for Pandora: "In this wreath many beasts of the earth and sea were wonderfully portrayed, almost as if they were alive. . . ."[39] Perhaps the most ingenious examples of Hephaistian artfulness are furnished by the female(-like) servants in his house: "Golden maidservants. . . .They looked like real girls and could not only speak and use their limbs but were endowed with intelligence and trained in handwork by the immortal gods."[40]

The wife of Hephaistos, both in the *Iliad* and in Hesiod, is Aglaia, the youngest of the Graces. Her name means "the glorious," and Kerényi asks if she might not be a *living* work of art, for "grace" (*charis*) means also the "delightfulness of art."[41]

Through Hephaistos, the great forms of nature image themselves forth in art. His cousins the Telchines were the first creatures to build images of the Gods.[42] The springs of creativity, which are rooted in the depths of the Great Mother, take a turn in Hephaistos from concrete child-bearing and body-centered sexuality toward the realization of the cosmos as imagination and symbol.

The Hephaistian configuration remains deeply situated in the feminine mysteries of childbirth and fertility and has little to do with the labors and efforts of masculine heroism. The forges and fires of Hephaistos are in the earth, in the womb of nature. The furnace itself is an "artificial uterus," as Eliade has pointed out;[43] the smith stands in the service of the metallurgic processes that occur in the furnace just as the Idaean Daktyloi served the Great Mother in her labor. Whereas the heroes of solar masculinity perform great tasks to free themselves from bondage to the maternal background, Hephaistos remains always in the service of the feminine. And the Hephaistian passion for creative work is deeply of the Mother.

This intimacy between Hephaistos and the feminine world finds mythic expression through an incident of his boyhood. When Hera flings him in disgust from the gates of heaven, the crippled child falls into the sea and is rescued from drowning by the sea-nymphs Thetis and Eurynome, who take him home with them and nurture him for nine years. The Greek word for where they take him is *"mukos,"* which means "the innermost place," "the secret place," but also "the women's apartments in the house." During this sojourn in the women's quarters, the young Hephaistos puts his talented hands to work for the first time and fashions for his surrogate mothers many beautiful articles of jewelry. These nine years in *mukos* represent, of course, a second incubation period for Hephaistos, and it is during this period that he learns of his ability to create. Years later, when Thetis comes to the master-craftsman and begs him to fashion a shield for her son Achilles, Hephaistos forges the work that demonstrates the vast scope of his resonance to the primordial creative processes within the Great Mother herself.

Shifting for a moment from the archetypal background of the Hephaistian configuration to more personal psychological considerations, it is not hard to see that a man whose ego-consciousness is strongly influenced by the Hephaistian pattern will experience certain characteristic problems and proclivities. He will presumably find himself rather an outcast from a conventional world that requires ready adaptation to patriarchal and masculine dominants; he will be moody and given to swinging between inflation and depression; he will appear both to himself and to others, especially to the analyst, rather unheroic and uninterested in overcoming his close attachment to the world of women and mothers; indeed, he will cling to feminine circles and company, fascinated by the mysteries of creativity and often lost in a world of inner images and fantasy, bound hand, foot and soul to the excitement and anguish of tending the "underground forges." He will seem to be quite anima-possessed, smoldering and crippled.[44]

Emma Jung, writing of the image-producing effect of the anima, describes a state of masculine ego-consciousness which is close to Hephaistian consciousness in a man:

> The transmission of the unconscious contents in the sense of making them visible is the special role of the anima. It helps the man to perceive these otherwise obscure things. A necessary condition for this is a sort of *dimming of consciousness*; that is, the establishment of *a more feminine consciousness,* less sharp and clear than man's but one which is thus able to perceive in a wider field things that are still shadowy.[45]

The analytic 'treatment' of such a case of Hephaistian determination will be considered in connection with his association to Dionysos; for now it is sufficient to point out that the creativity of Hephaistos depends absolutely on his intimacy with the feminine world, for it is only as he is able to resonate to the deep maternal creative movements within the Mother that he can realize his creativity.

To the feminine ego the Hephaistian constellation may appear perhaps even more problematical and threatening. Hephaistos connects to her deepest feminine-maternal impulses, yet wants something other than simple maternity. The Hephaistian animus represents a subtle undermining threat to simple, natural feminine creativity, in that he tends toward creating the symbol that mirrors the creative process of nature but produces an artificial product which at once represents and substitutes for "the real thing." Hence the monstrousness of *Hephaistian* creativity for the feminine psyche: Hephaistos goes *contra naturam* (his feet are turned the wrong way round!) in a way that profoundly threatens to undermine or rechannel the essence of purely natural feminine creativity. Hephaistos may be, therefore, a monstrous offense to feminine naturalism, a sick-making disharmony in the tones that vibrate between feminine ego-consciousness and the Great Mother.

*

Returning to the Hephaistian configuration itself, we find in the contrast between the brothers Ares and Hephaistos several important points of differentiation that go far toward further clarifying the Hephaistian pattern. We come here upon a highly complex set of stories and motifs. The mythic links between Ares and Hephaistos pass through three nodes: their birth to Hera, both without paternity; the love triangle among Hephaistos, Aphrodite, and Ares; and the rite of passage episode when Ares tries by force, unsuccessfully, to bring Hephaistos back up to Olympus.

Like Hephaistos, Ares is born to an angry, jealous Hera. Zeus has offended her deeply, this time not so much by his promiscuity as by the affront of performing within himself the maternal task of bearing a child, Athene, and thereby demonstrating the superfluousness of womankind. This hermaphroditic act on the part of Zeus stimulates Hera to action: she does likewise. Her first effort results in the birth of Hephaistos; later attempts bring forth the monster Typhon and Ares, God of furious warfare and battle-rage. Hephaistos proves unsatisfactory in this competition because he measures up so unfavorably to Athene: "Without me he has born Athene," laments Hera, "who is glorious amongst all the immortals, whilst my own son, whom I bore, Hephaistos, is the least of all of us."[46] Dwarfish, lame, grotesquely comical, Hephaistos just will not do at all. But Hera's judgment of his inadequacy relates also to his deeper meaning: this animus of introverted *contra naturam* creativity, bound to the maternal depths and

75

committed to a symbolic imitation of feminine creativity, simply does not begin to answer the extraverted challenge of Athene with her ear-splitting battle cry in a way that would satisfy the jealous rage of Hera. And yet, in a subtle way unseen by Hera, Hephaistos is a precise response to Athene, from hermaphroditic femininity to hermaphroditic masculinity. If, as W. F. Otto says, "Athene is a woman, but as if she were a man,"[47] Hephaistos is a man, but a bit as if he were a woman.

Because she sees in Hephaistos a failure, Hera tries again and produces, finally, Ares. Whether or not Ares satisfies her is not said, but he certainly does reflect his mother's ferocious, battle-crazy animus. Ares, in contrast to the dwarfishness of Hephaistos, is gigantic;[48] the epithet "*artipos Ares*" ("swiftfooted Ares")[49] calls attention to his further physical superiority over Hephaistos, who bears the epithet "*apedanos*" ("the weakly").[50] In temperament, too, the brothers are very unlike, Ares thriving on strife and drinking deeply of the bloody waters of mortal combat, Hephaistos rather the peace-maker who tends to shy away from conflict.

But Ares is more than the split-off battle-thirsty animus of Hera, though he is surely that. He is also the fructifier, the masculine impregnator.[51] It is this underlined masculinity of his that distinguishes him sharply from Hephaistos, whose masculinity, in the sense of an aggressive, outwardly-fructifying flow of libido, is clouded by his intimate associations with the world of women. The crippled feet give an obvious clue of problematical sexuality in the Hephaistian configuration, feet having definitely a phallic significance.

The famous episode of the triangular relation among Hephaistos, his wife Aphrodite, and Ares her lover leads toward similar conclusions. Hephaistos, it is told, won the hand of Aphrodite as a reward for freeing Hera from the chains with which he had bound her. What sort of marriage this was remains in the dark, but it seems quite clear that Hephaistos spent much of his time on Lemnos with his smithy-friends, leaving the voluptuous Aphrodite home alone to mind the house. Her affair with Ares, begun during these interludes and carried on while Hephaistos was introverting at his underground forge, is marked by high erotic intensity: it is as though in the coming together of Ares and Aphrodite two sexual opposites meet which were simply not present in the Hephaistos-Aphrodite combination.

Not that Hephaistos is at all effeminate and soft. The many drawings and paintings of him show generally a robust specimen of the masculine sex with heavily muscled arms and thick neck. And he is, after all, God of smiths and craftsmen ('hardhats'!), probably the least effeminate elements in the population. When Hephaistos' temper flares, the volcanoes rumble in the distance. With the strength of his arm, he turns his furnace on Ares and sends him flying back to Olympus when the war-God comes to force him home, and his mighty deed in the Trojan War, scalding the river Xanthus with his dazzling flames, defeats any notion that Hephaistos is second-best in battle. But the masculine, fructifying libido in the Hephaistian configuration, unlike that in the Ares constellation where it shoots actively and aggressively outward, instead moves in a kind of incestuous motion back toward the Mother, toward the subterranean forges on Lemnos.

Ares plays a secondary role in a story that tells of Hephaistos' return to Olympus and of a curious connection between the young smith and Dionysos. Angry at Hera for rejecting him, Hephaistos seeks revenge by constructing a throne for her that will bind her fast and levitate when she sits down on it. After the trap has sprung successfully, and Hera has suffered a while the mortification and discomfort of hanging suspended in mid-air on this trick chair, the Gods send brother Ares down to bring Hephaistos back to Olympus by force. But Hephaistos drives Ares off with several blasts from his fiery furnace. Next the Gods send down Dionysos, and this God uses a cunning ruse instead of trying force: Hephaistos has neither seen nor tasted wine before, and Dionysos tempts him to try a bit. The smith drinks deeply, again and again, and soon suffers himself to be led away. Dionysos returns to Olympus, leading Hephaistos, who is drunkenly draped over a donkey, behind him. But Hephaistos is not so witless that he fails to bargain for the freedom of his mother: loosened chains in return for the hand of Aphrodite. This mythic link between Dionysos and Hephaistos comes at an exceedingly important moment in the 'development' of Hephaistos: the crippled child has been cast out of heaven, has sulked and sought revenge, has learned of his creative gifts, but has not yet found his maturity. His return to Olympus represents a rite of passage to maturity, to taking up a position within the Olympian hierarchy. The agent provocateur of this passage is his binding of Hera; the bonds he has applied to his mother provoke the crisis and force the issue. But his maturity depends on loosening the bonds with which he has tied her. This act of 'loosening' is effected through Dionysos and his intoxicating wine. As Hillman has pointed out, "Dionysos was called *Lysios,* the loosener."[2] Obviously he is the right God to send on this mission, for loosening is precisely what is called for—not only the loosening of Hera from her chains, but the prior loosening of Hephaistos from his *idée fixe* which is bent on revenge against his mother. The hardening of Hephaistos in this attitude of irreconcilable bitterness toward his mother would spell absolute disaster for both, for it would leave the mother suspended and suffering in midair and the son cut off from the creative energies that flow into him through his contact with the Mother. Caught in his own trap, Hephaistos would wither in the self-destructive heat of resentment. A sort of anarchistic self-directed pyromania takes over in such cases, an attitude utterly devoid of creativity, rejoicing only in conflagration, even courting visions of martyrish death in the flames of its own kindling. The fire in the earth becomes an erupting volcano, and Hephaistos takes on the most terrifying aspects of his brothers Ares and Typhon. Only in Hephaistos this anarchistic violence would be directed not outward, as with Ares, but inward against himself, against his own body and soul.

Dionysos comes, then, to save Hephaistos from himself, from suicide. The two Gods have several things in common. Dionysos was also born hermaphroditically, from the thigh of Zeus; one story tells that Hephaistos was born from the thigh of Hera.[3] Moreover, both Gods have deep linkages into the world of women. Even more than Hephaistos, Dionysos is "a man, but as if he were a woman." But whereas Hephaistos tends to tie down and fixate (a kind of compulsion to 'show them'), Dionysos is the God of dismemberment, dissolution, and loosening. It is unclear where Hephaistos is when Dionysos comes to him, but one must suppose that he is still in the watery home of the sea nymphs where he fell when Hera threw him from her. So Dionysos comes with his wine, with his spirit of drunkenness and eros, to free the fire of Hephaistos from its fixated imprisonment in water. By separating with his spirits the fire from the water, Dionysos frees Hephaistos from his submergence in the bitterly resentful negative anima; he frees the fire to follow its natural tendency upward, and by loosening Hephaistos' fixation frees him to touch yet more profoundly the creative energies in the core of the primordial Great Mother.

Loosening means separating without cutting off, rather healing and freeing to take a new look, to sink more deeply, to rise higher, to become flexible and plastic. For Hephaistos the solution to the mother 'hangup' is not a heroic, aggressive battle against the maternal monster, but a kind of unfocused Dionysian intoxication which dissolves his claims upon her. Hephaistos rides back to Olympus, drunken, on a donkey, that phallic animal, and at the moment of entry into the Olympian gates his claim 'transfers' from mother Hera to erotic Aphrodite. From this latter union, by some accounts, the God Eros was born.

The loves of Hephaistos, which begin with Aphrodite, tend to conclude in disappointment. Behind these disasters in love lies the incestuous, Mother-directed motion of his libido. Already somewhat apparent in his triangular relationship with Aphrodite and Ares, this pattern is dramatically stated in the story of his love affair with Athene.

The mythic ties between Hephaistos and Athene show, both in their quantity and profundity, a deep-going association between these two figures. More than Aphrodite, Athene is the 'soul-mate' of Hephaistos. Yet a kind of cloudy mysteriousness shrouds their relationship; no single tradition was ever clearly established on this subject, and so what confronts us is a blurred image based on rumors and conflicting reports.[54] Despite this welter of tales, a few points seem fairly clear, and the general outlines of a myth emerge.

Hephaistos was undoubtedly present at Athene's birth: many drawings and paintings attest to his presence there.[55] With his hammer he performed a midwife role, releasing the Goddess from the head of Zeus with a mighty, rending blow. It is highly significant that the contrasexually-colored Hephaistos should be the instrument of Athene's birth, for she is to masculine Zeus as Hephaistos to feminine Hera: the product of a hermaphroditic birth process decisively marked by the contrasexual parent. The birth of Athene heralds a significant development on Olympus, for she represents that inner space and capacity for reflection within the masculine world which is capable of containing affect and the chaos of conflicting, ambivalent feelings.[56] That she is a *contra naturam* content is clear, first because Athene springs (fully armed) from the *head* of her *male* parent, secondly because Hephaistos is her mid-wife and the essence of Hephaistos is a spiritual imitating of the procreative processes within the Great Mother. The Hephaistian configuration would seem to have a liberating effect on the Athene-pregnant head of Zeus: the Mother-tuned, introverting Hephaistian attitude works on the dominant masculine attitude to release, loosen, free the Athene anima.

Immediately Athene springs forth with her "far-echoing battle-cry,"[57] Hephaistos falls into desperate love with her. In other versions he first loves her when she comes to his shop for a spear, but always it is love at first sight on his part and a distinct coolness towards him on hers: Whether, as in some versions, he marries her or not, the outcome is the same: Hephaistos seeks impetuously and passionately to make love to Athene; at the moment of climax she pushes him aside, and his semen falls to the earth where it impregnates Gaia; the child of this misadventure is named Erichthonios. The marriage of Athene and Hephaistos and the fruit of their union were celebrated annually by the Athenians in a fertility festival named the Chalkeia.[58]

This story of Hephaistos' semen missing its intended mark and fertilizing instead the Great Mother tells of the introverted, incestuous course of his libido, and the offspring, Erichthonios, symbolizes the outcome of this movement. Erichthonios is closely associated both in art and story with snakes: in some accounts he is himself a serpent below the waist or has serpentine feet;[59] in other stories he is guarded by snakes which curl around him in "a covered, round basket, probably such as those which are used in the Mysteries";[60] in some versions he is even altogether a serpent.[61] "*Chthonios,*" the stem of his name, means "sprung from the earth," and an epithet often applied to him is "*gaygenays,*" meaning "born of Ge," of the earth. The claim of the Athenians to being *autochthonous,* i.e., indigenous to their soil, rested on their connection to Erichthonios, for after his birth Athene takes him up and cares for him, and when he comes of age, places him on the throne of Athens, founding the royal line that culminates several generations later in the famous hero Theseus.

Hephaistos, then, not only mimics and transforms the creative energies in the dark, maternal, earth-bound background of the psyche, producing his art and culture-building artifacts, but also impregnates the Mother with the incestuous, introverted turnings of his libido. And this impregnation of the psyche's fecund, inchoate background gives birth to an image of "natural man," unsplit between instinct and spirit, Luna and Sol, animal and angel—of man whose familiar is the snake. Perhaps it is to an intimation of this image of original man— at home with the earth, integrated, intact, intuitive, at one with himself, undivided by religion, unspoilt by civilization, creative, wise as the serpent, simple as his father "fire" and strong as his protectress Athene—that the Marxists have sung their paeans of praise. This Hephaistian turning of the libido back into the psychic depths fathers the birth of the ancestor-spirit fantasy (that "two million year old man")[62] and activates the symbol, the numinous images of the Gods.

1   Homer, *The Iliad*, Bk. I, 605. All quotations from the *Iliad* are taken from the translation by E. V. Rieu, Harmondsworth: Penguin Books, 1966.
2   Ibid., Bk. I, 590–600.
3   Ibid., Bk. I, 585–87.
4   Ibid., Bk. I, 600.
5   C. Kerényi, *The Gods of the Greeks*, London: Thames and Hudson, 1951, p. 72.
6   Ibid., p. 86.
7   Ibid.
8   Ibid., p. 189.
9   Cf. René Malamud, "The Amazon Problem," this volume. Also, cf. Kerényi, op. cit., p. 84.
10 Kerényi, op. cit., p. 211.
11 Ibid., p. 87.
12 Ibid.
13 Ibid., p. 158.
14 Malamud, op. cit.
15 M. Eliade, *The Forge and the Crucible*, (London, 1962), p. 105.
16 Kerényi, op. cit., p. 86.
17 Malamud, op. cit.
18 Kerényi, op. cit., p. 84.
19 Ibid., p. 88.
20 Ibid., p. 156. Cf. also W. H. Roscher, *Ausführliches Lexikon der griechischen und römischen Mythologie*, (Leipzig, 1916–24), vol. I, 2, p. 2037.
21 Ibid., p. 2038.
22 Ibid., pp. 2037–38.
23 Kerényi, op. cit., p. 156.
24 Ibid.
25 Ibid.
26 Their names meant "thunder" and "lightning." Ibid., p. 18.
27 Cf. for interesting amplification and interpretation of the Cyclops, Philip Zabriskie, *Odysseus and the Great Goddess*, unpublished Diploma Thesis, C.G. Jung Institute, Zürich, 1972, pp. 16–27.
28 Kerényi, op. cit., p. 212.
29 Ibid., p. 84.
30 Ibid., p. 211.
31 In some stories, Prometheus stole the fire, which he gave to man, from the Hephaistian forge on Lemnos (cf. Kerényi, p. 216). On the connections between Hephaistos and Prometheus, cf. Kerényi, pp. 212–13 and Roscher, pp. 2050–51. Like Prometheus, Hephaistos is a "phosphoros" ("lightbringer"), but the heroic and "tricky" features which are so prominent in Prometheus are clearly lacking in Hephaistos, who is as "simple as fire itself" (Kerényi, p. 212).
32 Kerényi, op. cit., p. 219.
33 Ibid.
34 In the story of Deukalion and Pyrrha, too, the identification between Pandora and Mother Earth is made: Deukalion, the son of Pandora, is told to throw the "bones of the mother" over his shoulder in order to create a new race of men; he obeys this command by throwing "stones" over his shoulder (cf. Kerényi, p. 229).
35 Erwin Panofsky, *Studies in Iconology*, (New York: Harper Torchbooks, 1962), p. 38.
36 Ibid.
37 *The Homeric Hymns*, translated by Charles Boer (Spring Publications, 1979), pp. 84–5.
38 *Iliad*, Bk. XVIII, 610.
39 Kerényi, op. cit., p. 217.
40 *Iliad*, Bk. XVIII, 417–20.

41 Kerényi, op. cit., p. 72.
42 Ibid., p. 88.
43 Eliade, op. cit., p. 52.
44 P. E. Slater, in his book *The Glory of Hera*, Boston: Beacon Press, 1968, includes under the general heading "Mythical Defenses Against the Maternal Threat," a chapter entitled "Self-Emasculation: Hephaistos." Slater discovers in the Hephaistian configuration a defense mechanism: the son, rejected by a jealous, authoritarian father (Zeus) and a narcissistic mother (Hera), "emasculates" himself by elaborating the style of fool and jester, thereby taking himself out of competition with his father, saying, "You have nothing to fear from me, nor is there anything about me which should arouse your envy or resentment" (p. 193). The industry of Hephaistos belongs also in Slater's view to the defense, here against his mother: since he cannot present *himself* as an adequate object for "maternal display," he can create objects which will function as substitutes in this regard" (p. 199). This, it seems to me, is the view of Hephaistos obtained by looking at him through the eyes of Zeus, through the paradigmatic grid of a heroic, "mature" ego. This view certainly has its validity, but it is onesided and ultimately betrays the potentialities inherent even in the "weakness" and "inadequacy" of the child Hephaistos. What Slater fails to see, only because his method cannot cope with the inherent depth and subtlety of myth, is the pattern of meaning and movement within the Hephaistian configuration itself, and this reflects a fundamental failure of imagination. Instead of looking at and "explaining" myths through the concepts of an ego-building psychology (a psychology governed, it seems to me, by Zeus and Apollo), we are trying to let myth instruct our psychology, to broaden and deepen its visions, and to move us out of our narrow preconceptions of "what it means to be a man."
45 Emma Jung, *Animus and Anima* (New York and Zürich: Spring Publ., 1957/72), p. 25.
46 *Homeri Hymnus in Apollinem*, 309; quoted by Kerényi, op. cit., p. 151.
47 Quoted by Malamud, op. cit., p. 7.
48 Kerényi, op. cit., p. 150; cf. also *Iliad*, Bk. XXI, 400.
49 Roscher, op. cit., p. 2039, quoting *hy. in Ap. Pyth.*, 138.
50 Ibid.
51 Malamud, op. cit.
52 J. Hillman, "Dionysus in Jung's Writings," *Spring 1972*, p. 203.
53 Kerényi, op. cit., p. 155.
54 Cf. Kerényi, op. cit., pp. 123–26.
55 Cf., for example, Kerényi, ibid., p. 119, and Roscher, op. cit., p. 2062.
56 Cf. Malamud, op. cit.
57 Kerényi, op. cit., p. 120.
58 Roscher, op. cit., p. 2070.
59 Ibid., p. 2063; also Kerényi, op. cit., pp. 125–26.
60 Kerényi, op. cit., p. 125.
61 Ibid.
62 C.G. Jung, "Fragments from a Talk with Students," *Spring 1970*, pp. 177–81.

POSTSCRIPT ON HEPHAISTOS

I should like to address a question generated in part by the attention this article has received since first published some seven years ago. What is the value, and what are the dangers and limitations, of relating personal psychological material to mythical figures and themes?

In our psychological interpretation, Hephaistos represents a possible pattern of self-organization, hence of human identity, with a characteristic set of complexes, inner dynamics, and internal relations among various inner figures ("imagos"). The Hephaistian mythologem, including the various figures in the story as well as the tales, themes and images clustered about them, may lead the psychologist to insight into individual psychology, as well as certain aspects of group psychology (e.g., labor-management relations and struggles). The mythologem presents psychological structure and in relation to groups, social structure. The "architect" of the Hephaistian mythologem, at work long ago in ancient Greece, is presumably identical to a psychological factor which continues to design and erect the same structures in the modern psyche.

Besides giving voice to the depth of experience and relating separate pieces of experience into a configuration, the connection of personal experience to myth can produce or consolidate a psychological inflation (assimilation of the ego by an unconscious, often archetypal, content). The individual is unconsciously living a myth rather than a life. More accurately, an unconscious content is living him, rather than he it. Without going into the dynamics of inflation, it should be said that one telltale clue is the individual's inability to reflect in novel ways on his experience, his thoughts, and behavioral patterns. Inflation closes the doors to such reflection; and the person becomes "locked in" to a restricted field of vision. Suffering from inflation, a person has difficulty registering and responding to signals in the world around him. More and more rigid and maladapted, he misses nuance and complexity and gets lost in the simplifications of a monomaniacal vision in which there is only one interpretation of experience, only one perspective, only one complex through which the world is screened and filtered.

It is a great gain for consciousness to be able to identify the pattern(s) in which one lives, through which one sees and interprets the world, by which one "handles" and "deals with" life. A mythical figure or a mythologem can be the means by which such a pattern of self-organization is raised to consciousness. Making such a connection to myth may then burst an inflation by creating a "gap" between the ego and the pattern with which it is identified.

But making a mythic connection may increase or consolidate inflation. When a pertinent archetypal pattern is named and claimed as "my myth," tacit identification already extant but somewhat unconscious, may be given added strength. Tendencies of action, perception, feeling increase intensity, and the "I" becomes more assimilated to a mythic (or archetypal) pattern. Finding a myth to live by may increase the grip of neurosis by justifying and rationalizing and aggrandizing it.

While the individual thus becomes further assimilated to an archetypal (mythic) pattern of feeling, understanding, and perceiving, the archetypal content itself is reduced to personalist terms and is thereby drained of its richness and complexity. This is the other side of inflation: myth is drained of its archetypal resources, of its complexity, its power, its otherness. "Hephaistos" becomes a mere I, "Hera" becomes my mother, "Zeus" is my father or the boss, the "Olympian Circle" is the circle of colleagues closed to me, etc. In Jungian terms, the myth becomes a "sign," rather than retaining its force as a "symbol." The great archetypal structures and powers are squeezed into the limits of personal life patterns and character traits. While the complexity of real persons is reduced to stereotyped roles, the numinous otherness of mythic Persons collapses into family drama and suburban soap. Behavior and perception become stilted, monochromatic and distorted as the grip of the archetype gets stronger (as in inflation), and the archetypal figures depleted.

This leads me to suggesting another use of mythic sensibility, one which frees consciousness from its identification with a complex, releases it from an archetypally determined pattern, opens it to greater complexity of insight, yet preserves respect for archetypal forces.

The archetypal patterns of self-organization reflected in mythical images and tales lie in the unconscious background of the psyche and act like psychological "magnets" that draw fantasy, behavior, and perception toward specific forms. The awareness of archetypal (or mythic) patterns and connections should consequently be present as a background, and used for insight. As a force, the archetype is honored and respected, occasionally obeyed (consciously), with the twin intention of maintaining awareness of it and preserving or gaining a certain degree of distance from it. This can allow the "I" to recognize a typical way the consciousness in which it is embedded gets organized. When the "I" is able to see beyond such patterns and the role it plays, to see into the pattern of tacit assumptions, relationships, and forces at work behind the conscious structures, it is (as we say) on the way to "becoming psychological." This reflection on the archetypal background of consciousness, using mythical figures and tales, does not dissolve or even necessarily alter the constellating archetypal content and its force. It does produce a dual or reflexive consciousness, with some distance between the "embedded I" and the "reflective I." It is this distance that allows for "seeing through" our behavior, our cognitive structures, and our emotional action and reaction patterns.

The organizing force behind these personal dynamics and structures should be honored. It has a meaning for the person in whom it is constellated. The archetype has answers to the questions it poses. The Hephaistian pattern, for instance, shows a way of working through the problem of a negative, rejecting mother and a remote indifferent father, which have contributed to a crippling, self-demeaning attitude. Following the pattern through makes good therapeutic sense: the unconscious is wiser in most cases than consciousness. But the archetype is best and most therapeutically honored when honored at a distance, as a numinous force that both blesses the individual with its presence and inflicts itself on his life as a curse. The type of reflexive consciousness referred to above allows for this kind of honoring: it both participates, with the "consciousness-embedded I" playing its part in the constellated pattern, and monitors this participation, with the "reflective I" as interested observer. Without this dual consciousness, the participatory "I" is simply a puppet of the archetype. When that is the case, I have found, the pattern tends simply to repeat itself rather than lead to release and working through—Hephaistos keeps getting thrown out of Olympus, keeps trying to suspend his mother in midair, keeps on suffering humiliations at the Olympian banquets, keeps on withdrawing to Lemnos, on and on without resolution. The individual keeps on cycling through the pattern, deepened into the myth however far he may be.

How to create this necessary distance? A first step is realizing that living mythically is pathological. It is a state of inflation—of possession, unfreedom, onesidedness, and stereotypy. It is the very contrary of "wholeness," which is complex, made up of heightened tensions and contrary forces, of a mixture of myths complementing and contradicting one another. The pathology of archetypal possession is indicated as well by the fact of repetition without resolution. Finally, the pathos of this situation indicates pathology—the soul is in critical suffering. If this pattern of repetition and suffering is rationalized as "meaningful" by forging a connection to mythic patterns and figures, it becomes more deeply intractable.

An instinct for the pathology of identification and inflation is the key to developing dual consciousness and the necessary psychological distance from archetypally determined constellations of consciousness. Another vital acquisition is *suspicion*. Most good psychological analysis is rooted in the impulse to suspect our unexamined states of consciousness. This leads to asking such questions as, Suppose my "absolute knowledge" is not absolute but rather the opinion of one figure in an archetypally constellated field? Does the "I" cling to and need a certain state of affairs, complete with allies and enemies, to feel at home in the world? Who or what creates the psychological world in which I live?

The intuition of pathology and cultivation of suspicion can lead quite profitably to the act of *repudiation*. Identification with an archetypal content needs to be repudiated. Repudiation does not, of course, destroy or repress the repudiated; it creates a new sort of tension in the relationship with it. It creates alienation, hence distance.

Finally, the sense of pathology and attitude of suspicion, combined with the act of repudiation, may well lead to unfaithfulness. The bond of loyalty to the One, the True, the Only is severed as the state of inflation and possession is seen through, and this leads to a quest for new Gods, new sources of meaning, new myths. Out of this disloyalty and alienated quest, leading as it does into the desert of liminality, is born the ability to see from a distance—like a son who, having left his family's values for other values and powers, one day returns and looks upon his father and mother in lower case letters, and places them beside other significant figures in his life. This does not dispossess them of their parenthood, any more than it disposses an originative constellating archetype of its historical centrality, but it does strip them of their commanding *mana*. As obedience gives way to reflection as a primary virtue, psychological monotheism gives way to psychological polytheism.

Having said this about the necessary distance from archetypally sponsored inflation and possession, it is important to recall that archetypal consciousness does enrich experience. But its proper function is not to confirm pathology by providing a sophisticated rationale. Rather it is to enhance the value and importance of human experience. For the psychotherapist, the understanding of mythic connections and the development of archetypal consciousness can furnish important hints for ways of working through certain types of psychological impasse. Finally, archetypal awareness can dignify certain forms of intractable and irredeemable human suffering, serving the therapeutic function of releasing a suffering soul from blind meaninglessness.

V

RED RIDING HOOD AND GRAND MOTHER RHEA:
Images in a Psychology of Inflation

David L. Miller

Folg nur dem alten Spruch und meiner Muhme, der Slange!
Dir wird gewiss einmal bei deiner Gottähnlichkeit bange.

("Just follow the old word and my cousin, the snake!
Your godlikeness will one day make you fear and quake.)

Goethe, *Faust*, I. 2049f.

It's an odd bit of information the Devil gives the student in Goethe's poem. One might have thought that it would have been just one's "godlikeness," the image of God within, which would be a salvation, saving a person from anxiety. But Mephistopheles says it is exactly the opposite.

Jung agrees, and for good psychological reason. He uses the poet's *Gottähnlichkeit* ("godlikeness"), borrowing it as he says from Alfred Adler.[1] Jung means for the term to name a particular problem in life and in therapy.

Sometimes a person will identify almost completely with a social role, a piece of literal ego-history, a *persona*-mask. At other times there may be an unconscious identification with some universal pattern, an archetypal configuration, a collective and primordial image. The problem is that the person is, in fact, neither some social role nor an archetype. To view a personal situation in one of these ways, as Goethe's Devil says, may indeed make one feel godlike, but the self-deception involved leads to anxieties and frustrations that may become unbearable. So Jung says that when a person thinks himself "godlike," he attempts "to fill a space he normally cannot fill" by

appropriating to himself qualities and contents which properly exist for themselves alone and should therefore remain outside our bounds. What lies outside ourselves belongs either to someone else, or to every one, or to no one.[2]

A sense of "godlikeness," however unconscious, causes, as Jung puts it, "exaggeration, a puffed-up attitude, loss of free will, delusion, and enthusiasm in good and evil alike."³ If it is a case of losing oneself in a social role of ego's history, a megalomania and simple obnoxiousness may occur. But if it is a case of identifying self with collective archetypal fantasies, at best there will be neurosis and, at worst, psychosis.⁴

What is surprising in this problem of "godlikeness" is (as Jung notes) that it happens "inevitably" in *successful* analysis. A person in therapy may discover that what were assumed to be personal problems are in fact complexes produced by family psychology or social history—or alternatively that what was formerly viewed as "me" or "mine" is now experienced as belonging to archetypal aspects of self. In either case one begins to sense a collective dimension, whether social or archetypal, in one's makeup.

This is, of course, often thought of as a breakthrough, and the release from anxiety or guilt may be such a relief one may be tempted to view self as totally these others—*personae* or archetypes. One will have swayed from a Charybdis of projecting self onto other to a Scylla of introjecting the other into ego.⁵ In this way a collective archetypal psychology may produce in the person a sort of spiritual pride at being no one and/or an inflation at being everyone.

But a psychological mistake is still present. It is ego's error of *personalizing* what has been experienced as *personified*.⁶ Ego still wants to see what he or she *is* (an important *persona* or some God or Goddess), rather than suffering the humbling which Jung commends explicitly, of "putting clearly before him [the 'godlikeness'] as *that which he is not*."⁷

This phrase may be crucial in dealing with this "piling up of energy in monomanias that the ancients called a 'god.'"⁸ We shall return to this formulation a few pages later. For now let us simply observe that Jung shifted his terminology concerning this problem.

In early essays the use of the word "godlikeness," was consistent ("New Paths in Psychology" [1912], "The Structure of the Unconscious" [1916]). This term was to disappear from Jung's writings. In later editions of these same works it was replaced by the word "inflation" (see "On the Psychology of the Unconscious" [1917, 1918, 1926, 1936, 1943], and "The Relations between the Ego and the Unconscious" [1928, 1935, 1938]).⁹

Had Jung come to feel that, in an understanding of the psychology of "inflation," the term "godlikeness" itself leads to inflated thinking? Or perhaps Jung was demythologizing his psychology, employing a more abstract language for theoretical work whose ideas he would later remythologize through what he called the "poetic myth" of alchemy.[10] He said of his thinking in this period: "I had not yet found the right language."[11]

Whatever may have been the case for Jung, this question of language at least raises the possibility that, not only in living life, but also in "doing" psychology, whether in the practice of therapy or in the making of theory, "godlikeness" is a devilish matter.

Take the example of Mother.[12] In contemporary theories of mythology, religion, literature, anthropology, and psychology, it has become a commonplace in English to name the Mother-goddess by the phrase, "Great Mother."[13] Why? Apparently this terminology is meant to translate the Latin words *Magna Mater*. But "Grand Mother" would have been as linguistically precise as "Great Mother." And is there not in the use of the term "Great" already a subtle implication, in sound and connotation, of inflation?

What is the difference between "Great" and "Grand"? Is it that the phrase "Great Mother," implies a judgment about Mother, even an inflated idealizing of some one who is wife to a man and a mother to their children? Does not the phrase "Grand Mother" (as in "grandmother") connote a less inflated image of one who is mother to both wife and husband, that is, to beings who themselves now have children as she had a generation ago? Is she ("grandmother") not often seen as confidante of the children of her children, a bit removed from immediate family messes? After all, she is also a Mother-in-Law, the butt of so many jokes. She has already suffered the Mother-business and, knowing how seldom it seems Great, she is simply Grand. To say Great about Mother may already represent an inflated perspective.

Perhaps, then, we could for the moment stay with *images* of Mother, in order to attempt to get at the larger issue of "godlikeness" and the *concept* of "inflation." Such strategy takes its cue from Jung's observation; "Concepts are coined and negotiable values; images are life."[14]

Swallowing the Grand Mother

One of the livelier images of Mothers occurs in the folktale "Little Red Riding Hood," or "Red Cap" (*Rotkäppchen*), as it is known in the original German version.[15] Perhaps this story will furnish some insight into the concept of "inflation." Certainly no little psychological attention has been given to the tale.

For instance, Sigmund Freud, analyzing a dream of a young man with a strong father-complex, indicates a parallel between the dream and the story of "Little Red Riding Hood." The patient's actual father had, it seems, engaged from time to time in what Freud calls "affectionate abuse." In the process the father was remembered by his son as having said, "I'm going to eat you all up!" Freud concludes that the figure of the wolf in the patient's dream and in the folktale serves as a father-surrogate. It becomes a case, simply, of infantile fear of the father.[16]

Erich Fromm sees the story a bit differently. From his perspective the tale signals intimations of the onset of menstruation ("red cap") and an accompanying female fear of being devoured by the male. The stones in the wolf's belly, placed there by the women, are a sign of male sterility and of a victory by women (Mother, Daughter, Grandmother), all of whom hate men. They are threatened by what comes to them in the "trip" through the "forest" of puberty.[17]

To Eric Berne the matter is more obvious, though hardly less reductive; it relates one of the "games people play." Red Riding Hood, or LRRH as he calls her, is playing "Rapo" with the wolf. She tells him precisely where he can find her, namely, at grandmother's house. Grandmother, it seems, lives alone and leaves her door open! In fact, everyone in the story is a bit stupid and surely is suspect in motivation. What is the hunter really up to, playing around as he does with old women and young girls? The wolf is too heroically ambitious, chasing "chicks" instead of bunny-rabbits; Mother sends the girl into the forest where the wolves are; And how can anyone imagine LRRH really thinking that someone with those eyes, ears, and teeth could be grandmother? Surely, after talking to the wolf, Little Red should have said to herself, as Berne thinks, "that son-of-a-bitch is going to eat up my grandmother if I don't get some help fast." Berne goes on:

> The truth of the matter is that everybody in the story is looking for action at almost any price. If the payoff at the end is taken at face value, then the whole thing was a plot to do in the poor wolf by making him think he was outsmarting everybody, using LRRH as bait. In that case, the moral of the story is not that innocent maidens should keep out of forests where there are wolves, but that wolves should keep away from innocent-looking maidens and their grandmothers; in short, a wolf should not walk through the forest alone. This also raises the interesting question of what the mother did after she got rid of LRHH for the day.[18]

Perhaps it is an interesting question, but what has happened to the story and its images in these psychological commentaries? The folktale, though it may not be Great, was nonetheless a Grand story before the analysts brought it into their consulting rooms. The story of a Grand Mother getting swallowed by a wolf is itself in danger of being devoured by a process of analysis which reduces lively images to abstract concepts.

Yet this very reduction may be precisely an example of "inflation" in psychological theorizing. It may correspond in thinking to what in life and therapy has been called "negative inflation." This happens when making something "too small," as Jung puts it, has the same psychological function as making it "too big."[19] One is, in either case, still focused on personal- and ego-meanings. By conceptualizing the story of "Little Red Riding Hood," I think *I* know something about the images. Meanwhile, the story itself may have been Grander-er than *my* Great ideas about it. Something sizeable has been swallowed by something smaller.

Otto Rank, on the other hand, uses an entirely different psychological strategy with regard to the folktale. Whereas Freud, Fromm, and Berne reduce the story's size, Rank amplifies it mythically,[20] arguing that the clue is to remember the Greek God Kronos who (according to Hesiod)[21] ate his children. His wife Rhea gave him a stone to swallow in place of their youngest child, Zeus. This suggests that the German story is not so much about fear of the father, women who hate men, or "games people play." Rather, these neurotic perspectives are varieties of a Kronos-archetype. The folktale does not signify literal behavior of a single complex; rather, literal life and complex are amplified in and by myth.[22]

But once again the story is lost, now swallowed by the mythology of an old culture. Grand Mother, is, as it were, digested by the Great Greek Gods. So it may be that archetypal amplification can become just another sort of psychological "inflation" through a technique of seeing "godlikeness." The point is that the story, with its fascinating images, is already profoundly mythical and complicatedly archetypal—before interpretation. Yet we forfeit exactly this Grand-eur when, in the ego-perspectives of our psychologizing, we think *we* know something, whether by means of the *personae* of our reductive ideas or by the archetypes of our mythological amplifications.

The question is: how can we rediscover that which is Grand, even if not so Great? Once again, we return to images of Mother for help.

91

The Rhythms of Grand Mother Rhea

We have mentioned the Goddess Rhea in connection with Red Riding Hood's Grandmother. There is good reason to intuit that her storied image may have something to do with a psychology of inflation. According to tradition,[23] Rhea, the Grandmother of Dionysos, saved him when he was torn to pieces by the Titans (that is, by the titanic, an inflation sent by the Great Mother, Hera). The imaginal association between Titan and inflation is intriguing enough to warrant asking the question, who is this Grand One who can save the Grand Son?

Most storytellers (for example, Hesiod[24] and Apollodorus[25]) say that Rhea is born by the coming-together of Heaven and Earth, making her daughter to Ouranos and Gaia. Out of this conjunction, her sisters are Tethys (Disposer), Themis (Law), Mnemosyne (Memory), Phoebe (Bright Moon), Dione (Divine Queen), and Theia (The Goddess). These names indicate an extraordinary group—Great Ones! In fact, the brothers of these women are the very Titans from whom Rhea came to save Dionysos. She herself wed one of them, Kronos, whom Rank linked to Red Riding Hood's wolf. So goes the traditional account—not a little inflated itself.

But behind this story is quite a different one. According to Orpheus' song (so says Apollonius of Rhodes[26]), Kronos and Rhea replace, not Heaven and Earth, the very entirety of the world, but Eurynome (Wide Wandering, the "wide" suggesting Grand rather than Great) and Ophion (Moon Snake, the serpentine association linking not with the Great light, the Sun, but with the Grand one which comes during the periods of darkness). Robert Graves believes this Orphic account to be pre-hellenic and pre-homeric, connecting as do its images, with earthy, chthonic matters.[27] It is as if the later and now standard story cloaks, like Little Red's Riding Hood, a real Grand Mother.

In the non-heroic, Orphic mood, Rhea is linked with the oak tree,[28] with Pandora and her box,[29] with Cybele and the Orient,[30] and with a daughter whose name, Pluto, suggests a "wealth" whose treasury is in the depths, since this name is also an alias of Hades who rules the Underworld.[31]

The dimension of depth, with its inevitable darkness, is also indicated in an odd line in the Orphic Hymn dedicated to Rhea. The phrase in Greek is *pseudomenē sōteira*.[32] It means "deceitful savior," as if some sorts of salvation may have to come from a kind of trickery.

This hermetic quality, usually reserved for the God Hermes, may refer to Rhea's part in the plot to get her husband-brother-titan Kronos to swallow a saturnine stone in place of the Great God Zeus. Since in the Orphic perspective the round stone, like the egg, represents the world, one might think of Kronos-Saturn as suffering the world interiorly as the heroic Atlas does exteriorly. The point in any case is that Rhea's grace is of an underhanded kind.

Nor is the line in the Orphic Hymn the only connection to Rhea's manner of helping in an interior and underworld way. She gave life to Pelops in his death.[33] For Jason, she brought a spring of water out of a rock.[34] She assisted the Telchines in their task of giving Poseidon a trident for his watery depths.[35] It was her persistence in keeping her five fingers in earth that made possible the creation of the Dactyls.[36] But perhaps most relevant of all is Rhea's role with regard to Persephone, Queen of the Underworld.

Persephone, hitherto an innocent maid, suddenly finds herself in Hades. The bottom had fallen out of her innocence. Swallowed by the abyss, she suffered the depths deeply; never again could it be the same for her. She had tasted the soul-food of the Underworld, the tough, niggling little seeds of the pomegranate. Demeter, the Great Mother, wanted her back in the light of life while her abductor and king, Hades, wanted her constantly in the depths. But Rhea had a Grand-er vision than either—some of the time in the light, and some in the dark. It is as if Rhea knows we belong to both realms.

But how can she manage this sort of solution where Great Zeus fails? How does she accomplish this back-and-forth between "inflation" in one direction (Demeter) and "inflation" in the other (Hades)?

The traditional story does not help with these questions, itself puffed-up to Heaven (Ouranos) on one side and to the whole Earth (Gaia) on the other. Bringing us a little closer, the Orphic tale offers a view of Rhea as the child who carries the breadth (Grand-eur) of the "wide-wandering" Eurynome and the wisdom (as opposed to Great promethean knowledge) of the "moon snake," Ophion. But there is yet another clue in Euripides' play, *The Bacchae,* and in the Orphic Hymn that speaks of Rhea as a "deceitful savior."

In Euripides' drama, Rhea has a drum in her hand[37] (drums are said to have been her invention.)[38] To quote the Orphic Hymn, "Drum beating, frantic, of a splendid mien,/Brass-sounding, honor'd, Saturn's blessed Queen."[39]

The drum-motif, not only pre-hellenic and pre-homeric, as Graves guesses, is also specifically shamanistic. The motif connects with Eurynome, who was a dancer, but it locates the dance and the rhythm in a particular space. The eighty-sixth Orphic Fragment suggests that Rhea's drumming takes place at the door of the dark cave of the God whose name is Night.[40] It is right on the threshold. And it is implied that the go-between rhythms of Rhea are a salvation which comes from below:—soul's beatings. Such rhythms are primordial, like African drumming or the throbbing bass of Handel's "Hallelujah Chorus," and the Rolling Stones.

In shamanism the profound drummings are contexts for the magic of healing. Native American dance drumming makes possible a total transformation of *persona,* from pacifist to warrior to pacifist again. The drum induces ecstasy,[41] one which takes the shaman flying not up and out, but down and in to another sense of self. The healing magic happens, or so says the shaman, because the drum is made of wood from the World Tree (remember Rhea's connection with the oak.)

Among some "primitive" groups the drum is an altar, its hourglass shape suggesting the reversibility, and the intimacy, of upper and lower worlds.[42] The drum *is* the world itself for the shaman. Perhaps one could imagine that whereas Kronos swallowed the world, Rhea played upon it and danced to its beatings.

If one could see things this way, then it would be in her drumming rhythms that Rhea is Mother to so many Gods, being in her way Grand rather than Great, as were Athena, Aphrodite, Hera, and Artemis. Ever close to the titanic, even loving it in Kronos, Rhea does not totally identify with either Demeter or Hades, life or death, ego or self, *persona* or archetype. Her deeper sense of timing dances between these beats. Her way seems to acknowledge inflation without succumbing.

On Not Taking the Name of God in Vain

One could easily become enthusiastic about the perspective represented by Rhea in relation to the psychology of inflation. But there is a problem just at this point in seeking the "godlike" image of a particular psychological idea. Jung warned that "enthusiasm" may be itself symptomatic of inflation.

How can we *not* use the names of Gods without presumption, without puffing up our ideas mythologically, without overstating some mortal sense of things, without beginning to feel that *we know something?* Is it not always a danger-signal of soul when something Grand seems Great?[43]

James Hillman has spoken forcefully about this danger in archetypal psychology. He warns against "reducing archetypes to allegories of disease" (negative inflation?) and against making "a new nominalism" of the Gods of Greece, a "new [or old] grid of classificatory terms" (positive inflation?). "We are not," he says, "looking for a new way to classify . . . but for a new way of experiencing. . . ." Hillman reminds us that mythic thinking, like dream-knowing, is indirect, metaphoric, and poetic. The Gods are not "things" and *we* are not the Gods. "They are *likenesses* to happenings," he says.[44]

This warning is reminiscent of the difficulty Jung had with language. Behind his term "inflation" was the notion of godlikeness, and later he would develop a perspective on alchemy as poetic myth. This shift in Jung's diction allows the hypothesis that a poetic way of seeing, as in the case of alchemy, could be a way of steering a middle course between an inflation which may happen, on the one hand, if the myths of the Gods become a new nominalism, and on the other if the terminology of psychology denies the Gods in becoming abstract and unimaginal (this latter being the "negative inflation" of reductionism).

The mistake in both instances is a lurking ego-perspective that seems to want rational knowledge and psychological control. Thinking or saying, "She is into Hestia," is no better than declaring, "He has an *anima* problem," if by either I feel *I* know something. A mythological depth-psychology deficient in poetic sensibility is no better than the behaviorism of ego-psychologies. Viewing poetically, as Jung seems to imply, puts the emphasis where it belongs, that is, on likeness, even as one speaks of Gods in relation to self. The attitude in this perspective denies to so-called "ego" the certainty and clarity on which the "I" prefers always to center.

Some pages earlier we called attention to Jung's phrase "as that which he is not." Perhaps this formulation is now apt. One begins in life or therapy to see collective sides to self—whether *persona*-role in the social order or archetypal complex of primordial nature. One wrestles it, as Jacob did the angel, not as identical to oneself, but as an other, "as that which he is *not.*" But the "as" here is as crucial as the "not." That which I am not is nonetheless a likeness, a metaphor, a poem of the soul. What I *am* not is precisely what I am "like." In Sanskrit, instead of using "like" or "as," similes are typically formed with the negative particle. "My love"—or so it would seem—"is not a red, red rose."[45]

Poets seem to understand these things. It is they who have long concurred with religious traditions in being wary of "naming the Gods," lest it be in vain.[46] Hölderlin writes:

Shall I name the High Ones then? No God loves what is unseemly;
To grasp him, our joy is scarcely large enough.
Often we must keep silence; holy names are lacking;
Hearts beat and yet does speech still hold back?
But lyre-music lends to each hour its sounds,
And perhaps rejoices the heavenly ones who draw near.[47]

The poem seems to say that to speak of the Gods at all may be an unseemly inflation, afflatus, a *flatus vocis*. "Our joy is scarcely large enough"—Great, perhaps, but not yet Grand. We (that is, our ego-views) are therefore silenced. Yet the beat continues on its own, according to the poet, and with heart too. "Lyre music"—a poetizing perspective—gives the needed sound. For, indeed, the Gods are near. They are likenesses of soul.

The Church Fathers spoke of the task implied by this perspective. They called it turning image to likeness. The Book of Genesis had said that God would create man "in our own image, after our likeness" (Genesis 1:26). But when God actually created man, the Bible says only, "in his image," neglecting to mention "likeness" (Genesis 1:27). So Origen, for example, writes: "Man received the honor of God's image in his first creation, whereas the completion of God's likeness was reserved . . . for his own earnest efforts."[48]

These efforts toward likeness are not an easy work for soul. But perhaps Rhea can be of help, as she was to Dionysos and Persephone, to Poseidon and Jason, to Pelops and the Dactyls. She encourages us to see in the images, not literal identifications, neither some actual "this" nor a really real "that," but the rhythm between "this" and "that," between ego and self, between *persona* and archetype. These betweens take one deep into the beatings drummed in underworlds of soul.

Putting matters this way may allow Rhea's "rhythmic" to modify a bit the "fear and quake" of which Goethe's Mephistopheles speaks. "Godlikeness," in the context of Rhea's *mythos,* may seem more Grand than Great. Her perspective, though it be divine, focuses less on some

"God" and more on a poetizing "likeness." Rhea's view seems closer to that of the Chorus at the end of the faustian drama than it is to the Devil at the beginning. After Goethe's hero has thoroughly been introduced to the realm of the Mothers, the Mystical Chorus says: *Alles Vergängliche/Ist nur ein Gleichnis* ("Everything that passes before you is just a likeness.")[49]

What is given us are images and the images are archetypal. They are images of Gods. Soul's task is to let the variety of imaginal experience in life become metaphor, listening for the likenesses. Then therapy and life itself begin to be sensed as underworld poetry, not psychology but psychopoetics,[50] and one connects with the many imaginal likenesses, not as ego's literal identifications, but "as that which he is not."

In order to arrive at what you are not

You must go through the way in which you are not.
And what you do not know is the only thing you know
And what you own is what you do not own
And where you are is where you are not.[51]

1   C.G. Jung, *Collected Works* (*CW*) VII, §224; compare §111f., 240, 389, 454, 460, 464.
2   Jung, *CW*, VII, §227.
3   Jung, *CW*, VII, §110.
4   "It must be reckoned a psychic catastrophe when the ego is assimilated by the self. . . . However, accentuation of the ego personality and the world of consciousness may easily assume such proportions that the figures of the unconscious are psychologized and the self consequently becomes assimilated to the ego." Jung, *CW* IX, ii, §45, 47.
5   Jung, *CW* VII, §466–470, 110.
6   See James Hillman, *Re-visioning Psychology* (New York: Harper and Row, 1975), Part One.
7   Jung, *CW* VII, §112. The whole sentence is as follows: "The only person who escapes the grim law of enantiodromia is the man who knows how to separate himself from the unconscious, not by repressing it—for then it simply attacks him from the rear—but by putting it clearly before him as *that which he is not.*" Compare §269: "The aim of individuation is nothing less than to divest the self of the false wrappings of the persona on the one hand, and of the suggestive power of primordial images on the other."
8   Jung, *CW* VII, §111.
9   Most of these essays now appear in Volume VII of the *Collected Works*. For example see §476, where the formulation is "acceptance of 'godlikeness,'" and §260, where the same sentence is changed to read, "acceptance of inflation," etc.
10 Jung, *Memories, Dreams, Reflections* (New York: Vintage Books, 1965), p. 282.
11 *Ibid.,* p. 188.

12 The example of Mother, along with those of Magician and Savior, is an instance of "godlikeness" given by Jung. See *CW* VII, §377ff.
13 Some examples are: Erich Neumann, *The Great Mother* (New York: Pantheon, 1955); Robert Briffault, *The Mothers* (New York: Macmillan, 1927); J. J. Bachofen, *Myth, Religion, and Mother Right* (Princeton: Princeton University Press, 1967).
14 Jung, *CW* XIV, §226; compare *CW* XIII, §75; "Everything of which we are conscious is an image, and that image is psyche."
15 Jacob and Wilhelm Grimm, *Kinder- und Hausmärchen,* #26; *Grimm's German Folktales,* trans. Magoun and Krappe (Carbondale: Southern Illinois University Press, 1960), pp. 102ff.
16 Sigmund Freud, "The Occurrence in Dreams of Material from Fairy Tales," *On Creativity and the Unconscious* (New York: Harper and Row, 1958), pp. 79ff. See also: L. Veszy-Wagner, "Little Red Riding Hood on the Couch," *Psycholoanalytical Forum,* I (1966), 399–415, and Elizabeth Crawford, "The Wolf as Condensation," *American Imago,* XII (1955), 307–314.
17 Erich Fromm, *The Forgotten Language* (New York: Grove Press, 1957), pp. 235–240.
18 Eric Berne, *What Do You Say After You Say Hello?* (New York: Bantam Books, 1973), pp. 42–46.
19 Jung, *CW* VII, §227.
20 Otto Rank, "Völkerpsychologische Parallelen zu den infantilen Sexualtheorien," 1912; compare Freud *op. cit.,* p. 83.
21 *Theogony,* 453–506.
22 See David L. Miller, "Fairy Tale or Myth?," *Spring 1976* (New York: Spring Publications), 157–164.
23 See Robert Graves, *The Greek Myths* (Baltimore: Penguin, 1955), I, 118f., 104.
24 *Theogony,* 116–153.
25 *The Library of Greek Mythology (Bibliotheca),* I, 1–44.
26 *Argonautica,* I, 480–511.
27 Graves, *op. cit.,* I, 27, n. 2.
28 Pausanias is the source of this. See *ibid.* I, 39.
29 Aristophanes, *Birds,* 971. See Graves, *op. cit.* I, 148.
30 Euripides, *The Bacchae,* 79.
31 Graves, *op. cit.* I, 310–311.
32 *Orphic Hymns,* XIV, 8.
33 Graves, *op. cit.,* II, 27.
34 *Ibid.,* II, 226.
35 *Ibid.,* I, 188.
36 *Ibid.,* I, 185.
37 Euripides, *The Bacchae,* 127.
38 *Ibid.,* 59.
39 *Orphic Hymns,* XIV, 3f. This translation by Thomas Taylor is found in Raine and Harper (eds.), *Thomas Taylor the Platonist* (Princeton: Princeton University Press, 1969), p. 230.
40 See Graves, *op. cit.* I, 30f.
41 See Mircea Eliade, *Shamanism* (New York: Pantheon, 1964), pp. 168ff.
42 See: J. E. Cirlot, *A Dictionary of Symbols* (New York: Philosophical Library, 1962), p. 85, and James Hastings (ed.), *Encyclopedia of Religion and Ethics* (New York: Scribners, 1912), V, 89–94.
43 It may be worth a footnote to call attention to the *linguistic* difference between the terms "Great" and "Grand." The former comes into English by way of Dutch (*groot* = "thick") and from Old High German (*groz*). Originally this word may have been Slavic. "Grand," on the other hand, has a Southern history. It comes into English from Latin by way of Spanish and French. Its origin is Indoeuropean (the root *grad-,* meaning "strong"). "Great" is Northern; "Grand" is Mediterranean. So, to say the name of the

country England, in French, one utters the phrase, *Grande* Brétagne, whereas in Anglo-Saxon speech one says *Great* Britain.

44   Hillman, *op. cit.*, p. 101.

45   See: Julián Marías, "Philosophic Truth and the Metaphoric System" in Hopper and Miller (eds.), *Interpretation: The Poetry of Meaning* (New York: Harcourt Brace, 1967), p. 46f.

46   Recall the Jewish taboo against speaking the name of God. "Thou shalt not take the name of the Lord thy God in vain; for the Lord will not hold him guiltless that taketh his name in vain" (Exodus 20:7). See Stanley R. Hopper, "On the Naming of the Gods in Hölderlin and Rilke" in Michalson (ed.), *Christianity and the Existentialists* (New York: Scribner's, 1956).

47   The poem is titled *Heimkunft* ("Homecoming"), and this translation is found in Martin Heidegger, *Existence and Being* (Chicago: Gateway, 1949), p. 241; see also the essay by Heidegger on the "naming of the Gods" in this same volume.

48   Origen, *Peri archōn* ("On First Principles"), III, vi, 1; also *Contra Celsum*, IV, 30; Irenaeus, *Ad. haer.*, V. 6; and Clement of Alexandria, *Stromata*, II, 38, 5. On seeing the "likeness" of "images" see also Hillman, "An Inquiry into Image," *Spring 1977*, pp. 62–88, and "Further Notes on Images," *Spring 1978*, pp. 152–182.

49   Goethe, *Faust*, II, 12104f.

50   See David L. Miller, "Hades and Dionysos: The Poetry of Soul," *Journal of the American Academy of Religion*, XLVI, 3, 331–335. In this essay a poetic way of seeing is linked to perspectives of humor not unlike the way Jung views a sense of humor as a principal enemy of "inflation," *CW* VII, §227.

51   T. S. Eliot, "Four Quartets," *The Complete Poems and Plays 1909–1950* (New York: Harcourt, Brace, 1952), p. 127.

VI

HESTIA:
a Background of Psychological Focusing
Barbara Kirksey

I

The appearance of an imaginal figure as a connection to the fantasy ongoings of our individual lives differs distinctly from an intellectual acquaintance with that figure. This is especially true of a mythic persona. Though a classicist may know quite well the persona's entire development and its cultural/religious value [for the society], such knowledge does not always guarantee the *experiencing* of mythical figures and the possibilities they give. What must happen is an encounter with a figure on a level of psychological experience rather than conceptual thought: one might say a close encounter of the soul kind. When this occurs, a pattern of images, a certain preference for an imaginal inscape, and a personal, random history of images suddenly emerge as 'making sense.' There is a focusing, and the connection to that figure becomes the occasion of awakening to psychological experience.

Our initial image then is one of gathering, weaving together (integrating), and centering randomness. We are already within a certain psychic domain—a place at a center which integrates and weaves together random strands of our lives. Fantasies of 'the center' have prevailed throughout the tradition of Jungian psychology. Jung himself devoted much labor developing those concepts which revolve around a center. The 'Self,' mandala imagery, and the circularity of alchemical processes have a content of centeredness or the quality of movement within a circle. In later Jungian thought, however, centering became co-equal with fantasies of harmony, wholeness, spiritual development and integration, fantasies which failed both to differentiate sufficiently the various experiences of centeredness and to keep the imagining of centeredness distinct from literalisms of 'the center.'

For an excellently documented and comprehensive account of the mythology and cult of Hestia, see the article by Stephanie A. Demetrakopoulos, "Hestia, Goddess of the Hearth: Notes on an Oppressed Archetype" in *Spring 1979*, pp. 55–76, which appeared since the present paper was written.

Recently some authors have moved to do away with fantasies of centeredness altogether, since so much of what has been put 'in the center' is more seconding of theology than phenomenology of soul. Yet the movement to find a center is not so easily eradicated from the psyche's concerns, and this desire for centeredness manifests itself in the most diverse and insistent ways. One of the most common yet most subtle is the choice of a single theme, figure or symptom about which to write. Such a choice gives a centrality to the theme, figure, or symptom. We also exercise the function of centering when we concentrate on psychic contents and pay attention to them; we focus on them and find a place for them in life, or a dream is viewed as 'central' to some complex in therapy. Occasionally some imaginal figure comes to bring things together for a while or engulf us into his center. Then a mini-cosmos presents itself in the imaginal realm, and the drama begins. We describe the event as a central experience in our life or a central point in the course of therapy, a 'peripateia' in the psychic drama.

All of these are ways centering is an inherent part of life, and yet they seem humbler than the glorious fantasies which accompany the 'Self' in its spiritual aloofness or as literal pivot in a picture. Here we are presenting the center as a style of consciousness, a natural movement within the structure of consciousness insofar as consciousness includes *concentrating* or *focusing*. If the center is inherent, fantasizing about its various kinds seems imperative, so that they may gain an imaginal depth, even in their most mundane forms. One way to begin such fantasy is to find a God whose realm is characterized by centeredness.

When I begin to imagine a central figure in Greek mythology, the immediate tendency is to move to Zeus since he is the father of the Gods and the organizational genius of Mount Olympus. In addition, he stands as the epitome of many cultural values which the western world cherishes, such as power, effective action, and managerial prowess. However, if we ask the question, "What is the center for the Gods and for the Greeks themselves?" then another figure who has remained relatively obscure in mythology as well as in archetypal literature emerges. This is Hestia, who was worshipped at the center of the city and the center of the Greek household, and who was presented as a heap of glowing charcoal which became the *omphalos* (navel) at Delphi, the Greek center of the world.[1] Almost no notice is awarded her in archetypal literature, and yet Kerényi points out, "she obtained as her sacred place the central point of the house, the hearth—which is also the meaning of her name."[2] Hestia occupies a place at the center of dwelling, and thus she must be central to psychic life. Furthermore, her character is bound up with the center, and thus centeredness is part of her realm. What the quality of that centeredness is and what are its possibilities for the soul will occupy the remaining discussion.

II

Hestia is simultaneously the oldest of Kronos' and Rhea's children and the youngest, since she was the first he swallowed and the last to return from his stomach. Thus she is the first Olympian, but almost paradoxically the most obscure; there are almost no stories about her, and she does not appear as a personal Goddess. Ovid writes, "Long did I foolishly think that there were images of Vesta: afterwards I learned that there are none under her curved dome."[3] Her image and her place are identical. There were no statues of her in her temple. There was only the sacred fire on the hearth. Because she chose not to marry, Zeus gave her the privilege of receiving the first and last sacrifices at any ceremony. In the Homeric hymn to her, we find the claim that "Without you, mankind would have no feasts, since no one could begin the first and last drink of honey-like wine without an offering to Hestia."[4] The worship of a sacred fire was common in several ancient religions, particularly the Zoroastrian cult in Persia. But the *lack of personification* is consistent throughout her history, and Ovid advises, "Conceive of Vesta as naught but the living flame."[5] This is a strong admonition, though curiously it is this same author who produced the one story of antiquity we do have concerning Hestia.

Despite the lack of myths, we repeatedly find Hestia in the center of Greek life as the *hearth*. The Homeric hymn says she is in the dwellings of Gods and mortals, and like Hermes she protects and gives good things to man.[6] Significantly, she seems more connected to the life of mortals than the other Olympians by virtue of her place, the hearth; yet she takes no part in the wars, grievances, or affairs between Gods and mortals. She stays on Mount Olympos far removed from mortal goings-on. Her relation to Apollo is important because of her place, as coals, at Delphi, and also because Apollo (as well as Poseidon) was her suitor.[7]

In the Roman world her name was Vesta. Ovid writes: "Vesta is the same as the earth . . . under both of them is a perpetual fire; the earth and the hearth are symbols of the home."[8] Her priestesses at the temple in Rome were the famous Vestal Virgins, who took a vow of chastity. If the vow was broken the guilty priestess was punished by being buried alive, since she had contaminated the earth. Needless to say, there were few offenders in the many years of this cult. Her temple in Rome was described by Ovid as similar to the shape of the temple of old and this shape was based on Vesta's association with the earth. The shape was round and there were no projecting angles in it; a dome over the temple protected the interior from rain.[9] Her temple was a further expression of Hestia's kinship with the primordial feminine deity, Earth. The architecture of the temple manifests Hestia in a way which statues manifest the more personalized deities of Greek and Roman myths. Thus her *image is architectural*. This is supported by her role as a guardian of homes, and as the deity who first built a house.[10]

We must be careful to differentiate Hestia from other "earth Goddesses." She is a virgin Goddess, and one of the three who are immune to the power of Aphrodite.[11] The seriousness of her chastity is reflected in the Vestal Virgin's pledge of virginity. She cannot be associated with (or reduced to) the fecundity and productivity of Gaia or Rhea without losing her specific and unique place among the pantheon.

In order to reflect further on Hestia's psychological significance two unique aspects of her character require elaboration. The first is her peculiar lack of personified images: she resists personification as a human-like figure. This is not to say that she has no personal quality; rather she resists becoming an object of imagining in a bodily way as occurs with other mythic personae. But when imagined, Hestia appears as the hearth and the contained fire upon it. She is the domestic fire without which there could be no feasts for men, as Homer stated. Hestia appears as a particular aspect of the world which is 'nobody' (without body) but which gathers men together and enables soul to have a place. It is as if when we gather we are in her body and so cannot see her *as* a body; place becomes her body.

This is no discrete location, as Descartes' placing the soul in the pineal gland, nor do I suggest the concrete fireplace or hearth guarantees an experience of soul, though this material level facilitates her epiphany. Bachelard, for instance, gained access to Hestian imaginal realities by dwelling with the image of the fireplace in his *Poetics of Space*.

Hestia's value in psychological life is her ability to mediate soul by giving a place to congregate, a gathering point. And through this point the psyche and world merge. Hestia allows *spaciality* to be a form of *psychological reality*. The Greeks never forsook this truth for a purely geometric view of space. Spaciality had a divine aspect. According to Rollo May, "We Americans have very little sense of sacredness of space."[13] May quotes De Tocqueville as saying, "In the United States, a man builds a house in which to spend his old age, and he sells it before the roof is on. . . ."[14]

But the ancients knew that the circularity of the hearth was the expression of sacred space, in accordance with the nature of a specific Goddess. The space echoed the roundness of the earth, but this roundness was domestic and tied to man's cities and homes in a way that nature's circularity was not. It is through the mediumistic presence of Hestia that the abode of man's world is psychological. Imagining, which is the psychological activity *par excellence*, is not severed from the world and retained within an individual body. The imaginal does not equal a literal interior space; and the world, especially the dwelling spaces, reflect back to us an indication of our soul condition. The dwellings we create and in which we abide (interiorly and exteriorly) manifest an aspect of our soul. The 'places' of dreams and fantasies, the dwellings—high-rise apartments, old haunted mansions, basements, hallways, and bedrooms—tell us much about where our soul is at the moment. To quote Bachelard, "All great simple images reveal a psychic state. The house, even more than the landscape, is a 'psychic state' and even when reproduced as it appears from the outside, it bespeaks intimacy."[15] The day-world dwellings speak of our soul's place: they reveal an intimate side of one's psyche.[16]

Because the psychology of Hestia is a revisioning of soul in terms of spatial metaphors, the pathology of the soul through Hestia's language contains phrases related to space. 'Off base,' 'off-center,' 'unable to find a place,' 'can't settle down,' 'spaced out,' and 'off the wall' are related to Hestian values, and remind the wanderer of her power to bring the soul into a state of dwelling. Ever since antiquity, pathology has been fantasized as a 'wandering' phenomenon (*e.g.,* delirium, deviate). Cicero proclaimed that a sick soul was one which could not attain or endure and was always astray, The soul, gone astray, is a soul without psychic connection to this Goddess and her centeredness. The soul can't come home for there is no place for the homecoming. This specific lack of having a place is not equal to being an abandoned child or to the wanderings of the puer. The child may still find a home and a place to nurse its abandonment within other dwelling places. But the loss of Hestia is a more severe threat to the total psyche with its multitude of images and their influence. Without Hestia, there can be no focusing on the image, and there are no boundaries to differentiate the intimacy of the inner dwelling and the outer world, for there is no psychic house to give protective walls. There can be no joyous feasts, no celebrations of life, no food for the soul.

Certain transient disorders in psychosis, particularly of the schizophrenias, could be understood as Hestia's absence in the psyche. There is no centering containment so what is 'in here' is also 'out there' and what comes from 'out there' cannot be protected against because there are no barriers to the 'in here.' This disturbance has a peculiarly spatial aspect. With no separation between the spaces of dwelling and the spaces of wilderness there is no permanence either, so that the whole psychic world is experienced as transient and fleeting. Bachelard expresses this more eloquently: ". . . the house shelters daydreaming, the house protects the dreamer, the house allows one to dream in peace."[17] If Hestia does not build her house there is no protection or peace for the dreamer. Jung's description of the schizophrenic's state echoes many of the images of which we have spoken. He states:

> . . . the latent schizophrenic must always reckon with the possibility that his very foundations will give way somewhere . . . that his ideas and concepts will lose their cohesion and their connection with other spheres of association and with the environment. As a result, he feels threatened by an uncontrollable chaos of chance happenings.[18]

This deep and 'foundational' disturbance refers to the dwelling space whether imagistically presented as the earth or as a building. Jung goes on to cite examples of dream imagery which appear in the 'latent' schizophrenic patient. Images, such as the earth turning to water, the end of the world, the ground under the patient's feet heaving, or the walls beginning to bulge and bend are characteristic, he says, in the nightmares of these persons.[19] Jung sums up the phenomena by stating that "these images bear witness to a fundamental disturbance of relationship, that is, of the patient's *rapport with his surroundings*."[20]

I believe that this weak cohesion and insecurity relate to the absence of Hestia's mediating abilities which gather and center random events into a common space. She is non-personified because she, like the Moirai, is *a priori* to the experience of soul. Thus she is the first-born and the last—a kind of alpha and omega figure for the psyche. And her absence threatens the entire psychic 'structure' of the personality with chaos. She acts as a mediator for psychological integration analogous to Hermes' mediating activities as connector and mover of soul. She has a cohesive function in the soul, which preserves the element of wholeness, allowing the individual to image 'in peace.'

The second crucial psychological aspect of Hestia's character is her chosen virginity. She is one of the three great virgin Goddesses who have nothing to do with the erotic realm of experience. She is immune to Aphrodite's power and consequently to Eros' arrows. This immunity is a further elaboration of her presence as a stabilizing and foundational aspect of soul because it resists the onslaught of Erotic and/or Dionysian mania.

Within her pristine position, Hestia is able to *guard images*. My supposition here derives from this account in Ovid. The Palladium, an image of Athena in war dress, was guarded by Hestia in the Vestal Temple at Rome. It was stolen from Troy and believed to be the image which preserved the empire. Apollo had decreed that this image of Minerva would "transfer with herself the seat of empire."[21] After it was carried off to Rome, it was kept at the temple of Vesta because "she [Vesta] sees all things by her light that never fails."[22] Hestia is made guardian of that image which holds the empire together. The guardianship is given to her because of a power of illumination which never fails, sees all things, and which also fosters all things. Hestia's strength is unlike the other two virgin Goddesses. Both Athena and Artemis find their strength in forms of assertive action. Hestia illuminates. Her illuminating provides protection and fostering of the image. It guards the image, and by doing this, keeps the empire protected. This reverberates off the former association to Hestia's stabilizing and centering influence. She is protectress of the empire in psychic life, *i.e.,* the seat of imaginal activity.

What is the quality of Hestia's illumination? From the original image of her we gain a clue to her specific lightbringing power. Hestia's illumination is the light from the hearth and its flame. Ovid tells us that the word for hearth in Latin is *focus* and "the hearth (*focus*) is so named from the flames, and because it fosters (*fovet*) all things."[23] Because this word exists unchanged in the English language as it appeared in Latin, a discussion of the usage of this word can amplify the quality of Hestia's guardianship of images.[24]

III

A long history of the word "focus" is given in the *Oxford English Dictionary,* and the usage raids many disciplines. Johannes Kepler employs it in 1604 in its first modern scientific usage. The reason for his choice is not apparent; conjectures are that the optical sense (burning point of a lens or mirror) which is easily derived from the literal, was probably already in existence and would account for his selection of the word in his experiments with parabolic mirrors.[25] Kepler's use connects seeing, mirrors, and a burning point into a single constellation. Again, burning point emphasizes the place where illumination happens. Here is Hestia, guardian of illumination where light is most concentrated, protector of images through light.

The word "focus" is used in optics in a similar way. In this branch of science the focus is the point at which rays meet after being reflected or refracted, and also the point from which the rays appear to proceed. Newton used the word in 1704: "the point from which the rays diverge or to which they converge may be called their focus."[26] The point from which separation or convergence occurs—one's starting point or final point—is the focus. The origin of this starting point is expressed by the mythic figure, Hestia.

Reawakening the original meaning of the word profoundly alters the contemporary fantasies of perception. If the focus is a point of both beginning and ending, perception is not only a linear process of absorbing stimuli from the outside world. The archaic image contained in the word "focus" relates to circularity and to a point which is originating source and destination point. Focusing, which in common usage means the ability to perceive clearly, is an achievement of a circular process. It involves the ability to allow a circular relationship between the one who focuses and the object focused upon. Linearity, however, is not excluded from the origin of this word and the historical uses of it. The employment of the word in plane geometry relates both circularity and linearity as aspects of space and therefore as aspects of "focus."[27] The scientific tradition has so narrowly adopted and uniformly expanded the image of linearity that now only this aspect of perception predominates to the relative exclusion of the other.

The scientific definitions of focus are revealing; yet they are embedded within the specialized imaginings of science so that the fantasies these definitions produce are for only those with a deep appreciation of the scientific style of consciousness. Two other definitions of "focus" connect it more closely to psychological life.

The first comes from the modern theatre. In the theatre the focus is "the best illuminated part of the stage."[28] Those characters who appear in our psychological experiences as brightly illuminated or more illuminated than the others are the focus of psychological experience. We may say Hestia is in charge of the lighting during the drama. She is backstage, but necessary to the production. The drama of psychic life contains a focus, a point of illumination where figures may be seen. And if we take seriously the ancient belief of guardianship through illumination, it is necessary to give illumination and center stage to those figures in our scenes of consciousness. Focusing on the character allows the psychic drama to be played out; by doing this the image is preserved, given due reverence and protected.

Another fantasy-laden definition for focus is "that point or position at which an object must be situated in order that the image produced by the lens may be clear and well-defined."[29] Bringing an image into its focus situates it at a place where it produces itself definitively. The image places itself by remaining 'out' of focus until its position has been established in its own terms. The notion of image-precision is, in part, an inherent quality of the image.

However, the other part involves our finding the place where an image is sharp and well-defined—to a burning point. Then the image is 'in' focus and thus has clarity *from within*. Focusing is antithetical to interpreting the image because the action of focusing relies upon the image to direct it from the place where it is. Our language deceives us. We speak as if the image is moved to a new position in order for it to be seen clearly. But when we say that we 'bring' the image into focus, is it not the lens rather than the image which has moved? Ours is the adjustment. The image maintains its own space, and it is the process of focusing which brings the individual into a definitive relationship to the image whereby the image gains illumination and clarity. Returning to the image again and again from various directions is an attempt to focus—an attempt to find the fire of the image. This is imagining in a Hestian mode.

Amplification also touches upon this way of imagining. It is a kind of focusing where the image is a point at which all rays emerge and converge, beginning and ending at the point of the image itself and its place. When a complaint comes that the image is 'off'—it is imprecise or even inappropriate—this complaint reverts back to the intuition that images have a focus, a place where they manifest themselves to burn and illuminate, where they are protected and active.

The spatial qualities of a focus are geometric *and* imaginal. They belong to perception *and* imagination. Although imagination and perception have been severed and contrasted before, a common connection unites them. Hestia is a gathering point; her domain re-connects the differences. This connection is through "focusing" as a form of behavior.[30] Consequently, focusing transcends the conceptual distance which has been constructed between perception and imagination. It is a quality and a qualification of both.

Another etymological connection to Hestia comes through hospitality. Because Hestia gives the images a place to gather, she provides them with hospitality rather than hospitalization. The images gather as guests around her hearth. The words "guest," "ghost," "hospitality" and "hospital" share a common root etymologically, suggesting further fantasy about Hestia's focal position for psyche. The image as ghost is transformed into a guest by allowing it to enter the area of the hearth. A ghost is also "a piece of dead coal that instead of burning, appears in the fire as a white lump."[31] Images refusing focus are ghostly remains, haunting us in their smoldering graveyard, deadened to fire. Conversely, images have ghosts even at their brightest point, and not even in the most focused area can perfect illumination be achieved.

Yet if transformation from ghost to guest is possible, how might it happen? The definition for guest gives a clue. A guest is "a person or thing *personified* that comes and is entertained. . . ."[32] Personification enables images to become guests at the focus. Altering the image is not the question here. A guest and a ghost originate from a common etymological and imagistic source. There is no need to change the image, only to personify it. Personifying is a way of knowing (as James Hillman has said), and this way of knowing is hospitable toward images, getting to know them as guests when they visit, inviting them toward the warmth of the fire.

The word "focus" alludes to a foundational principle of life. Hestia, found as Earth, promotes fantasies of underlying foundational structures and central disturbances. This continues in medical fantasies where the focus of disease is "the principal seat [in the body], also a point where its activity is manifest."[33] (In German, the word *Herd* refers to hearth, as well as to focus and seat of disease.) Whatever is "focal" is also principal, manifest and central. Conversely, when the word "focus" is used, this word hints at the special value of the occasion for soul. Disease is one such important occasion. This value emerges also from the Greek word *Heschara* for our Goddess, which means "burned place," the English word for which is scar. Whereas focus is too easily imagined as vision and distance, scar reverberates throughout the body, even to that small inconspicuous mark at the center of our body which is the trace "of attachment of some structure that has been removed."[34] The omphalos is not so far from us, and contemplating one's navel is not so removed from psyche. . . . Reminiscent of a former attachment, the navel is so well-healed that it is almost inaccessible to consciousness. And yet psyche still speaks of "birth trauma," reminding us of the origins of the scar.

In English, the scar is both wound and sign of healing. It also remains unchanged in its verb form suggesting that *action* can be *wound,* and that forms of behavior may be scars. Scars are marked places, separated from surrounding areas by means of the wound. They are a different tissue. Scarring leaves a new kind of sensitivity so that when touched, the scar feels 'different' from other places. Our scars might well be the points marked out in the soul's life. These are the places where once a fire burned—where illumination occurred, or is occurring still. Hestia gives an archetypal depth to these wounds, transforming them from personal ashes to sacrificial fires.

The final etymological excursion with Hestia as focus is where the center of activity is. A focus is also "the center of activity or area of greatest energy, of a storm, volcanic eruption, etc., also a center or 'hot bed' of intrigue, sedition, etc."[35] The center is not a place of harmony or integration. This center contains pathology. There is betrayal and sedition at the center and eruptive storms which demand a focus—a place to burn and smolder. Pathology is a demand for re-adjusted focus. Psychic storms demand that we remove ourselves from center stage so that the other characters may enter. We must move in relationship to the pathological image to adjust to its "focus," so that the image has central importance. This adjustment of focusing is a movement of soul. It is not a journey to the underworld with Hermes, a Dionysian frenzy, or a Panic-stricken flight. Inherently more subtle, focusing is the slight movements toward and away from those burned–burning places of soul. It is a way of 'finding place' for one's illnesses and wounds.

Obtaining a focus after the experience of scarring requires adjustment. We adjust a lens, a microscope or any number of machines. But we also adjust to life, to our limitations, and to those which fate brings. Adjustment is not only an ugly bourgeois word, maligned by puer enthusiasts. It does not only connote stagnation and compromise. It is part of the psychological activity of focusing. It involves a movement of soul to find centered places for diseases, images, dramatic characters, and energies. Adjusting is what we are involved in when we want to find a center as a place of illumination and energy. Also adjustment has its part in the process of healing and wounding. Adjustment is the movement from one to the other: feeling when a wound should become ash and when it should flame. As part of the archetype of the journey home to the hearth, focusing is the experience of and connection to Hestia, builder of the house, so that the soul may dream in peace.

1   Barbara Koltuv, "Hestia/Vesta," *Quadrant 10* (Winter 1977), p. 57.
2   Carl Kerényi, *The Gods of the Greeks* (London: Thames & Hudson, 1951), pp. 91–92.
3   *Ovid's Fasti,* translated by Sir James Frazer (Cambridge: Harvard University Press), p. 341.
4   *The Homeric Hymns,* "The Homeric Hymn to Hestia," translated by Charles Boer (Spring Publications, 1979).
5   *Fasti,* p. 341.
6   *Op. cit,* p. 140.
7   Kerényi, p. 91.
8   *Fasti,* p. 339.
9   *Fasti,* p. 339.
10 David Kravitz, *Who's Who in Greek and Roman Mythology* (New York: Potter, 1975), p. 119.
11 *The Homeric Hymns, op. cit.*
12 Victor Drury, *The World of the Greeks* (Geneva: Minerva, 1971), p. 33.
13 Rollo May, *Power and Innocence* (New York: Norton, 1972), p. 57.
14 *Ibid.,* p. 57.
15 Gaston Bachelard, *The Poetics of Space* (Boston: Beacon Press), p. 72.
16 The hearth is a heavily laden symbol of which architects are aware. In a lecture at the University of Dallas (April 7, 1978), the distinguished architect Christian Norberg-Schulz devoted a long discussion to the importance of the hearth. He quotes Frank Lloyd Wright as saying that it comforted him to see the fire burning in the masonry. Schulz pointed out that it was Wright who reintroduced the concept of the hearth as the center of dwelling in contemporary architecture. He also cited etymological connections between the words "stove" and "house."
17 Bachelard, p. 6.
18 *CW* 3, §559.
19 *Ibid.,* §559.
20 *Ibid.,* §559 (italics mine).
21 *Fasti,* p. 351.

22 *Ibid.*, p. 332.
23 *Ibid.*, p. 341.
24 For a full presentation of the value and practice of psychological etymologizing, see Robert Kugelman, "Etymology as a Psychological Operation," *Dragonflies,* I:1 (University of Dallas, Fall 1978), pp. 43–63.
25 *The Oxford English Dictionary* (1914), 4:377.
26 *Idem.*
27 The focus is "one of the points from which the distance to any point of a given curve are connected by a linear relation." *Idem.*
28 *Idem.*
29 *Idem.*
30 I use the word "behavior" purposely, though it is a word easily misconstrued. I do not mean a measurable and visibly observable gesture so much as a *form of engagement* with that which is other than 'ego.' Focusing is not an activity of the ego nor a property of it either. This "engagement" is not subsumed under the ego; rather the ego depends upon it as a relatively autonomous function for its coherence as was mentioned above in regards to schizophrenia. "Arche-types are typical forms of behavior which once they become conscious naturally present themselves as ideas and images . . . (*CW* 8, §435). Focusing is archetypal behavior. Experientially and linguistically, this behavior is not limited by the differences between imagining and perceiving. It is an important aspect of both.
31 *Oxford English Dictionary,* Vol. 4, p. 149.
32 *Ibid.*, p. 488 (italics mine).
33 *Ibid.*, p. 377.
34 *Ibid.*, v. 13, p. 182.
35 *Ibid.*, v. 13, p. 377.

VII

HERMES' HETERONYMOUS APPELLATIONS*

William G. Doty

> Le bon Dieu est dans le détail.
> —G. Flaubert
> Only the exhaustive is truly interesting.
> —T. Mann

I. Names and Deities

How useful it is to have so many names!" Cario remarks to Hermes in Aristophanes' *Plutus* (l. 1164), after the latter has bargained for admittance throughout a half-mocking litany in which there are references to his roles as watcher-near-the-door, guide, presider-over-the-games, and God of thieves, commerce, and intrigues.

Gods and Goddesses who become most manifest through a long series of epithets have a significance and a lasting power less easily descried in more monotonic deities. Whether it is truly "useful" (or good, fortunate, serviceable—*agathos*) to the deity to have a number of forms is not something we can know; but as a carrier for projected human values, it seems obvious that a deity known heteronymously under many aspects will have a greater usefulness to us than one who sanctifies only something like the hearth or warfare.

At the level of primary diction, names are images, symbols; they are magical; knowing the names of a deity implies that one knows which appellations to use ritually to resolve particular problems or needs. Among the American Navajo, for instance, the deities 'must' come to a ceremonial when their picture-boards are correctly set forth; a specialist-diviner will be called in before the ceremonial to insure the right match between deity and need.

The Orphic Hymns, those strange Hellenistic attempts to cite every possible divine appellation (cf. the Egyptian and Tibetan Books of the Dead), as well as two epigrams in the Greek Anthology that

---

*Heteronymous: "different names or terms . . . having correspondence or interrelationship; for example *master* and *mistress*" (*American Heritage Dictionary*, 1975). From an ongoing series of essays on myth, and on Hermes, this is a first attempt to organize a mass of heteronymous materials. It was published earlier in *Archē* 2 (1978), 17–35, and is presented here in revised and expanded form by permission of the Center for Archaic Studies. A brief general presentation of Hermes' aspects, and of the power of the mythologem today, in response to K. Kerényi, *Hermes Guide of Souls*, transl. M. Stein (Spring Publ., 1976), is available in my article in the *Journal of Analytical Psychology* 23/4 (1978), 358–64.

give dozens of epithets of Dionysos and Apollo in alphabetical sequence (*A.P.* 9.524–5), betray that their authors are no longer in a living relationship with the deities; i.e., they no longer presume that identifying one specific aspect of a deity (with the history of its first-naming) is crucial. Perhaps it is not beside the point to refer to the contemporary dissatisfaction with monotheism and the consequent turn to a "new polytheism" in theology (see David L. Miller, *The New Polytheism,* 1974). Appropriately, at any rate, Hera, Adonis, and the Fates/Moirai are *polyOnymos,** "many-named" or "worshipped under many names" (Orphic Hymns 16, 56, 59), which may be the earlier equivalent of our "heteronymous" (first used in 1734, according to the OED).

In an illustrated presentation on "Hermes: Changing Manifestations of a Mythic Trickster," I develop some eleven of Hermes' aspects, and relate them to Hermes-like figures in other culture areas (Egypt, Africa, the ancient Americas, Haiti, Japan, Northern Europe). Some of the impact of that presentation depends upon the visual layering of images, which is not possible in this purely discursive essay, where you may select your own verbal layering. Neither space nor focus allows traveling into the fascinating territories ruled by the mystagogue Hermes Trismegistos, in gnostic and occult wisdoms, nor by the medieval form, Mercurius, who as transformative spirit was crucial to alchemy, and the patron of all the arts. (Iconographic similarities between alchemical illustrations and title pages of 'straight' medieval books make me wonder if 'the arts' were not actually comprehended as the alchemies of the soul, as alchemy proper was of the abstract spirit.) Touch a mythical or archetypal figure at the point of any one image, and others seem to clamor, like minority groups in American politics, for equal time.

II. Methodology

My procedure has pretty much shaped itself: (a) compiling lists of epithets as I followed references to Hermes in the primary and secondary literature; these were entered on index cards with examples of usage (no attempt to be exhaustive); (b) organizing the epithets so obtained into master groupings—here the taxonomic sensitivities of

---

*Greek words are transcribed as is customary, except that I use capital letters for the long vowels instead of a superscript line; the second vowel in this word therefore is 'big-o,' *o-mega,* usually transcribed -ō-.

the analyst are most involved, but presumably the materials them-selves will lead (and indeed did so, as I classified and reclassified); (c) cross-checking the groupings with my own and others' characteriza-tions—here the 'regulatory' aspects of the task are evident: were so-and-so's categories sufficient? how should appellations of Hermes be distinguished from those of another figure? (d) synopsis and interpre-tation—which in this instance falls mostly outside the scope of this report, which emphasizes the methodology and the raw data.

The bulk of what follows, then, is scarcely more than an index or word list; it is the sort of project a computer would facilitate greatly, although as in most computer-assisted projects that have been com-pleted to date, the crucial element is the codings. Ironically, we need the *epitheta deorum*, the concordance, in order to do the coding of the concordance itself. Nonetheless, we are faced like Psyche with a mountain of mixed grains, and must trust to the kindly ants/instincts to help us restore order.

And I am sometimes less interested in the beauty of the final product than in what may be learned along the way of following the task itself. In the course of my listing and charting of appellations (originally begun several years ago, as a means of finding my way around unfamiliar Greek nomenclature), several benefits to mytho-graphic exploration of Greek and other mythological figures showed themselves.

First, the approach gives us a way out of the dilemma of 'the text.' Instead of arbitrarily deciding that only such-and-such a version of a myth is *the* normative form, when authors such as Apollodorus or Ovid are at worst derivative, and at best mythopoetic in their own right, this approach seeks appellations throughout the range of extant materials, and, in its scope, reaches even into the Middle Ages (since I have combed the Greek Anthology, which does not get its final contours until the fourteenth century C.E., and the Orphic Hymns, approximately third century C.E.). I have tried to remain aware of the relative chronology of the epithets, but I consider the history-of-im-pact (*Nachgeschichte*) as important as any originating layer of tradition. The problems of contemporary semiotics remind us of the absolute necessity of combining the lexical-etymological (metaphor, synchrony, syntagm) with the history of utilization (metonym, diachrony, para-digm).

My hermeneutics leads me to emphasize *what a mytheme sets in motion* as much as how it originated, or when. The evolutionary bias that the earliest is the purest may be appropriate where we deal with a closely controlled text, but it is less helpful than the other eighteenth- and nineteenth-century monomythic approaches when we are dealing with the rich polytextuality of something like classical mythology. Charting appellations wherever they occur contributes to a manipulable meta-text, which, however, must also be cross-examined carefully when there is something of a quasi-canonical text that has claims to authority, as here, the Homeric Hymns to Hermes. (It may seem too coincidental, but I had never made my way systematically through the Hymns until I was preparing this paper: I found few appellations I had not already encountered elsewhere. Likewise, I used the lists of Carter and Eitrem—see Resources, below—only after making my own.)

A second benefit of this approach is that it may disclose variations or aspects of the mythic figures we would not otherwise have sighted, whether these lead to new overall perspectives or only to lesser clarifications. Dedications of kitchen utensils to Hermes, in the Greek Anthology, for example, gave me an expanded sense of Hermes' role as servant and God of commerce; inscriptions on harborside herms (bust-topped square stone pillars, often with erect phalli on their fronts, dedicated to or representing Hermes) showed me that the Hermes-Priapus link had a sea aspect as well as an agricultural one; and I had not suspected the association with Law and Justice (section J. in Part III).

This may be especially important when polyvalent deities are exhibited in their full range of ascribed features. In the Greek Anthology (*A.P.* 9.783), a statue of a hermaphrodite in a bathhouse carries an inscription which begins "To men, I am Hermes, but to women, appear as Cypris [Aphrodite]," suggesting that the positive/negative, good/evil, masculine/feminine identifications we make are matters of personal and cultural projections. "Beauty lies in the eye of the beholder": yes, but we have to be aware that in other situations "beauty" is not figured solely on the basis of our Western, masculine, logos-oriented aesthetics. The full range of meta-textual comparison may retard our seeing nothing but the reflection of our own custom in objectively-other materials.

A third benefit of this mythographic approach is that comparisons of epithets applied to a *number* of mythic figures might disclose statistically that certain shared terms are applied more frequently to one or another deity; correspondingly, it might give us a typology of deities according to more appropriately ethnopoetic standards—how the

Goddesses and Gods were actually experienced and described in the culture being studied, rather than in terms of schemata we impress upon it. As a sort of Confucian 'rectification of names,' this might serve to insure that we truly practice that phenomenological 'abeyance' by which we filter out our own signals and fine-tune both what the texts *were* saying in their own contexts and *are* saying within our own contexts today.

A quick example: I was intrigued to find a large cluster of epithets referring to wings, wing-footed, and the like (section Q. in Part III). I had wondered if this traditional representation of Hermes/Mercury in art were something read backward from the late Hellenistic erotes, which became the chubby, winged cupids of medieval paintings. Evidently it was not, given so many epithets of apparent antiquity; and my wondering led me to the remarkable phrase in *Odyssey* 17.57 that is translated "that arrow didn't hit its mark," but which is literally "speech/myth was to her [Penelope—who cannot trust Telemachos' wondrous hint that Odysseus is near] without wings": words which are not winged, which have no spiritual component, "don't connect." Awash in a sea of words, it may be crucial for us to re-member the effect-ual dynamic power of mythos/word as we learn to poeticize, to 'make' our own meanings.

Finally, the approach outlined and demonstrated provisionally here is but one path toward reconnection with the archai, the archai roots that have not withered away, but have often had heaped upon them mounds of mythological handbooks. Somehow we must regain the sense of the fictiveness of all our constructs—*fictio,* that which is made, constructed; not the ir-real, but the supra- and super-real. Somehow we need to touch the objective otherness of these roots and let them activate stronger self-imaginings.

Puzzling through the interconnections among many appellations is a game that knows few boundaries. It may even be the game that leads us down false byways and into cul-de-sacs. But it also shatters the assured consistencies of the handbooks in ways that challenge our social constructions of reality and lead us toward the creative image-play that Hermes, the shifty/turn-god/gamester/trickster/guide, never tired of: coming into the midst of a gathering—where that awkward silence has shaped itself, in the midst of superficial role-playing—bringing the new idea and interplay: *HermEs epeiselEluthe,* "Hermes has entered into our midst" (archaic and contemporary Greek proverb).

III. The Appellations

General Comments

1. The categories are not exclusive; I have made cross-references, but have not tried to note all the possibilities.

2. Nuances are not always clear from the brief definitions; I have usually placed an epithet in a category on the basis of its contexts, which could also be cited here. Associations with other figures could also be mentioned only occasionally.

3. Some of the epithets apply (also) to herms.

4. Arrangement within each section follows the order of the English transliterations, not the Greek spellings; hence *achnous* precedes *aglaos* in section A, though the opposite order would be expected from the Greek.

5. Strictly speaking, some of the epithets are adverbial rather than nouns and adjectives; I have not ruled them out if they are used as recurrent characterizations.

6. I have not traced here Latin epithets (PWK, *Realency.*, Suppl. II, or elsewhere, e.g., *C.I.G.* 5953). I did not have enough Greek and academic Latin to track all the references and modulations in Georg Kaibel, *Epigrammata Graeca.*

7. The lists do not indicate frequency or range of usage.

8. Abbreviations used: ep. = epithet/s; H. = Hermes; L-S = Liddell-Scott-Jones-McKenzie, *A Greek-English Lexicon*; mag. pap. = magical papyri; l. = line; pl. = plural; esp. = especially; freq. = frequent(ly); poet. = poetic; fr. = fragment; usu. = usual(ly).

9. "See A," etc., following a Greek ep. in parentheses, means that the main entry is in the section indicated.

A. APPEARANCE, DESCRIPTIVE

achnous beardless [on a herm by the racetrack; but there are just as many bearded representations, since H. is both youth and old man, below]

aglaos beautiful, famous

alkimos brave, stout

chlamydEphoros one who wears the chlamys (short cloak) [freq. ep. of the *epheboi*, and of heralds]

chrysophanEs shining like gold

(chrysopteros) see Q.

chrysorapis with wand of gold

diaugEs radiant

diprosOpos two-faced [see *tetra-* group below]

eriboas loud-shouting

eriphyllios many-leaved [probable reference to garlanded herm]

euphrOn cheerful, merry

eurrapis with beautiful staff

euphrengEs brilliant, shining

euskopos keen-sighted, watchful [esp. as compound with *argeiphontEs;* see S.]

eusphyros with beautiful ankles [usu. of women]

glischrOn niggard, greedling [adj.: sticky; penurious]

gymnas naked, trained; exercise [not an ep., but said H. delights in *gymnas* and deceit, and he is freq. represented as naked]

ischys the strong [as father, with Brimo/ Phoibe, of Brimos, "the strong"]

(kouros) see U.

kranaios of cornelian cherry wood [transference from herms made of such perhaps one of the connections to identification with the Minoan Master of the Animals, as Jacqueline Chittenden argues: hence he is master of Circe as Mistress of the Animals, and both are magical figures]

kratus mighty, strong

leukos bright, clear [cult ep., Tanagra]

neos young

pais child, youth

perikallEs very beautiful (like Apollo)

phaidros bright, beaming; cheerful

pheristos, phertatos bravest, best

philokertomos fond of jeering

presbys old man, elder

sOkos stout, strong one

sparganiOtEs child in swaddling clothes

sphEnopOgOn with wedge-shaped/ pointed beard

tetraglOchin four-square, -sided [transference from herm base]

tetragOnos the same

tetrakephalos four-headed

trikephalos three-headed [as before; Suidas explains as from facing three crossing roads]

B. ATHLETICS, GAMES, MUSIC (EXTENDED, ORIGINAL, SENSE)

(achnous) see A.

agOnios presider over games [athletic and musical contests]

aphetErios of the race track [on a herm, along with a statue of the Dioskouroi]

brabeutEs judge [at games]

dromios of the race-course [cult ep., Crete]

enagOnios of games, judge of contests [esp. in dedications by victors]

gymnasiou of the gymnasium [dedications in a palaestra: H. was frequently coupled with Herakles]

harmateus chariot-driver [cult ep., Erythrai]

nEniochOn chariot-driver

(kOrophilos) see U.

lyraios lyrist [as constellation; H. as overseer of the Muses]

mousopolos serving the Muses, poet, musician, minstrel

(paidokoros) see U.

(palaistritas) see U.

philaethlos fond of games, competitor, lover of sports

porsynOn provider [of athletic winners]

strophiouchos wearing boxing gloves [possibly also "wearing priest's headband"]

(tychOn) see C.

C. BENEFICENT TOWARD HUMANS; LUCKY

agathapoios beneficent [like the Agathos Daimon, snake-context]

areskomenos pleasing, agreeable

(charidotEs) see R.

charmophrOn heart-delighting, joyous-hearted

dOtEr giver [of good; cf. *dOtor' eaOn,* E.]

enkardios in the heart, close to one

epiphorOtatos most favorable

(eriounios) see S.

(euvangelos) see T.

eukolos good-natured, easily contented, easy-going, unexacting [cult ep., Metapontum]

eunoustatos most well-disposed, benevolent

hetairos comrade [of a feast; also: of black night]

klytoboulos famous in counsel

lysimerimnos one who frees us from care

masErios searcher

megalodOrotatos most munificent

meilichos gentle, kind [note: Zeus Melichios, represented as a great serpent, cthonic connection]

OphelOn helper, profitable one

phaesphoros light-bringer [context: Dionysiac rite]

philandros man-loving

philanthrOpotatos most loving of men [also used of Prometheus]

philios friendly [as God of words]

ploutodotEs giver of riches [hence iconographic trait, the purse full of gold; or earlier, acc. to Robert Graves, the crane-skin bag containing the letters of the alphabet]

prophrOn gracious

proxenon patron

pyriinous fire-minded, fiery one [on magical apparatus: note H. relation to the fire-sticks for making fire]

selaEphoros light-bringing

synopaOn companion

terpOn cheerful one

tychOn luck-bringer [love, trade, art, esp. music, athletics]

xeinodokos host, one who receives strangers [a festival in Achaia—*theoxenia*; H. served as host to other deities in his festival, the Hermaia]

D. CHTHONIC ASPECTS, THE DEAD, PSYCHOPOMP

adakrytos tearless [in leading souls to isle of the blessed]

amyEtos uninitiated [probably a joke, misunderstood by Hesychius; note that H. gets *initiated* before descent to Hades in Aristophanes, *Peace*, l. 374—ironic. A proverb quoted by Clement, *hermEs amyEtos* = "teach your grandmother!" Farnell, 5.16 n. b]

(angelos) see T.

archedamas tamer of powers [as guide of the dead]

chthonios chthonic [as conductor of souls; also in curse formulae and magic spells; iconographic: H. associated with serpent]

(daimOn) see F.

erichthonios (intensified from *chthonios*, above) [cult ep.]

eutaphiastEs good burial (?) [cult title, Metapontum]

heilissOn whirler [around Tartarus: mag. pap.]

(hetairos) see C.

(katachos) see L.

katachthonios infernal. subterranean God

kataibatEs one who descends

kinEsis mover [of spirits]

koiranos lord, ruler [*thnEtOn:* of the deceased]

(naiOn) see K.

nekropompos conductor of the dead

nekyEgos, nekragOgos, nekyagOgos same as *nekropompos*

nychios belonging to night, the nether world

(pompos) see H.

propompos escort, conductor [of the dead]

psychagOgos leading departed souls to the nether world

psychopompos psychopomp

psychostolos escort of souls

psychotamias keeper of souls

(sotEr) see O.

tamias steward, master [of souls]

E. CRAFTS, COMMERCE

agoraios of the market place [also: oratory, law, education]

charidotEs joy-giver

dEmiourgikOs workman-like, of a craftsman [in art, H. wears a worker's short chiton]

dOtor' eaOn giver of good things

eleopOlou oil-seller [at entry to shop]

empolaios commerce, trade [esp. as H. = God of weights and measures]

emporikos of or for commerce, mercantile

eparOgos helper [in work]

epipoliaios (uncertain) [prob. similar to *empolaios*]

heuretEs inventor or discoverer [cf. Eureka!—"I've found it!"; the verb may be etym. related to the name H.]

kerdemporos profiteer

kerdeOn bringer of gain, profit, advantage

kerdOos gain-bringer, gainful [H. as tradesmen's God, and as God of lucky find, the *hermaion* or *heurEma*

kyllEnios Cyllenean [as God of smiths]

mEchaniOtEs contriver, artificer

palinkapElos retailer of imported produce

(ploutodotes) see C.

poneumenos industrious

poristEs supplier, procurer [financial; but also a term robbers used of themselves]

poristikOtatos most able to supply or procure

F. DEITY, STATUS AS A

aidios eternal

askopos invisible

athanatos immortal

daimOn divine power [in the strong sense; esp. with *Ge*, "of the nether world"]

diotrephEs cherished by Zeus

hagnos holy, chaste

hedas abiding/seated one

makar blessed, happy [typical of deities, as opposed to mortals: cf. pl. *makares* = "the blessed dead"]

olympios Olympian

ouranios uranian, of heavenly origin

sebas revered

theos a God

theskelos marvelous, set in motion by a God, God-inspired

G. FAMILIAL

autadelphos brother [of Apollo]

genethlon offspring [of Dionysos; often H. is paired with D. in art, esp. in ritual scenes; a famous motif: H. carrying the infant D.]

gonos offspring [male; of Maia]

huiOnos grandson [of Kronos]

huios son [of Zeus, Maia]

kasignEtos brother [of Apollo]

Maidas huie son of Maia [*maia,* good mother, etc.: cf. *MaiEios, Maiadeus*;

probably originally a parallel form to Anatolian *Mâ,* "the Mother"]

nymphagetEs leader of the Nymphs

nymphios bridegroom [of Aphrodite]

pais son, child

patEr father [of Pan, *et al.*]

patrOios father

teknon son, child [of Zeus]

tekos son, child [poet.]

tokos offspring [of Z. and M.]

H. GUIDE

diaktoros guide, messenger

ithuntOr guide

kathEgEtOr, kathEgemOn leader, guide, teacher [cult ep., Delphi]

pompaios escort

pompos guide, wayfarer

(propompos) see D.

I. HERDS, ANIMALS; VEGETAL; FERTILITY

agrotEr rustic, hunter

auxidemos increaser of the people [apparent fertility aspect]

boElatas cattle-driver, -raider

boossoos ox-driver also used of a gad-fly!]

boukleps ox-stealer [contracted from *booklopos,* from *bouklopos*]

boukolos herder of cattle [note secondary meanings: cheater, deceiver, "bucolic" poet, worshipper of Dionysos]

bouphonos ox-slayer [also: priest!]

(charidotEs) see R.

elatEr driver [of oxen]

epikarpios guardian, bringer of fruits [unique at Amorgos (*I.G.* 12.7.252)—H. is not usu. a God of vegetation]

epimElios guardian, keeper of flocks

(eriounios) see S.

episkopos guardian, overseer [on a statue overlooking a goatfold]

epithalamitEs) see N.

euglagEs giver of milk [goatherd's dedication

kandaulEs dog-throttler [usu. = wild dogs threatening flock, or referring to Argos. The dog, however, is also Hecate's emblem, she who "along with H. . . . has power to make the animals on

the farm multiply," Hesiod, *Theogony,* l. 444]

kriophoros ram-bearer [also an aspect of Apollo; roots in Ancient Near East]

ktEnitEs belonging to cattle

kunagchEs dog-throttler [see *kandaulEs,* above]

mElossoos sheep-protector, guardian of sheep

nomaios shepherd

nomios protector of flocks, shepherd

(nymphios) see G.

oiopolos shepherd

phalEs phallic

phallos phallus [H. *as* the phallus; no ep. as ithyphallic, but so described, e.g., Callimachos, *Iamb* 9.199]

phytalmios producer, nourisher [vineyard inscription. but unusual]

poimEn shepherd

sOritas giver of heaps of wheat [usu. ep. of Demeter]

spElaitEs of the cave [Laodikeia; pastoral context]

tachygounos yielding fruit quickly

tyreutEr of goatherds and goat cheese

J. LAW, JUSTICE

(agoraios) see E.

dikaios just

dikaspolos law-giver, judge

ennomos just, within the law

peithodikaiosynos obedient to or pleading the cause of justice

thesmios law-giver

K. LOCAL AND PERSONAL NAMES

aerios = Thoth-Chu; also "aerial" vs. chthonic

aigyptios Egyptian [= H. Trismegistos]

aipytos Aipytos [Arcadian earth deity; assimilated to H.]

ainiOn God of Aenus [in Thrace; see *perpheraios,* below]

akakEsios Acacian [also: gracious, painless—which is secondary? Pausanias says of the temple of H. Acacios that only a tortoise in stone remained]

anoubis = Anubis, with face half-black, half-golden

arkados Arcadian [also simply *arkas*]

el Lukeio Lycian [cf. Apollo L.]

epaktios on the shore [cult ep., Sicyon]

epipoliaios uppermost [above entryway; at Rhodes]

(harmateus) see B.

helikOnios Heliconian [usu. of Poseidon]

(hermanoubis) see V.

hyperboreios Hyperborean

imbrios, imbramos Imbrian [Pelasgian H.]

(kadmilos) see P.

kadmos Cadmean [cult ep., Samothrace]

kOrykiOtEs Corycian

ktaros [treated as personal name, Lycophron, *Alex.* 679, but perhaps also "procurer," "possessor"?]

(kyllEnios) see E.

laphrios Laphrian

naiOn dweller near Cocytus, river of the dead]

nOnakriatEs Nonacrisian [in Arcadia]

oreios of the mountains [hunter]

parammon Parammon

pautnouphis [in inscriptions, as Egyptian rendering in Greek of Thoth]

perpheraios Perpheraios [ep. in Thrace; fisherman's herm was divinized when it proved indestructible by fire and was 'passed around,' Callimachos, *Iamb* 7.197]

pheraios = preceding entry?

polygios Polygian

prognOstEs prescient [of physicians and astrologers]

pterseus the destroyer [of H. and Perseus]

stilbOn Stilbon, name of the planet Mercury

syngonos native

L. MAGIC, ORACLES, DREAMS

(alexikakos) see O.

(chthonios) see D.

(epipempOn) see V.

hypnodotEs sleep-giver; var. *hypnodOtis*

katochos spellbinder [inhibiting or binding souls in graves—magical tablets; also in magical curses]

klEdynios omen-giver [later *klEdOn;* an oracle by chance: the first words heard after unstopping the ears, following a dedication to the God]

(klepsiphronos) see R.

klEros of the oracle, lottery

kosmokratOr lord of the universe [in mag. pap. and late Hellenistic mysticism]

mikrodynamos little-power [magical and astrological references to the planet Mercury]

oneiropompos guide of dreams

oneiros God of the dream [see *hEgEtor*, O.]

ophthalmos eye [mag.: "the great eye of the world," as chariot-driver of the sun]

(paredros) see O. [use in magical inscription]

pempOn sender [mag. pap.]

prognOstEs prescient [of physicians, of astrologers]

prostatEs guardian [of sleep]

psithyros, psithyristEs whisperer [magic spell; but also as God of love, in connection with Aphrodite]

M. PRAISE, FAME, BELOVED

(aglaos) see A.

ainetos praiseworthy

aristaios valorous one [cult title of H., Zeus, Apollo]

eratos beloved

eratos beloved

erikudEs glorious

eudokimos famous, glorious

euklEs famous

klytos renowned, glorious

kydimos glorious, noblest [= *kydalimos*]

logismos notable, famous

megas great

megistos greatest

Ormidion dearest, darling [mocking]

pammegistos greatest

pantokratOr almighty

periboEtos famous, notorious

phaneros illustrious; visible, manifest

philos beloved, dear

philtatos dearest

trismegistos thrice-greatest

N. ROADS, BOUNDARIES, JOURNEY, ENTRYWAYS

enodios (einodios) by the road [H. as guardian of crossroads, gates, and springs; note Hekate as *enodia,* and Artemis *einodiE*]

epitermios at the boundary

epithalamitEs bridal-song singer [from location at the door of the bridal chamber]

geitOn neighbor, borderer

hodios of the journey, road

hodoiporos wayfarer

(opOpEtEr) see R.

phylax guard [of the road]

polistrophos hinge of the city [cf. doorhinge image]

pronaos before the temple [a sort of religious prophylactic against evil]

propylaios of the gateway [where strangers, wayfarers, enter]

prothyraios before the door [like Artemis and Hekate]

pylaios at or before the gate

pylEdokos watching at the door

pylEtEs dwelling at the gate

pylios at the little gate [at the *pulE* both of the customs house and the underworld]

pylostrophos gate-turner

(strophaios) see R.

strophiouchos at the doorway

temenouros guardian of a *temenos* (sacred area) [on a boundary marker]

thalassios of the sea [later formulation, modeled on *hodios* and *enodios*]

thuraios at the door

O. RULER, LEADER, GUARDIAN, SAVIOR

agEtOr leader [freq. iconographic motif, hieratic significance]

alexikakos evil-averter, savior [usu. ep. of Apollo: chthonic and phallic associations]

anaktOr lord, master [cf. *anax*]

anassOn lord, master [vocative contracted to *O ana,* "O Lord"]

archEgetEs founder [esp. late Hellenistic mysticism: "creator of all the magic arts"]

(archos) see R.

(auxidemos) see I.

despotEs master, despot

diopos ruler, captain

ephoros guardian, overseer, ruler

hEgemonios guide [leader of the host to war]

hEgemoneus governor

hEgEtOr chief, commander [also "marshal of dreams," recalling that the last libation of the night was dedicated to H. (a nightcap might be called a *hermEs*), and that beds would be arranged to face his image in the bedroom]

(koiranos) see D.

kosmEtEs orderer, magistrate, director

kosmEtOr commander, marshal

(kosmokratOr) see L.

kreiOn lord, master

laossoos stirrer of the nation [to war]

medeis guardian, ruler

medeOn the same

palmus king [= *basileus*]

paredros coadjutor, assessor [administrative]

(phylax) see N.

proedros president, presider

progonos founder

promachos champion [war]

promos chief, warrior [by night]

proxenon patron [of the land]

rhytEr, rhytOr deliverer, guardian, defender, savior [of the field, of cattle]

sOtEr savior [tomb inscriptions]

timaoros avenger, tutelary God

P. SERVANT, MINISTER

diakonos ministrant [of Zeus; of a leader (tyrant) of youth]

epopteuOn steward, overseer [of Zeus]

homostolos attendant [of Maia]

hypEretas, -tEs servant, subordinate [of the Gods]

kadmilos, kasmilos minister [also a personal name, associated with the mysteries of the Kabeiroi; reflects H's role as the divine sacrificer]

katharophonos purifier [as gloss on Ar-geiphontEs]

latris servant

leukophontEs whitener [as gloss on Ar-geiphontEs]

mageiros cook [parallel to *kEryx* in function of preparing sacrifices]

oinochoos cupbearer

opEdos attendant [upon the Muses]

propolos attendant [of the greater Gods]

sakophoros shield-bearer, porter [esp. in art, carrying a gold-filled purse]

Q. SWIFT, WINGED

aellopodEs swift-, storm-footed

akichEtos swift, not to be overtaken

apteros swift [unspoken, because of great speed]

eupteros well-winged, plumed

chrysopteros with wings of gold

Okydromos swift-running

Okypedilos swift-footed

Okypous swift-footed

Okypteros swift-winged

Okys swift, fleet

pherepteros winged

podarkEs swift-footed [succoring with the feet, running to the rescue]

ptanos winged, swift-footed [associated with thievery]

ptEnopedilos with winged or flying sandals

pteroeis winged

pteropous wing-footed

tachinos swift [poet. for *tachys*]

tachys swift, etc.

tanypteros long-winged

tanysipteros long-winged

thoos quick, hasty

trochalos swift-running

R. THIEVERY, TRICKERY, WILES, DECEIT

amEchanos irresistible, irrepressible, unmanageable, inexplicable [dream-context]

anaideEn shameless one

aproidEs invisibly, unforeseen [connected with *akichEtos*, as a way H. comes into a house]

archos leader, chief [prince among robbers]

charidotEs joy-giver [Samos festival of H. CharidotEs, where there was license to steal; also fertility aspects]

dolios crafty

dolomEtEs crafty, devious-minded

dolophradEs wily-minded

EperopeutEs deceiver, cheat

exapatas deceitful

haimylomEtEs of winning wiles

haimylos wheedling, wily

hodoikoros waylayer

kakomEdEs contriving, deceitful

kakotechnos artful, lascivious, using evil practices

keraistEs plunderer, thief

kerdeOn most crafty, wily, cunning

kertomos mocker, sharp-tongued

klepsiphronos,-rOn stealthy-minded, dissembling

kleptEs thief, trickster

lEistEr robber

merimna nuisance [to gods and humans]

opOpEtEr spy [at the gates, by night]

127

orchamos leader/prince [of thieves]

pansophos most clever

periplokos intriguer

phalantheus the fallacious one [lit. bald one]

phElEtEs, philEtEs thief, trickster

phOrios furtive

psydros [hypothet., from the month *Psudreus*, Liar's]

poikiloboulos wily, clever, "of changeful counsel"

poikilomEtEs full of various wiles

poikilomythos of various discourse, skilled

in words

polymEtis of many counsels, devices

polytropos many-turning, shifty, versatile [cf. *versipellis*, of Mercurius]

(poristEs) see E.

(poristikOtatos) see E.

(ptanos) see Q.

sophos clever [Aristophanes: "wisest"— ironic, as freq. in A.]

strepsaios twisty [see following entry]

strophaios shifty (door-hinge God) [hence H.'s image on keys]

toichOrychos housebreaker, burglar

S. UNIQUE, UNUSUAL

argeiphontEs slayer of Argos? serpent slayer? the brightly-shining one? [freq.; many associated adjectives, e.g., *kratus,* "strong," *euskopos,* "keen-eyed"]

chelyklonos resounding with sound of tortoise shell [one of the few eps, referring to his patronage of music; tortoise: cf.

akakEsios, K., above]

dionysophoros carrier of [baby] Dionysos

eriounios (uncertain) bringer of blessings, clever one, luck-bringer, profitgiver, helper, quick one, etc. [hence associated in art with the cornucopia]

T. WORDS, ORATORY, MESSENGER

(agoraios) see E.

agornios speaker

angelos messenger, courier, "angel" [note *C.I.G.* 5816 and *Orphic Hymn* 1.407, messenger *of Persephone*]

eiremEs speaker, pacifier [Plato refers to this as one of the etymologies of *HermEs*]

euangelos bringer of good news

hermeneus, hermEneus interpreter [folk etymology connected with *hermEneuein,* to interpret]

hoplon instrument, weapon [Carter, in Roscher, Supp. I, reads as vocative and hence an appellation; Athanassakis gives a better English sense (*Orphic Hymns* 28.10): "you wield [among men] the dreaded and respected weapon of speech"]

kEryx herald, ambassador, messenger [even: sacrificer—note this role in Ho-

meric Hymns; esp. in phrase *kEryx megiste*]

lalos loquacious

logios skilled in words [applied to Demosthenes as an example of H. Logios; related to dialectics]

logos word, utterance [vocative: "O Hermes, you prophetic word"]

peisinous persuader of the mind [oratory; hence H. grouped with the Charities, in sense of the grace needed for the skill; he often leads them in iconography]

philologOtatos most talkative, learned

phlyEsiOn overflowing with babble, prater

(poikilomythos) see R.

prophEtEs interpreter, herald, prophet

StOmylos talkative, wordy

trochis messenger (of Zeus) [The *tongues* of sacrifices are offered to H. as the herald, God of words.]

U. YOUTH-SPONSORING, -LOVING

(chlamydEphoros) see A.

(diakonos) see P.

ephEbos ephebe [adolescent, over 18 years old]

(gymnasiou) see B.

kechrEmenos stained [i.e., with ashes: playing bogey-man to a disobedient child]

kOrophilos friend of youth [palaestra context]

kouros youth [applied to H. himself, in an appeal to Maia to send help by means of H.]

kourotrophos child-rearer [usu. of females and Goddesses; used esp. of H. caring for infant Dionysos]

maia [male] midwife [to Beroë/Amymone]

paidokorEs child-nourisher [cult ep., Metapontum]

paidokoros guardian of boys, "he who cares for boys"

paidotribEs gymnastic master [note that *paidagOgos*, "pedagogue," is not used of H., as modern meaning would anticipate; the actual usage is with reference to the slave who led children to the school; there were such who made dedications to H.]

(pais) see A.

palaistritas of the palaestra

philotekne friend/lover of children

syntrophos companion (of), familiar (to ephebes) ["zeal for learning," *eumatheia*, while "given by H.," is not used as an ep.; Callimachos, *Iambi*, fr. 221]

V. RELATED TERMS, PHRASES (SELECTED)

aguieus guardian of streets, at the street door: of Apollo's pointed pillars similar in function to usage in our category N., but not applied to H.

doneOn murmuring [listed as ep. by Carter, but not used appellatively of H.; refers to the bees from which he learned an art of prophecy]

epipempOn (dream-) sender: oracular and oneiric in context, but not used appellatively

euermia luck [lategrammaticians; cf. *euermeO*, to be fortunate or "favored by H."; *euermEs*, fortunate]

hermaia Hermaea [the festivals of H., sometimes characterized by license to thieve, or by exchange of master/servant roles; held on the fourth day of the month, which was (along with the seventh, Apollo's day) considered lucky]

hermeiae melesthai to practice gymnastics or oratory

hermaioi lophoi, or *hermax* [heaps of stones dedicated to H.; then heaped stones beneath herms; also applied to Roman milestones; later legends say H. was the first road-maker]

hermanoubis [Graecized form of Anubis]

hermokrapElia H.'s Market [a group of shops]

hermou spondai feast of H. [such as the yearly comic festival at Crete]

kErykeion H.'s staff or caduceus [sometimes it, or its two entwined serpents, were embossed on the sides of herms—often the easiest way to distinguish a herm of H. from an icon of Dionysos]

koinos hermEs "the H.-find gets shared!" [something like our "Halfers!" when something of value is come upon unexpectedly; more formally: "Half-shares in treasure trove"]

pseudreus [a month, prob. dedicated to H. as liar]

IV. The Hybris of Naming

In the process of compiling these lists, I sometimes felt I lost sight of where the hermetic work might be going, overwhelmed by the lexica, word lists, and critical editions. I took solace in an epigram on a herm, cited in the Greek Anthology (*A.Pl.* 16.187): "A man prayed for help to a herm made of wood, but Hermes remained wooden [i.e., unresponsive]. Then, taking up the herm, the man threw it on the ground [cf. the fairy tale motif of throwing the ugly frog or monster against the wall], and the statue broke open, and gold poured forth."

But the last line of the epigram is the best: *hybris pore pollaki kerdos*, "Outrage [or however you prefer: "pride," "surpassing chutzpah"] often produces profit." Perhaps we learn from this that hybris is not always "the tragic flaw," that forging ahead against the apparently non-productive task at least refines the gold which may later be crafted into shining vessels. Perhaps hybris now refers to an over-reliance upon the monothetic and the univocal.

For wherever one goes, hermetically, one is led into prolixity and *Mannigfaltigkeit*. Hermes reduces to "herald of the Gods" no more than a human being is only "clerk at the town hall." Rather Hermes is all the attributes, as the person is infinitely more than the job. And the discovery of the pathways of meanings comes into focus both as the therapy's task and as that which can be taught and heeded as a form of soul-growing.

Each of us is many; but few of us automatically honor the chance find, the stumbled-over discovery that makes life-music (Hermes stumbles over the poor creeping tortoise, and from its hollowed-out shell, makes the first lyre, which his brother Apollo will later covet: note the brotherly pairing of and tension between the Apollonic and the Hermetic). There is a truly hermetic training in the arts of the impossible possibilities, one that requires the hermetically-sealed vessel of self-attention, one that mirrors the flashing opposites, the sudden ups and downs that refuse to level out as vanilla-gray.

And Hermes goes all the way down—into Hades, if you will, certainly into the depths of sleep and psychic movement—before he returns leading the soul-messages (Persephone, Eurydice) back where they can lend insight into the daylight tedium and entrapments. That course of movement-downwards can, if we heed the tradition's iconography, be a winged, swift flight across the usual boundaries and limits.

It requires the deceit and trickery by which the common everyday—or the parents' sway—is momentarily ignored. It is a divine game, a contesting for meaning; it is a skillful craft which must be carefully and attentively practiced. And it is a matter of exploring the tyranny of words, in order to give insights to their etymological surprises—a hermeneutical poiesis. This enterprise, it seems, is a fertilizing one, even a wealth-bringing one.

The tasks begin when we set out from the here-at-home, when we are underway on the road, when our goal is Kafka's "truly immense journey," with its destination "away from here" (in his parable *Das Ziel*). The tasks concern entryways and byways, springs and kitchens, markets and libraries—all the boundless multiplicity of the cities and employments of humankind.

The connections and re-connections of the herald come repeatedly, each time in different guise, nor is there any iconographic monotheism that will refine the multiplicity into the perfect or single One. And yet the polynomy we have been tracing ciphers The Experience of Hermes, the many-in-the-one (an epigram on an ancient herm, *C.I.G.* 6745):

> I was not, I came to be.
> I was, I am not: that is all.
> And who shall say more, will lie:
> I shall not be.

Just that unique mercurial compression can also indicate having-lived, having-experienced more fully, having-seen-through the false stopping points of "maturity" or the single "identity."

And, having been touched by the magical staff, we now see differently: Herakles, in his descent into Hades, draws his sword against the menacing Gorgon—only to learn from Hermes that it is only a *kenon eidOlon,* an empty phantom (Apollodorus 2.5.12). Following the many opalescences of the hermetic images, we gain from this friend of our continued youth tutoring as to what is effectually phantasmic, and what *should* be feared and avoided, how to turn the shadowy deficit into gainful strength. Hermes the Thief was also invoked as a prophylactic *against* thieves.

We take up the Hermes-movements with an essential and lively self-craftiness that mocks the Apollonic listing of the Hermes-names, which can only be benchmarks toward the initiatory experiences Hermes sponsors as he guides our souls between the realms, bringing the dreams of more than reason. Where we go with the dreams, the messages, the gold coins of Hermes' purse, is up to us. The fable-maker Babrius has the God himself give voice to the dilemma and possibility (cited from Jane Harrison, *Mythology,* p. 9):

A stonemason made a marble Herm for sale
And men came up to bid. One wanted it
For a tombstone, since his son was lately dead.
A craftsman wanted to set it up as a god.
It was late, and the stonemason had not sold it yet.
So he said, "Come early tomorrow and look at it again."
He went to sleep and lo! in the gateway of dreams
Hermes stood and said "My affairs now hang in the balance,
Do make me one thing or another, dead man or god."

References and Resources

1. Articles on Hermes in the technical German-language encyclopedias are a gold-mine, but so densely and technically written and abbreviated that they are very difficult to use: S. Eitrem, in Pauly-Wissowa-Kroll, *Realency* (8:1, 1912), cols. 738–92; Suppl. III (1918), 1124–6; W. Fauth, in *Der Kleine Pauly* (2, 1967), cols. 1069–76; C. Scherer, in Roscher, *Lexikon,* 1:2, 1887), cols. 2342–2432.
2. Classical texts (a very limited selection): Aristophanes' dramas, especially *Peace, Plutus,* and *Frogs,* where we see the problematic re-visioning of the classical pantheon in tension with the growing self-confidence of human spirit.
Apollodorus: a Hellenistic compendium which gives an inkling of how the myths would have been taught in a course on "Introduction to Our Heritage" in the first century C.E.; an excellent modern translation is Michael Simpson, *Gods and Heroes of the Greeks: The Library of Apollodorus* (1976); valuable for its notes, if often outdated, is J.G. Frazer's translation in the Loeb series (1921), 2 vols.
The Greek Anthology: text and translation in five volumes by W.R. Paton, in the Loeb series (1916–18); texts and notes in two volumes by A.S.F. Gow and D. L. Page (1965); and text, notes, and translation in two volumes (1968).
Homeric Hymns: text edited by T. W. Allen, W. R. Halliday, and E. E. Sikes, second edition (1936); translations: prose, by N. O. Brown, in *Classics in Translation*; blank verse, by Thelma Sargent (1973); free verse, by Charles Boer (1979) and Apostolos N. Athanassakis (1976).
The Orphic Hymns: text, translation, and notes by A.N. Athanassakis (1977); those addressed to Hermes are 28 and 57.
Pausanias, *Description of Greece,* translation in four volumes by W.H.S. Jones and H. A. Ormerod (1918–35); companion volume by R. E. Wycherley, revised edition (1955); all in the Loeb series.
3. Lists of appellations: I found helpful the Epitheta Deorum sections in the supplements to W. H. Roscher, *Ausführliches Lexikon . . .* (1884–1937; J. B. Carter, Suppl. I, 104–111); in S. Eitrem, above; and the many citations of original texts in Lewis R. Farnell's five volumes of *The Cults of the Greek States* (1869–1909; see index).

4. Handbooks are helpful, but not always precise in linking citations or summaries to texts, and they do not usually give original-language references: Edward Tripp, *The Meridian Handbook of Classical Mythology* (the hardback edition was published as *Crowell's Handbook of Classical Mythology*) (1970); Robert Graves's two volumes of *The Greek Myths,* revised edition (1960); L. Preller and Carl Robert's two volumes, *Griechische Mythologie,* fourth edition (1964–67); H. J. Rose, *A Handbook of Greek Mythology* (1959).

5. Essays and monographs; too numerous to list here, let me just cite: Norman O. Brown, *Hermes the Thief* (1947), an amazing piece of scholarship, the work which first stimulated my interest in Hermes, years ago; and Kerényi (see first page of this essay).

6. Further bibliography: I am hopeful that my manuscript, *Mythography: The Study of Myths and Rituals,* will be published soon, for I have gathered many bibliographic resources there; John Peradotto, *Classical Mythology: An Annotated Bibliography* (1973), is helpful for finding editions and modern studies.

VIII

ARIADNE, MISTRESS OF THE LABYRINTH

Chris Downing

What I attempt in this essay can, at one level, be understood as an exercise in autobiography, a description of my own serpentine path to the center of a labyrinth. Thus I am following up on something suggested in an earlier paper in which I looked at *Interpretation of Dreams* and *Memories, Dreams, Reflections* as transformations of the genre of autobiography.[1] I propose there that if we have really attended to what Freud and Jung had to say, we can no longer tell our own stories in the same old way. To take the unconscious seriously means to acknowledge that telling my story truly and fully brings into view my participation in age-old, mythic patterns.

I should like to explore what Thomas Mann calls the becoming subjective of the mythical point of view, to explore it concretely, and therefore personally. In his beautiful essay, "Freud and the Future," he speaks of what it means to become conscious, "proudly and darkly, yet joyously, of recurrence and typicality." "The myth," he tells us, "is the legitimization of life . . . only through and in it does life find self-awareness, sanction, consecration."[2] I, too, am persuaded that the discovery of a mythical pattern that in some way one feels is connected to one's own life deepens one's self-understanding. At the same time, the discovery of the personal significance of a mythic pattern deepens our understanding of the myth and its variations. I am interested in how our own experience, opening us to dimensions of the myth to which we might otherwise be closed, helps us understand the shape of the myth; why the myth's several variations appropriately belong to it; and how all the different aspects of that myth necessarily occur together. Appreciation of the connection between a myth and my life seems simultaneously to make me much more attuned to the myth's unity and to help me understand how moments in my life, apparently accidental or fragmentary, belong to the whole. Indeed, we may thus come to recognize the *mythos*, the plot, the connecting thread, the *story* of our life. As we value the way in which all the variations, transformations, and elements that make up a myth are integral, necessary parts of it, we uncover its psycho-logic. Such attending to the psycho-logic of myth and the mytho-logic of the psyche's processes might be described as an exploration in *mytho-poeisis,* in soul-making, for we are trying to get some sense of how the soul, our soul, is given its shape through poetry, through images.

To do this, I believe, means to recognize our involvement in a number of different mythic patterns. As you may recall, one of Jung's primary accusations against Freud was that he seemed to be aware of only one archetype informing his life pattern and, by extension, the life pattern of all of us—the Oedipus myth. It was Jung's conviction that a psychology really attuned to the soul's processes admits our implication in a variety of myths. Similarly, James Hillman writes that archetypal psychology is polytheistic, is aware of the activity of many divinities in our soul.[3] Thus we are speaking of living *mythoi,* of being involved in several life stories, not just one.

We become more aware of the archetypal dimensions of our own experience by going deeper and deeper into a myth and, indeed, into *several* myths. It is my experience that the myths we enter most deeply are not ones that we choose out of some book of myths. Rather, in some profound way these myths choose us. I am intrigued by the importance of beginning, as we almost inevitably and necessarily do, with the most familiar, most recent versions of the myth. Only grad-ually, as we keep working with the myth, do we discover earlier versions, buried strata, different layers. The process is very similar to that of working with a dream, where we start with the manifest version and discover in time that it covers a story much more complex and unfamiliar—and therefore more informative and transformative. Because I am particularly interested in myths which illuminate women's experience, I focus on myths about Goddesses. It seems especially important with such myths to attend to the earlier strata of Greek traditions and not only to the classical versions which tend to represent the perspectives of a patriarchal culture.

Some years ago I wrote a paper in which I explored my lifelong relationship with the figure of Persephone.[4] Born on the first day of spring, I knew myself, as far back as I can remember, in some way or other to be Persephone, the Goddess of Spring. I tried in the paper to suggest the ways in which my sense of identification has changed during the more than forty years that she and I have been involved with one another. I now understand that connection very differently from my initial, appropriately naive and innocent, perspective. Gradually, I have come to appreciate features of the myth which at some earlier point seemed relatively insignificant or were sometimes not even visible.

Now another mythical figure has come forward to announce that it is time for a reckoning between us. Though Ariadne is again someone with whom I have long been involved, for more than fifteen years that relationship has been dormant. But recently several events helped me recognize the necessity of returning to her to discover who she might be for me now. First, while I was working on the Persephone paper, I found several passages in which Carl Kerényi refers to Ariadne as a Persephone figure. Never having thought of the two together before, I began wondering whether attending to one might demand a look at the other. Soon after, I taught a course on mythology in which, as I thought just by chance, I included both Dionysus and Theseus. Only when I was well into that course did I start wondering, "Now why did I choose just these two figures out of the whole range of Greek heroes and Greek Gods? Why *the* hero and *the* God who figure so importantly in the Ariadne mythologem?" It must be because some part of me is ready to confront Ariadne again. Finally, that spring I bought a house which, I discovered only after I had already recognized it as mine, stands at the intersection of Avenida Primavera (suggesting Persephone) and Serpentine Drive, the labyrinthine way. So, it was time to ask again: who is Ariadne?

Pursuing this question, I learned that my involvement with Ariadne is as important as the connection with Persephone, and that living more than one myth does not imply schizophrenia. Yet the relationship to Ariadne is quite different from the one to Persephone because it was originally another's projection on me, not a self-identification. Return to this myth, therefore, meant exploring the pertinence to me of another's view of who I am. In ways which we don't fully understand at first and to which we should attend, what another sees in us that may be invisible to us might be a clue to who we really are. Heeding the other's view may elucidate a hitherto puzzling connection between what Sartre would call the *en soi* and the *pour soi*, the "for others" and the "for ourselves."

This turning to Ariadne felt like a return or like *being* returned to a big dream that I might have had fifteen or twenty years ago—a dream that I had now redreamt or that was itself insisting on being looked at anew. Suddenly it was there. This time around, new things would be discovered in it. Otherwise, why would it need to appear again?

Years ago a dear friend communicated to me that I, in a way that felt very important to him, was his Ariadne. He meant by this that my being toward him as I was had given him the strength, the courage, the insight, the readiness to risk the exploration of his own labyrinth, his own soul, in a way that he felt would otherwise have been impossible. To say "Ariadne" was to say this more precisely and more fully than any other language available to him. It suggested also that the relationship between Theseus and Ariadne might be a paradigm for ours in ways not yet fully discernible to either of us. His description was not mine, however, as I understood what was happening between us in terms of *my* myth: I saw him as a Hermes who would appear whenever really needed and rescue Persephone from the depths. Strange . . . each saw the other as psychopomp, but he saw me as someone who would guide him into the depths and I saw him as one who would help me back out. (Only recently have I seen how Hades and the Labyrinth might represent two rather different imaginings about the realm of soul.)

I was moved, flattered, perhaps a little inflated, by what he had to say about my meaning for him. But I was also scared. For, though I didn't know very much about Ariadne, I did know that the story doesn't end with Theseus' safe return and then some variant of "They lived happily ever after." Myths don't seem to end like that. As Geza Roheim once remarked, though Eros may triumph in fairytales, Thanatos does in myths. I knew that Theseus had come from Athens to Crete as part of the Athenian tribute, and that for him and his companions to be free to sail back home he needed to penetrate the Labyrinth and slay the Minotaur. Ariadne's holding the thread enabled him not only to make his way into the Labyrinth but also to make his way safely out. I knew that and I knew one other thing about Ariadne and Theseus—the part that frightened me: I knew that Theseus, in gratitude to Ariadne, agreed to take her with him from Crete, and that on the very first night of their journey back to Athens, they stopped on the island of Naxos; early the next morning Theseus set sail, leaving Ariadne behind. I feared that if my lover and I were indeed living this myth, then that kind of desertion was a part of our story that was still to be lived.

And it happened: a separation that felt like a desertion even though at some rational level it was right and necessary. When we reflect on the story of Theseus and Ariadne, it's important to remember that integral to the story is the moment when Ariadne knows herself to be deserted. In Strauss's opera, *Ariadne Auf Naxos,* she first appears at that moment, the moment when she wakes up and finds that Theseus is gone. The music beautifully renders her sense of desertion and gives expression to the feeling: "I will never love again, and therefore in some sense, I will never live again." So in our story, there was that separation and it felt like betrayal, and like death.

Two years later in a way that seemed like a real gift, this man returned and our connection seemed immeasurably different. Literally a connection with the same person, at some more real level it was with another. The relationship was no longer colored with the confusions, possessiveness, and betrayals that are part of the love that we think of as mortal love. The only way I know to describe it is as an immortal love, though that suggests just the romanticism that had been left behind. Clearly, the renewed connection would be lived in an eternal kind of way, even though our literal times together would henceforward be very few and far between. What mattered was the feeling that our love no longer carried with it the danger of interfering with or disrupting our everyday lives.

More important was the sense that each of us now had our center in ourself. We were no longer dependent on one another for our connections to soul. I was very aware of the power of being with a man who, in touch with the 'feminine' in himself, didn't look to me to supply it for him. Only much later did I learn that in the myth of Ariadne something very similar happened. After Theseus deserted her, the God Dionysus appeared and made Ariadne his bride. At the time, that analogue between the myth and our relationship seemed 'interesting' rather than important. I understood what had happened between this man and me as just good luck, a blessing, not as mythologically inevitable. (I am still not sure how often the inner bond between Theseus and Dionysus is expressed through the same man playing both roles. But I do know that it is often difficult to distinguish between Theseus and Dionysus in ancient vase paintings, and there is frequent confusion between them in the mythological tradition: which fathered Ariadne's children, for instance, and from whom did she receive the crown that now adorns the heavens as *corona borealis?*)

But I have come to recognize that Theseus' desertion of Ariadne is the necessary prelude to her relationship to Dionysus. If Ariadne helps Theseus, then Ariadne must be left behind. That may sound a little odd at first hearing, but it is absolutely essential to the understanding of this myth. In the Ariadne/Theseus part of the story, Ariadne is an anima figure (though, of course, a very different one from Persephone: Ariadne obviously takes more initiative, which is why she has to be deserted rather than raped). What this story is suggesting here is that anima dependence must be overcome: Theseus can't stay with Ariadne. But it's just as important for Ariadne that she be left behind, so that she might leave behind her dependence on playing the role of the anima. Only after both of them have moved beyond their separation is there the possibility of a connection where each has his own soul. Dionysus enters here, because inevitably a man who has his own soul is psychologically androgynous.

Yet reading my life in terms of this myth was not part of how I was making sense of it during most of the last fifteen years. Only recently did those strange little things start happening which suggested to me that it was time *now* to discover my own relationship to Ariadne, not the other's relationship to Ariadne through me. That led me to understand much better than I had before why I had instinctively shrugged off, to some degree, the Ariadne identification when the Theseus figure had first proposed it. Something about that hadn't quite rung true to my sense of who Chris is, because the version of the myth that I had known then—the version which I would suppose is most familiar—is the man's version. Only as I came to penetrate to some of the myth's earlier strata, some of its buried aspects, did I come to my own connection to the myth.

The familiar version, just because it is the man's version, has some truth for us women, so long as and to the degree that we are defined by our relationships with men and by their relationships to us. Because the 'masculine' perspective is in a significant sense an ego perspective, it may also help us discriminate between those aspects of Ariadne which are human, which we may incarnate, and those other divine aspects from which we also must learn to differentiate ourselves. It is not only men who are in danger of being swallowed by a Goddess.

It's important, however, to see how this way of telling the myth grows out of the heroic, the Olympian, the male- and ego-dominated world. Indeed Theseus—perhaps especially in Mary Renault's retellings of the legends associated with his name, *The King Must Die* and *The Bull From the Sea*—really represents the emergence of the patriarchal perspective. In all the different stories that have been hooked onto the Theseus figure, one theme keeps recurring: Theseus is the male hero who continually finds himself in conflict with the matrilineal world, the "king must die" world. The hero most deeply aware of the danger and the appeal of the feminine, he spends his life battling against being taken over by it. Not only Theseus but also the heroes of many of the Greek myths that we know best—Orestes and Oedipus, for example—seem to inhabit precisely the moment of transition in Greek cultural history from the matrilineal to the patrilineal. In the earlier period the sacred was experienced most powerfully as feminine and political power was defined, if not in the hands of women, by one's relation to them; one married the king's daughter or stole his wife from him. This is still dimly evident in the received versions of the ancient tales, but the Greek myths as we get them from Homer and Hesiod, from Aeschylus and Sophocles, are myths written from the perspective of the patriarchal period, a perspective that issues in the reduction of ancient Goddesses into figures with whom men can safely deal.[5]

Thus each of the major Olympian Goddesses—Hera and Athena, Artemis and Aphrodite—is identified with one aspect of the feminine. One differentiates the feminine, cutting it up, separating it out into the wife and comrade, the elusive maiden and the generously available lover. Whereas one can deal safely with each isolated aspect, the whole panorama of femininity all at once is much too fearful. It is also safer if one humanizes. In the Homeric world there are female figures—not just Ariadne but also Helen of Troy, for instance—who were clearly once Goddesses, now divested of their overwhelming magic by being made human. Yet over and over again, even in Homer, we find clues that these women once had much more power, scope, significance than they do on the surface in the accepted versions.

There are hints in the *Odyssey* that Ariadne was once something much more than the helpful but clingy mortal girl whom Theseus took away from Crete.[6] His desertion of a simple maiden would not have been celebrated as something that Athena brought about to save Athens from contamination by overwhelming feminine power. The way in which Homer tells the story even excuses Theseus of any conscious cruelty. When he wakes up in the morning, he somehow has quite forgotten he had Ariadne with him and thus, in all innocence, sets sail back to Athens. When he remembers her, he is so griefstruck that he forgets to change the sails which would have assured his father of his safe return. (Freud could help us understand these two instances of forgetfulness.) Homer implies that he unconsciously leaves her because she has to be left. Theseus must abandon Ariadne, not just before he gets to Athens but immediately, before there is any opportunity for the consummation of their love—for afterwards, he might not be able to leave.

Events in myth are often overdetermined: Theseus' departure is associated not only with Athena but also with Artemis, who intervenes at Dionysus' instigation. He tells Artemis to make sure that Ariadne gets left—which suggests that the connection with Dionysus, not that with Theseus, is the one that gives Ariadne's story its shape. Ariadne belongs to Dionysus in her essence, not just, as some scholars have suggested, because of chance cult associations in a later period. Artemis' intervention reveals that Dionysus already has a claim, for she assails only the faithless.

I noted earlier that all the variations and transformations of a myth are meaningful. Thus, although one version asserts that Dionysus only appears in Ariadne's life after she's been deserted by Theseus, another suggests she already belonged to Dionysus before Theseus ever came into the story. It is as though she only recognized Dionysus' prior claim in her life after she had betrayed it. A tradition tells that already on Crete, before she got involved with Theseus, Ariadne had been Dionysus' betrothed. According to one version, the crown she gave Theseus to light his way through the labyrinth had earlier been given her by Dionysus. (This makes sense at the personal level: perhaps we can serve another as anima only because of our prior experience of the sacred. Clearly, even as mortal maiden, Ariadne knows much more than Theseus about encounters with the divine in its fearful aspects.) When Ariadne left with the Athenians, Dionysus sent Artemis to kill her as punishment for having turned from the immortal God to a mortal lover. Other stories in Greek mythology—for instance, the story about Koronis—are of a similar pattern, where a woman betrays a God (in this instance, Apollo) who has been her lover for the sake of a mortal. In that story, too, Artemis brings about the woman's death.

I believe it's not too difficult to have some understanding of what such a betrayal means and why one would commit it. Clearly, at times we are pulled to an involvement with a human other as an escape from a connection with the transcendent, a connection with a prior claim on us that is somehow too much. We flee to the heroic mortal

142

lover, escaping from the deeper experience. Kerényi says that in all of us there lurks an enemy of Dionysus as well as a devotee.[7] At the moments when what Dionysus represents is more than we feel we can handle or stay in touch with, we turn our backs on it.

In the Homeric version of the myth, Ariadne is killed by Dionysus or at his suggestion. In Hesiod, Dionysus appears to rescue and make her his bride, and then Zeus grants her immortality. Another tradition has Dionysus put Ariadne so soundly asleep on Naxos that Theseus cannot awaken her and so reluctantly has to leave her behind. There is even a version in which Dionysus kidnaps Ariadne, forcefully taking her from Theseus. She is both married to Dionysus and dies because of her connection with him. There is more buried here than the mythological version of an original conflict between two cults and its resolution through the absorption of the Ariadne cult by the one dedicated to Dionysus.[8] The relation between Dionysus and Ariadne cannot be reduced to an historical accident. It communicates an intuition about the relation between love and death: Ariadne is a bride of death. The Ariadne cult in Southern Italy seems to have consisted primarily of rituals intended as preparations for death. To go to death as bride was to go to death as enhanced life.

As we explore Ariadne's primary connection with Dionysus, we get closer, I believe, to Ariadne as women know her. She assumes an entirely new style of power and significance. If her relation to Dionysus is not just compensation for getting left by Theseus, then perhaps the clue to who Ariadne is would come from understanding the God for whom she is the female other. This I find intriguing—that Ariadne is *the* counterpart of Dionysus, *the* wife, *the* chosen one. Sarah Pomeroy in her book *Goddesses, Whores, Wives and Slaves*[9] says that in all of Greek mythology Dionysus is the only God who doesn't exploit females, the only faithful husband. And Ariadne is the woman to whom he is faithful.

This version of the story shows Ariadne made immortal, a Goddess, through her connection to Dionysus (as also happens to his mortal mother, Semele.) To know who she is thus depends on learning who he is. Though Dionysus is a complex God, one initial description is that he is the God of women. Dionysus is unique in Greek mythology in that his most frequent and characteristic worshippers were humans of the *other* sex; his primary attendants are always women, the maenads, and men are excluded from their rituals. Thus Dionysus is masculinity, male sexuality, as *women* experience it. Because he is a phallus at the disposal of women, he can be represented either as disembodied phallus or as an emasculated God. Dionysus is also the God of madness and ecstasy, the God of vitality, the God in whose realm everything is turned upside down. He means madness and mystery—"Madness not as sickness . . . but a companion to life at its healthiest."[10]

This God who comes to women in their most impassioned moments is a God connected with a visionary eroticism, an imaginal sexuality. We should not reduce these sexual experiences to narcissistic or masturbationary fantasies; they are lived as intercourse with another, a divine other. This is the sexuality of what Esther Harding[11] calls the virgin, the woman who has her center in herself, the woman who is able to indulge in her passion without thereby becoming dependent on relationships with others. For women to be thus in touch with their own life-giving energy inevitably provokes the opposition of Hera (the archetypal 'wife') and of husbands. Dionysus is the lover of women who are not defined by their relationships with literal men. The image of women yielding themselves to their own passion strikes fear in men, and even women know how close is such ecstasy to annihilation. The bride of Dionysus is the bride of death.

Dionysus is often called "the womanly one." His androgyny is suggested in many parts of his story. He is so able to bring men in touch with their femininity that he can even make Zeus into a woman: after Hera has caused the death of Semele, Dionysus' mother, Zeus makes his thigh into a womb which contains Dionysus for the last three months of gestation. To protect Dionysus from Hera's still unappeased wrath, he is raised as a girl. Later Dionysus goes to the underworld in search of Semele whom he wants to take to Olympus and make into a Goddess. On his way he is helped by a man who points out to him the gate by which he enters the underworld. In recompense he promises to serve this man as a woman on his return journey. (As it happens, by then the man is dead, so Dionysus has intercourse with an enormous wooden phallus instead.)

The emphasis on Dionysus' bisexuality suggests that Ariadne, as the fully appropriate consort, must herself be androgynous. Indeed, one of her brothers is called Androgeos. (That brother's death was what lay behind the Athenian obligation to pay the tribute to Crete.) Another brother is the Minotaur. We have already noted that she is a very initiative-taking young woman even in the episodes that link her to Theseus. And like Dionysus, Ariadne was sometimes given the power to bring men into touch with female experience: in the Cypriot rituals dedicated to her, men simulate the pain of childbirth. One of her sons is Thoas, King of Lemnos, the island which is taken over by women after they kill their husbands and sons.

Studying the mythological traditions associated with Ariadne much more carefully than before brought me in touch with hitherto unsuspected aspects of this Goddess; I began to understand why Ariadne might matter to me now. For the hidden Ariadne means woman in relation to her own powers, not defined by relationships with others and not afraid of her own sensuality or her own capacity for ecstasy. She is then an epitome of what Esther Harding means by "in-herself-ness." Now I began to glimpse the earliest Ariadne of all, the Ariadne who on Crete is identified as the Mistress of the Labyrinth. This Ariadne belongs to an ancient, matrilineal, mother-Goddess worshipping period. She is not just a mortal girl who is Theseus' beloved, nor is she just someone who is made a Goddess through her connection to Dionysus. She is an immortal in her own being. Rather than a mortal who becomes immortal, Ariadne is an immortal whom later traditions transform into a mortal. She is one of the pre-patriarchal Goddesses who blend in and out of each other in such confusing ways because they are women as women themselves experience their woman-ness. From that perspective the nice, neat, clear-cut differentiations don't quite work; we know we are each all of those things, at least in possibility.

Ariadne is one of the Great Mothers, a Great Goddess of Crete. As such she is called The Potent One, The Mistress of the Labyrinth, The Untouched One.[12] Asking who Ariadne is, to follow the thread all the way to its end, leads us to the center of a labyrinth where we find Ariadne herself. In the beginning there is Ariadne, a Goddess who is complete in herself, androgynous and self-perpetuating, creating out of her own being with no need of another. This Ariadne is superseded by another who is related to the masculine as something outside herself which is nevertheless her creation and entirely at her disposal. At this stage, Ariadne is represented as accompanied by a clearly subordinate male figure, the dying-rising male who is son and lover and, eventually, victim. It's clear then, as we pursue this story, that originally Ariadne was the important figure and Dionysus the necessary "other." Because Dionysus begins as a dying and rising God, he is still, even in the Classical period, the appearing and disappearing God. Even on Olympus, Dionysus serves to remind us of the time when Gods were sons and then lovers, then died and reappeared as newborn sons, became lovers once more and died, again and again.

As one of the ancient mother Goddesses, Ariadne is much more than just a vegetal Goddess.[13] The vision is much more profound and comprehensive than that. She is connected not just to animation, to natural life, but to anima, to the soul.

An all-important aspect of Ariadne is her relationship to the realm of death. Death in her world differs significantly from death in Persephone's. (The Persephone/Ariadne parallels, particularly the way in which each is related to both Theseus and Dionysus, must be fully admitted before we can appreciate the more subtle significance of the differences.) That in Crete the afterworld is associated with water, not with the underworld as in Greece, suggests a resemblance to Jung's unconscious more than Freud's—a source of continual renewal rather than a depository for what has been banished from the world of the living. Ariadne seems always to be linked to islands; death in her world takes one to the islands of the blessed, to the Elysian realm. In classical Greek mythology this becomes a privileged area within Hades ruled by Ariadne's father, Minos, where the specially favored don't really die but are allowed to live in death. The Cretans' vision of the life process—moving from life to death—differs utterly from the radical distinction the Greeks made between life and death. For the Greeks (although this, of course, changes when the mystery cults become important), life is life and death is death. Mortals die, but the Gods never die at all. On Crete, on the other hand, such a clear-cut differentiation neither distinguishes the divine and the human nor abruptly and finally demarcates life and death.

Ariadne's special connection with death is of course preeminently represented by the labyrinth from which most never return but some return transformed. In Argos, appropriately for a Goddess of death, her tomb serves as an altar. Most intriguingly, however, Ariadne herself suffers death in so many ways. Among these death stories is the one, already considered, in which she is killed by Artemis. Another story says that she simply dies of grief, and a third tells us that she commits suicide by hanging herself from a tree in despair at Theseus' departure.

Most interesting of all is the tradition according to which Ariadne dies just prior to giving birth. Some say that Theseus reluctantly left Ariadne in the care of midwives on Naxos (or Dia, another island that is often named in the Ariadne traditions instead) because her time had come. Artemis is reported to have killed her with the child still in her womb, which recalls the deaths of Koronis and Semele. But whereas Asclepius and Dionysus are rescued from their dying mothers' wombs just in time, Ariadne enters the realm of death with the unborn child still within her and then, the story continues, gives birth. This is the only account in Greek mythology of a birth in the world of the dead, a clue that something profound and fascinating is present here.

What does it mean for a child to be born in the afterworld, for birth to take place in the realm of death? Again, as so often in connection with Ariadne, the mythological suggestion is that birth and death, rather than mutually exclusive, are intimately intertwined. The child, like the thread, unites this world and the other, the outer and the inner, life and death. Birth is not opposed to death; they are not even to be understood as following one another sequentially. That this birth is only possible in death marks it off as entirely different from those of the other sons attributed to Ariadne (who are all related to Dionysus' more worldly side, to grape and vine and wine).

We need to attend to what the myth has to say about the identity of the father of this child and of the child itself. Clearly, the father is Dionysus; after all, Ariadne is killed because of her unfaithfulness to him. Kerényi believes that the child who is born must also be Dionysus.[14] (Confirming his suggestion are the many parallels between Ariadne and the other Goddesses represented as mothers to Dionysus: Semele and Persephone.) This fits in with the ancient son and lover motif, but more is here than is usual in the archaic pattern—the more suggested by the unique locus of the birth. Not a literal event occurring in the "real" world, this birth represents the fullness of what birth means when we understand it not literally but symbolically. To recognize birth as a mystery is to see it in relation to the afterworld. Intercourse with Dionysus when he is fully present, and not only there as God of wine and physical fertility, issues in a birth into death, into the imaginal, a birth in the soul, a birth of soul. Ariadne is the one through whom such birth is possible.

That returns us to where we began. Kerényi says that Ariadne represents "the archetypal reality of the bestower of soul, of what makes a living creature an individual."[15] Thus at the center of the labyrinth we come to the point where one returns back to the beginning. The serpentine way, to recall Eliot's words, returns us to the place where we started, and we know it for the first time. So we find ourselves now where we began, with Ariadne as anima, Ariadne as soul.

But this is so in a much, much deeper kind of way. Ariadne, no longer the anima waiting outside the labyrinth while another enters, means soul as what is at the labyrinth's center, the center of the self. Ariadne means soul, center, the Goddess, what I call *She*. As James Hillman has tried to convey,[16] anima, at its most important levels, has nothing to do with contra-sexuality. Neither the magically attractive, seductive, bewitching woman nor a man's feminine side, the anima is soul, to which we women need to relate just as truly as do men. The anima is "what gives events the dimension of soul," what attunes us to the imaginal significance of the experiences in which we participate.

When to know Ariadne as mistress of the labyrinth, I reject identification with her not because I don't want to be left behind, but because she is a Goddess and, at the center of the labyrinth, I find not myself but *Her*. And I begin to understand that at this point in my life I am being pulled back to Ariadne to give my devotion to her and to the child born in the realm of death, the child born in the realm of soul.

1 Christine Downing, "Re-Visioning Autobiography: The Bequest of Freud and Jung," *Soundings,* Summer 1977, pp. 210–228.
2 Thomas Mann, "Freud and the Future," in *Essays* (New York: Vintage Books, 1957), p. 317.
3 Cf. James Hillman, "Psychology: Monotheistic or Polytheistic," *Spring 1971,* pp. 193–208.
4 Christine Downing, "Persephone in Hades," *Anima,* IV:1, pp. 22–29.
5 Cf. E.A.S. Butterworth, "Some Traces of the Pre-Homeric World," in *Great Literature and Mythology* (Berlin: deGruyter, 1966).
6 Cf. *Odyssey* XI, 321–325. Other classical sources include: *Iliad* XVIII, 590–592; Hesiod, *Theogony,* 947–949; Plutarch, "Theseus"; Apollodorus, 3.1.2.
7 Carl Kerényi, *Dionysos: Archetypal Image of Indestructible Life* (Princeton: Princeton University Press, 1976), p. 241.
8 Cf. Martin P. Nilsson, *The Mycenean Origin of Greek Mythology* (Berkeley: University of California Press, 1972), p. 172.
9 Sarah B. Pomeroy, *Goddesses, Whores, Wives and Slaves* (New York: Schocken Books, 1965), p. 12.
10 Walter F. Otto, *Dionysus: Myth and Cult* (Bloomington: Indiana University Press, 1965), p. 143.
11 Esther Harding, *Woman's Mysteries* (New York: Bantam Books, 1973), *passim.*

12 Charles F. Herberger, *The Thread of Ariadne* (New York: Philosophical Library, 1972), p. 90; T.B.L. Webster, *From Mycenae to Homer* (New York: Barnes & Noble, 1960), p. 50.
13 Cf. Nilsson, *Mycenean Origin*.
14 Kerényi, *Dionysos*, pp. 108, 277.
15 Kerényi, *Dionysos*, p. 124.
16 James Hillman, "Anima," *Spring 1973*, pp. 97–132; "'Anima' (II)," *Spring 1974*, pp. 113–146.

IX

DIONYSOS IN JUNG'S WRITINGS

James Hillman

An examination of Jung's view of Dionysos and the Dionysian is the subject of this note. Some years ago,[1] I suggested with some detail that analytical consciousness has been governed by an archetypal structure that favors the masculine over the feminine, the principles of light, order and distance over emotional involvement, or what has, in short, been called the Apollonic over the Dionysian. I also then examined the notion of Dionysos, exposing prejudices in both classical psychiatry and Classical scholarship, prejudices which hinder the transformation of consciousness and resolution of fundamental analytical problems. I put the case that the fields of psychiatry and mythology—by using each other's arguments[2]—have been for the most part in collusion against the Dionysian, resulting in a repression, and thus a distortion, of all Dionysian phenomena so that they have come to be regarded as inferior, hysterical, effeminate, unbridled and dangerous. I suggested a rectification of our appreciation of this archetypal structure, and also a means to move toward this rectification. For, after all, Dionysos was the Lord of Souls (as Rohde called him), so that psychotherapy can hardly afford to labor under misleading notions of him.

This note is a postscript to that argument which, having taken some sixty pages to elaborate, can only be referred to here. But I ought to say that objections to the usage of "Apollonic" and "Dionysian" and to their opposition were there in part rehearsed, and I believe satisfactorily answered. We may therefore have a freer hand in using the term "Dionysian" for an archetypal structure of consciousness, much as Nietzsche introduced it in *The Birth of Tragedy* (1872), which Cornford called "a work of profound imaginative insight, which left the scholarship of a generation toiling in the rear."[3] We are also following Jung (who followed Nietzsche) in employing "Dionysian" as a term for a basic structure of consciousness (*CW* 6, §223–42; *CW* 10, p. 186n.)

Jung's long seminar, "Psychological Analysis of Nietzsche's Zara-thustra,"[4] usually referred to as the "Nietzsche Seminar" or "Zarathustra Seminar," which he held during the years 1934 to 1939, will not be included among the passages studied in this note for two reasons. First, the notes of the "Zarathustra Seminar" may not be quoted because they were not written by Jung, they have never been published, and because an authoritative version of the text has not been established. Second, the ten volumes form too large a body of material for inclusion in a short note. The reader should not, however, conclude that leaving out that material therefore leads to a one-sided presentation of Jung's notion of the Dionysian. On the contrary, my reading of those volumes indicates that Jung there reinforces with more detail the main ideas which I am here culling from the *Collected Works,* the published seminars, and his autobiography.

Moreover, the "Zarathustra Seminar," even if obviously relevant to the matter of this note, is less relevant to its purpose, which is to look closely into the fantasy concerning Dionysos in Jung's published and widely read writings so that we readers may be aware of what is going on and what is at stake.

The First Dionysos

The following selection of passages represents the dominant notion of the Dionysian in the *Collected Works.*[5] (Quotations are from the first edition, by section numbers, unless otherwise indicated.)

CW 12[2], 118: "Dionysus is the abyss of impassioned dissolution. . . ."
CW 15, 212: "Seldom or never have I had a patient who did not go back to neolithic art forms or revel in evocations of Dionysian orgies."
CW 5, 624: "No reason guides him, only the Dionysian *libido effrenata.* . . ."
CW 6, 908: "'Before dinner I am a Kantian, but after dinner a Nietzschean.' In his habitual attitude, that is to say, he is an intellectual, but under the stimulating influence of a good dinner a Dionysian wave breaks through his conscious attitude."
CW 5, 623: "The 'terrible Mother' is the *mater saeva cupidinum,* unbridled and unbroken Nature, represented by the most paradoxical god of the Greek Pantheon, Dionysus. . . ."
CW 7[2], 17: ". . . Dionysian orgies that surged over from the East. . . ."
". . . Dionysian licentiousness. . . ."
CW 7[2], 40: "He delivers himself up unresistingly to the animal psyche.

That is the moment of the Dionysian frenzy, the overwhelming manifestation of the 'blond beast'. . . ."
CW 13, 91: ". . . an outburst of bestial greed and the tearing of living
animals with the teeth were part of the Dionysian orgy." (cf. CW 11,
353.)

In Jung's alchemical writings, Dionysos is associated with the ape, and
the Black Mass (CW 12², 191), an atavistic identification with animal
ancestors (171), and the Lord of Darkness (devil) (119, 181). (Cf.
ETH Lectures, "Alchemy," Vol. 1, Jan. 17, 1941, p. 78 and June 6,
1941, p. 181, Edition 1960, privately printed, C. G. Jung Institute,
Zürich.) The association of Dionysos with the devil continues in both
Jung's alchemical study of transference and in his late opus, *Mysterium
Coniunctionis* (the former found in CW 16², 388: "The Church has the
doctrine of the devil, of an evil principle, whom we like to imagine
complete with cloven hoofs, horns, and tail, half man, half beast, a
chthonic deity apparently escaped from the rout of Dionysus, the sole
surviving champion of the sinful joys of paganism" and the latter in
CW 14, 420).

Another group of passages, fewer in number and lesser in power,
gives us another connotation, a second Dionysos. But these passages
we shall put off until later, because there is still more to say about the
first Dionysos in Jung's writings.

Despite the many references to Dionysos and the long "Zarathustra Seminar," Dionysos was never central to Jung's focus. Dionysos
had been given ample attention by Jung's earlier contemporaries in
both classical psychiatry and the history of religions, so that perhaps
this avenue of mythology and pathology was less open to original
exploration. Rohde and Nietzsche had forced Dionysos upon the
consciousness of Classical scholarship. Freud and Janet had done the
same for hysteria, which had already in the nineteenth century been
associated with Dionysos.[6] Then there was the literary-philosophical
psychologizing of Stefan George and Ludwig Klages, which Jung
would not go near and in which he saw a poetic cult of the irrational
in the name of Dionysos (CW 10, 375).

Thus, as Jung's attention was only peripherally engaged with hysteria (CW, 1, 3, 4, 6, 7, *passim*), likewise was he only occasionally
occupied with Dionysos. Schizophrenia and Hermes-Mercurius, however, received his full interest from the start and into his late work.
He wrote separate studies on both schizophrenia and on Hermes-

Mercurius (and Trickster), making extraordinary psychological contributions to both psychopathology and mythology. His basic insights into the nature of the psyche owe more to his work on schizophrenia than to hysteria and more to his investigation of the archetypal complexities of Hermes-Mercurius-Trickster than to those of Dionysos.

Although Dionysos was not in the foreground, Nietzsche was. There is probably a direct and causal relation between the presence of Nietzsche in Jung's consciousness and the absence of Dionysos, as if the more deeply Jung entered into Nietzsche, the more he was dissuaded from the Dionysian.

Jung says in his autobiography[7] that in his youth (around 1890), "I was unconsciously caught up by this spirit of the age, and had no methods at hand for extricating myself from it." This spirit he describes: "The archetypes of Wagner were already knocking at the gates, and along with them came the Dionysian experience of Nietzsche—which might better be ascribed to the god of ecstasy, Wotan" (*MDR*, 222). Jung displays already in his doctoral thesis his familiarity with Nietzsche's work (*CW* 1, 140–42). Jung was interested enough in Nietzsche to turn directly to the philosopher's family for checking some data (*CW* 1, 141). But it is Nietzsche as case—a subject of the long "Zarathustra Seminar" of the thirties—that seems, already in 1901–02, uppermost in Jung's mind. Jung writes that Nietzsche's "poetic ecstasy at more than one point verges on the pathological" (*CW* 1, 142).

Perhaps the history of psychiatry and of ideas will one day examine more closely the effects of the case of Nietzsche upon the spirit of the nineties and the turn of the century. It must certainly have been vividly felt in Basel, city of both Nietzsche and Jung, and especially in psychiatric circles, owing to the questions about Nietzsche's diagnosis and to the pathography on Nietzsche written by Moebius (who linked the God Dionysos with the concept of hysteria).

At least we do know that upon Jung the case of Nietzsche had a profound effect. During Jung's student years he harbored "a secret fear that I might be like him [Nietzsche], at least in regard to the 'secret' which had isolated him from his environment" (*MDR*, 105). And Jung imagined his "personality Number 2" to correspond with Zarathustra (*MDR*, 106). We must remember that at the core of Nietzsche's catastrophe was his identification with Dionysos-Zagreus. Evidently, the fate of Nietzsche was a *Vorbild* of possession by an archetypal power, neither the idea of which nor a means of extrication from which were then available to Jung. This power was called Dionysos, even if it should have been called Wotan. "In Nietzsche's biography you will find irrefutable proof that the god he originally meant was really Wotan, but being a philologist and living in the seventies and eighties of the nineteenth century, he called him Dionysus" (*CW* 11, 44).

Not only in Nietzsche's biography will we find this proof. *The Birth of Tragedy*[8] opens with a dedicatory foreword to Wagner in which Nietzsche relates his essay to the "German problem" and "German hopes." At the end (section 24), he warms again to his German theme:

> . . . in some inaccessible abyss the German spirit still rests and dreams, undestroyed, in glorious health, profundity, and Dionysian strength, like a knight sunk in slumber: from which abyss the Dionysian song rises to our ears to let us know that this German knight even now is dreaming his primitive Dionysian myth. . . .

The paragraph ends with Brunnhilde and Wotan's spear. This is not Greek, not antiquity, but the return of Wotan in modern Germany. The restitution of the Dionysian in modern Western consciousness was from the very beginning entangled in Wotan.[8a]

In 1911 Thomas Mann recapitulated the disastrous mess of this archetypal contamination by means of a dream which turns the fate of Gustave Aschenbach in the novella *Death in Venice*.[9] There we see Dionysos, Pan and the Maenads in a Germanic inscape informed by a Wotanic spirit. The facet of Dionysos that is revealed is altogether an "enemy to dignity and self-control." But is this 'stranger God' not more likely Wotan than the one depicted in antique vase-paintings, where he appears so dignified and self-possessed? Or, even if there is a Dionysos as obscene and exuberant as Aschenbach's dream, that obscenity meant a death of another sort than the one in Venice. For Heraclitus[10] pointed out in regard to the obscene Lenean rites of the Dionysian cult that they must be understood in the light of the unity of Hades and Dionysos. They may not be taken on the literal level of concrete enactment, but have an invisible meaning for the soul in terms of its death. Thus, though the images presented to Aschenbach seem authentically Dionysian, the structure of his consciousness in which they perform provides a stage for literalism that is Wagnerian, Nietzschean, Wotanic, and where Hades becomes literal death, rather than the invisible realm of souls. The case of Nietzsche repeats in Mann's Aschenbach where "Dionysos" means enantiodromia, disease and death.

Unlike Nietzsche, Jung saw through to the Wotan shadow of what Nietzsche called Dionysos (e.g., *CW* 5, 623; *CW* 10, 375, 391; *CW* 9:i, 442 & n). Yet, Jung insists that the "two gods have much in common." He speaks of them as "cousins" (*CW* 11, 44; cf. *CW* 10, 386). He brings them into juxtapositions which are mythographically strained, as, for instance, Jung's amplification of the horse and horse's hoof motifs (*CW* 5, 421) appropriate to Wotan, but where Dionysos is suddenly introduced by means of the *bull's* foot. Another peculiar—and Nietzschean—instance is the apposition of "Dionysian frenzy" and "blond beast" (*CW* 7^2, 40). It is as if, despite himself, Jung had difficulty extricating his perception of Dionysos from the Wotanic distortion shared by his generation and their transalpine, Germanic view of pagan Mediterranean culture. He observes this himself, saying: "Hence the Christian Weltanschauung, when reflected in the ocean of the (Germanic) unconscious, logically takes on the features of Wotan" (*CW* 9:i, 442). As Kerényi points out: ". . . in that which concerns the image of Dionysos, researchers and scholars have submitted to the influence of German philosophy to a much higher degree than they themselves realize."[11] In other words Jung's first view of Dionysos is distorted not only by the influence of nineteenth-century northern European scholarship, but also by a dominant in the background of that scholarship: Wotan. More specifically, Jung's view is crucially affected by the model of Nietzsche who not only was the first to formulate and thus give his personal stamp to what has become our popular notion of this divinity, but who also chose him as his God. Jung asks and answers what Dionysos signifies by means of Nietzsche. The first Dionysos of whom Jung writes is thus neither a figure of antiquity nor a figure in Jung's own life, but one who is vicariously known to Jung through Nietzsche. The key passage illustrating this is in *Psychology and Alchemy* (*CW* 12, 118):

It needed a Nietzsche to expose in all its feebleness Europe's schoolboy attitude to the ancient world. But what did Dionysus mean to Nietzsche? What he says about it must be taken seriously; what it did to him still more so. There can be no doubt that he knew, in the preliminary stages of his fatal illness, that the dismal fate of Zagreus was reserved for him. Dionysus is the abyss of impassioned dissolution, where all human distinctions are merged in the animal divinity of the primordial psyche—a blissful and terrible experience.

That Nietzsche's experience—eleven years of degenerating madness—should have provided the Vergil for the underworld descent in *Psychology and Alchemy* is of no minor importance for everyone who uses the model of individuation described in that book. Let us return to that text to see exactly where and how the Nietzschean Dionysos enters and how it affects the course of psychic movement.

The passage occurs at the end of Part Two, Chapter II. The initial dreams and visions of the case have led to a climax. An elephant, an ape-man or bear or cave-man with a club, and a man with a pointed beard appear. The text is accompanied by three terrifying pictures of a skeleton, a wild-man and a devil.

These visual images may be referred to "the Dionysian experience" as Jung does in paragraphs 118–119, but strictly they are not images of Dionysos. Mythographically, Dionysos was not a cave God (like Pan), not a bear, nor were the ape or elephant in his train. The vision finds its lysis in a voice saying, "Everything must be ruled by the light." Jung concludes that the *nekyia* is now reversing and that the light refers to that "of the discerning, conscious mind" (120). The chapter ends (121) with the "active intervention of the intellect" and the "symbols of the self." Immediately thereafter, we turn to the study of the mandala while the pictures accompanying the text turn from horrid images of human shapes to abstract contemplative forms.

Of course Jung was following material of a case and not his own visions and dreams—neither was the case one of his. Also, the accompanying pictures were not chosen and placed there by him. Yet the *selection* of the material, the *amplifications,* and the elaboration of the case into the *sequences* of the book are Jung's. How are we to understand this sudden return from the *nekyia* via the light of intellect to the mandala? Does not the pattern presented in this movement indicate a direct relation between the Dionysian and the mandala?

We may remember that in Jung's life the mandala played a similar role. Jung's discovery of it came toward the end of his own *nekyia*[12] when he "began to emerge from the darkness" of that long disturbance (1913–1919) (*MDR,* 186), which Ellenberger calls "a creative illness."[13] He had painted his first mandala in 1916 and began to understand it in 1918.

Something similar to the mandala coincided with this emergence from the darkness: *Psychological Types*. This work was the first major fruit to be published after this dark phase. (*MDR*, 185n; cf. Aniela Jaffé's paper, *Spring 1972*.) We may look at the typological system with its eightfold structure within the psychological context of Jung's life. *Psychological Types* is also a mandala, in conceptual form, performing a similarly ordering—and defensive—function.[14] Autobiographically in Jung's case, and in the sequence presented in *Psychology and Alchemy*, the mandala appears against the background of the "Dionysian experience" (i.e., Nietzschean Wotanic experience) and is a response to it.

The upshot of all this can be put in a series of conclusions. First, the experience—as Jung himself observes in several places that we cited—should not be named "Dionysian," but "Wotanic." Second, as Dionysos and Wotan differ, so must our psychological measures for connecting with them differ. A defensive order against Wotan may be appropriate; against Dionysos, it may be altogether inappropriate, as the tales of Lycurgus and Pentheus show. Third, although the mandala and typology may serve as useful defenses against Wotan and Nietzschean disintegration, these very same abstractions may block an appreciation of the "Dionysian experience." For psychotherapy to misperceive Dionysos would be worse than folly. After all, this God plays a central role in tragedy, in the transformational mysteries of Eleusis, in the instinctual and communal levels of the soul, and in the development of the kind of culture related to wine.[15] Moreover, there is the profound importance of Dionysos for the feminine psyche. Fourth, if this God is the archetypal dominant expressing life itself (*zoē*) as some commentators have said, then to misread his manifestations could seriously mislead the very processes of healing. Yet, until the ghost of Nietzsche be laid to rest, every Dionysian event in therapy will tend to be seen as a herald of Wotanic eruption. We will tend to protect ourselves and analysands in the manner of the movement to the self that is depicted in *Psychology and Alchemy*, which model, on closer look, may turn out to be a centering in flight from Dionysos.

The Second Dionysos

Nilsson and Guthrie[16] have said that Greek myths are described according to the personal bias of the writer and according to the spiritual horizons of a period. Dionysos, a most paradoxical figure, offers commentators upon him a variety of perspectives and attributes.

Which of these we choose to make our starting-point for understanding the "Dionysian experience" reveals, according to Guthrie, the writer's essential concern as much as it reveals the God's essence.

For instance: Nietzsche stresses the ecstatic, excessive, barbarian, titanic, even criminal aspects. Harrison, who considers herself in this regard a disciple of Nietzsche (Preface to the second edition of *Themis*), takes the suffering, intoxicated Dionysos first, but identifies him with Bergson's instinctual life force. Kerényi seems to go also along this path, pointing again and again to the wine, the vegetative life and zoē. Nilsson lays stress upon the child. Rohde emphasizes the connection with Hades, the mysteries and the cult of souls. Otto places the madness foremost but takes it as the expression of an inner antithesis: Dionysos, the God who holds life and death together. Grant considers him the "irresistible irrational" and integrates the tales and cult of him around this perspective. Dodds and Guthrie place freedom and joy in the foreground, forgetting oneself, one's station, one's differences. Jeanmaire combines joy with festivals, wine and an agrarian cult of the people by means of an archaic tree or vegetation cult. One could also start with the God's non-heroic bisexuality, or with his *thiasos,* i.e., he does not appear alone, but is a God with a community.

Jung stresses dismemberment, and draws attention to the dismembered Dionysos in the following additional passages so far not mentioned here: *CW* 7^2, 113; *CW* 8, 162; *CW* 11, 53 & n, 387, 400; *CW* 14, 365, p259n. In these passages Dionysos emerges less contaminated with Wotan, though Nietzsche still hovers in the background as exemplary of dismemberment; for it was with the dismembered Zagreus-Dionysos that Nietzsche was identified, signing himself "Zagreus" in his later letters (*CW* 11, 142). In *CW* 7^2, 113, Jung writes of the "divine punishment of being torn asunder like Zagreus" still with Nietzsche in view: "This was what Nietzsche experienced at the onset of his malady. Enantiodromia means being torn asunder into pairs of opposites. . . ."

But then dismemberment loses the background of Nietzsche and even of the rending by the opposites, and begins to take on a wider archetypal significance. Jung writes: "The classical world thought of this pneuma as Dionysus, particularly the suffering Dionysus Zagreus, whose divine substance is distributed throughout the whole of nature" (*CW* 11, 378). ". . . so his worshippers tore wild animals to pieces in order to reintegrate his dismembered spirit" (400). In *Aion* (*CW* 9:ii, 158n), dismemberment is again placed against the background of the

Neoplatonic Dionysos: "The divine powers imprisoned in bodies are nothing other than *Dionysus dispersed in matter.*" Thus, dismemberment becomes a way of discovering the puer spirit, for "Dionysus, youngest of the gods" belongs to the theme of the "renewal of the ageing god" (*CW* 14, 379).

The movement between the first and second view of dismemberment compares with crossing a psychic border between seeing the God from outside and seeing him from within his cosmos. In this respect Dodds speaks of black and white Maenadism, and Kerényi writes: "The God sends his madness, the dark counter-image of the Dionysian, not to his devotees who give themselves to his miracle, but to his enemies who defend themselves against him."[17] Although misperceptions of the God through Wotan may well produce the darker side, there is no surety that upon entering his cosmos all shall be well. As Dionysos supposedly comes into civilized Greece from "borderlands" (Thrace, Asia-Minor, Crete, Egypt), so as Kerényi says: ". . . where Dionysus appears, there appears also the border . . ." (ibid.). The Dionysian experience thus refers to a borderline state in which the black and white aspects of dismemberment meet.

If we leave the "malady" of Nietzsche as our model for dismemberment, we may also leave the view of it as only rending by opposites and violent enantiodromia. Instead we may understand the violence in a new light. If we take our clues from Jung's exploration of the theme in alchemy ("The Visions of Zosimos," passim, *CW* 13), dismemberment refers to a psychological process that requires a *body metaphor* (*CW* 12², 530; *CW* 13, 89; *CW* 14, 64). The process of division is presented as a body experience, even as a horrifying torture. If, however, dismemberment is ruled by the archetypal dominant of Dionysos, then the process, while beheading or dissolving the central control of the old king, may be at the same time activating the pneuma that is distributed throughout the materializations of our complexes. The background of the second Dionysos offers new insight into the rending pain of self-division, especially as a body experience.

Jung reminds us that Dionysos was called the divided one (*CW* 14, p. 259n.) His dismemberment was evidence of his divisibility into parts. In each part he lived as the pneuma dispersed in matter. Bits of the Dionysian spirit are like sparks shining in the *terra foetida* (*CW* 14, 64), or rotten stench of the decaying body as it dissociates into pieces. We experience this process in psychosomatic symptoms, in hysterical conversions, in specific sado-masochistic perversions, in cancer fantasies, in fears of aging, in horror of pollution, or in disintegrative incoherent conditions that have a body focus. This experience has its other side. The dismemberment of central control is at the same time the resurrection of the natural light of archetypal consciousness distributed in each of the organs.

Jung describes this organ consciousness in a footnote on Joyce's "visceral thinking" in *Ulysses* (*CW* 15, 112 & n.): ". . . an *abaissement du niveau mental* constellates what Wernicke calls the 'organ-representatives,' i.e., symbols representing the organs." The context for this remark is the *leitmotif* of body parts—kidneys, genitals, heart, lungs, esophagus, etc.—in each of the chapters of *Ulysses*. That each organ has a "psychic representative" is also mentioned in *CW* 12², 440.

From this perspective of dismemberment, our renderings can be understood as the particular kind of renewal presented by Dionysos. This renewal describes itself by means of a body metaphor. The renewal that goes by way of dismemberment is not a re-assembly of parts into another organization. It is not a movement from integration to disintegration to re-integration. Perhaps, it is better to envision this renewal not as a process at all. Rather, the crucial experience would be the awareness of the parts as parts distinct from each other, dismembered, each with its own light, a state in which the body becomes conscious of itself as a composite of differences. The scintillae and fishes' eyes of which Jung speaks in regard to the multiple consciousness of the psyche (*CW* 14, 42ff., esp. 64; *CW* 8, 388ff.) may be experienced as embedded in physical expressions. The distribution of Dionysos through matter may be compared with the distribution of consciousness through members, organs and zones.

Freud, who began his construction of psychology on the base of hysteria, used this kind of Dionysian metaphor. The *zoë* that is Dionysos, the child and the bisexuality that is Dionysos repeat metaphorically in erogenous zones and the polymorphous perverse child described by Freud. Adler, too, went in this direction when deriving character from organ inferiority. The structure of each individual's consciousness was intimately linked with the psychic representatives of particular organs. Ultimately, renewal (cure) for both Freud and Adler requires the redemption of pneuma from its libidinal cathexes in organ representatives. The fantasies of Freud and Adler find an archetypal background in the second Dionysos of Jung. Conceptual fantasies such as "visceral thinking," "erogenous zones" and "organ inferiority" refer on another level to the psychoid Dionysos. Here, we made a distinction between *zoē*, or life-force of the body, and the pneuma of that life-force. By attributing a 'God' to *zoē*, the life-force is given psychic interiority and a specific kind of consciousness which might partly be characterized as an awareness of self-divisibility into many parts.

Finally, if we draw the implications fully, dismemberment becomes necessary for awakening the consciousness of the body. The second Dionysos in Jung's work gives another meaning than Wotanic eruption and disintegration to that first "Dionysian experience," the Nietzschean. It means an initiation into the archetypal consciousness of the body. Through Dionysos the body may be re-appreciated as a metaphorical field and not only in behavioral interaction with the world of other bodies. Dismemberment severs the only-natural connections, the habitual ways we have 'grown up' and 'grown together.' It disconnects the body's habits at the animal-vegetable level, releasing a subtler appreciation of the members and organs as *psychic representations*. Religions speak of the resurrection of the flesh and the construction of the subtle body.

This movement seems possible only when the dominant organization lets go its hold. Then the *abaissement du niveau mental* results in the activation of the psychic life of the organs. Or, perhaps these events occur in reverse order: Dionysos constellates through the dissolution into parts, thereby bringing about what we subsequently call a lowering of the mental level. The aging God we call 'ego' loses his support in the body's organization as it dissociates. The Dionysian experience would then be essential for understanding what Jung meant with the fundamental dissociability of the psyche and its multiple consciousness. It also becomes clearer how this experience and that of the mandala could tend to exclude each other, since the latter would integrate what the former would loosen.

Dionysos was called *Lysios*, the loosener.[18] The word is cognate with *lysis*, the last syllables of *analysis*. *Lysis* means loosening, setting free, deliverance, dissolution, collapse, breaking bonds and laws, and the final unraveling as of a plot in tragedy.

*

Returning now to *Psychology and Alchemy* (*CW* 12², 117f), we may conclude that the voice's declaration, "Everything must be ruled by the light" may be understood in two ways. (Therapeutic considerations would not play a part in determining between the two ways, since Jung presents the material there not as a case but as empirical evidence for the centering process [CW 12², 45].) On the one hand, the light may mean changing consciousness through opposites, where the active intervention of the intellect, the symbols of the self and the mandala become the counterpoise to the Wotanic experience. As Jung's intention is to present precisely this kind of centering imagery, the light is understood in this way.

On the other hand, the light may mean the light of nature, and changing consciousness through sames where like works upon like. Then, fragmentation would be imagined not from within the viewpoint of centering, but from within Dionysian consciousness itself working within dissolution. The dispersed pneuma of the second Dionysos that emerges through dissolution would be the light called for by the voice, implying the lysis of the Dionysian experience.

Personally, I believe that if we miss the possibilities for light in experiences of dissolution, we then tend to emphasize, as a defensive compensation, centering and wholeness. So, it has seemed to me useful to work out this Dionysian background to the important idea of wholeness in Jungian thought.

1   "First Adam, Then Eve: Fantasies of Female Inferiority in Changing Consciousness," *Eranos Jahrbuch* XXXVIII/1969, Zürich, and in a revised, expanded version as Part III of *The Myth of Analysis*, Evanston: Northwestern Univ. Press, 1972; N.Y.: Harper Colophon Books, 1978.

2   Moebius, the psychiatrist, used for his diagnostic view of Dionysos Rohde's work in mythology, while Rohde's discussion of the wilder Dionysian cult, in turn, refers to the psychiatric work of J.F.K. Hecker on dancing hysteria and to Janet on hysterical dissociation. The books to be consulted are: P. J. Moebius, *Über das Pathologische bei Nietzsche*, Wiesbaden, 1902; E. Rohde, *Psyche*, London: Routledge, 1925⁸, pp. 305n9 and 595f; J.F.K. Hecker, *Die Tanzwuth* (Engl. transl. by B. G. Babbington, *The Epidemics of the Middle Ages*, 1846 and 1888). The material is in my *The Myth of Analysis*.

3   F. M. Cornford, *From Religion to Philosophy*, N.Y.: Harper Torchbook, 1957, p. 111n.

4   "Psychological Analysis of Nietzsche's Zarathustra," Notes on the Seminar given by Prof. Dr. C.G. Jung, edited by Mary Foote, in ten volumes (1934–1939) with Index volume (1942), privately mimeographed and distributed.

5   *The Collected Works of C.G. Jung* (Bollingen Series XX), translated by R.F.C. Hull and edited by H. Read, M. Fordham, G. Adler and Wm. McGuire, Princeton University Press, Princeton, and Routledge and Kegan Paul, London.

6   See *The Myth of Analysis*, section "Hysteria." Rabelais had already in the Renaissance compared the hysterics with Maenads. Moebius, op. cit. sup., p. 50, wrote: ". . . Dionysus is really the God of Hysteria. . . . This is already shown by the fact that (in his cult) women are in the foreground, altogether contrary to the usual Greek custom. Thus Nietzsche without noticing it chose the Patron of Hysteria for his Saint."

FACING THE GODS

7   C.G. Jung, *Memories, Dreams, Reflections,* recorded and edited by Aniela Jaffé, London: Collins and Routledge, 1963. Referred to in my text as *MDR* with page numbers.
8   "The Birth of Tragedy," transl. by C. P. Fadiman in *The Philosophy of Nietzsche,* N.Y.: Modern Library, n.d.
8a My view of Wotan here follows that of Jung which in turn follows that of Nietzsche and Wagner. But this is not the whole Wotan by any means; see M. Burri, "Repression, Falsification, and Bedeviling of Germanic Mythology," *Spring 1978,* pp. 88–104.
9   Th. Mann, "Death in Venice," in *Stories of Three Decades* (transl. by H. T. Lowe-Porter), N.Y.: Knopf, 1936.
10 Heraclitus, Fr. 15 (Diels arrangement): "If it were not in honour of Dionysus that they conducted the procession and sang the phallic hymn, their activity would be completely shameless. But Hades is the same as Dionysus, in whose honour they rave and perform the Bacchic revels." K. Freeman, *Ancilla to the Pre-Socratic Philosophers,* Oxford, 1948.
11 C. Kerényi, "Dionysus le Cretois," *Diogenes* 20, Paris, 1957, p. 4, translation mine.
12 Jung read the *nekyia* episode of the *Odyssey* during a sailing trip with friends on the Lake of Zürich. This is left out of the English version of *MDR,* but see the account in H. F. Ellenberger, *The Discovery of the Unconscious,* N.Y.: Basic Books, 1970, p. 670, and also the German original of *MDR,* pp. 103–04.
13 Ellenberger, idem., p. 672.
14 J.W.T. Redfearn says: "The need for the defensive aspect of mandalas [is] to be recognised and interpreted." ("Mandala Symbols and the Individuation Process," unpublished paper presented at the IVth International Congress for Analytical Psychology, London, 1971.) He, too, notes in connection with the mandala that Jung's theory of the four functions "developed at a time when chaotic psychotic forces were threatening him." Jung points to the protective function of mandalas in *CW* 9:i, 16, 710, and pp. 387–88.
15 On the cultural significance of wine, see Plato, *Laws* 672a–d where "the gift of Dionysus," even including "Bacchic possession and all its frenzied dancing," is made a source of music: ". . . the gift was meant . . . as a medicine, to produce modesty of soul, and health and strength of the body." This "gift of Dionysus" belongs with aging, for it shall be prohibited to "boys under eighteen," allowed moderately to "men under thirty." "But when a man is verging on the forties, we shall tell him, after he has finished banqueting at the general table, to invoke the gods, and more particularly to ask the presence of Dionysus in that sacrament and pastime of advancing years—I mean the wine cup . . ." (666a–b). Plato's most impressive dialogue—with a vision of love that has been the main cultural influence (excepting the Gospels) upon the eros of our Western psyche—is a drinking-party. The God ruling that dialogue, who is hinted at in the last episodes and through Silenos, is Dionysos. On the cultural significance of wine education and wine in education, see P. Friedländer, *Plato,* Vol. III, Princeton Univ. Press, 1969, pp. 397–403. Sparta was abstinent (*Laws,* 637a–b), and where there is no wine does this not mean a misperception of Dionysos and his entire significance, if not a ban against him? If so, Moebius was abstinent for most of his adult life, and so was Bleuler—and Jung too for a time at Bleuler's Burghölzli. (On Jung's enjoyment of drink in Basel, see A. Oeri, "Some Youthful Memories of C.G. Jung," *Spring 1970*).
16 Cf. *The Myth of Analysis,* section "Dionysus and Bi-sexual Consciousness," for references and quotations from Nilsson, Guthrie and other authors mentioned in this paragraph.
17 K. Kerényi, *Griechische Miniaturen,* Zürich, 1957, p. 133 (translation mine); for Dodds's references and a longer discussion of black and white Maenadism and the 'border' question, see *The Myth of Analysis,* "Dionysus Re-Imagined."
18 See W. H. Roscher, *Ausführliches Lexikon der griechischen und römischen Mythologie* (photomechanischer Nachdruck), Hildesheim: Olms, 1965, Vol. II, 2212, "Lysios."

164

ACKNOWLEDGMENTS

"On the Necessity of Abnormal Psychology—Ananke and Athene" was first delivered as a lecture at the Eranos Conference of 1974, Ascona, Switzerland, and revised for publication in the *Eranos Jahrbuch–43, Norms in a Changing World* (Leiden: Brill, 1977). The paper has been again expanded and revised for publication in the present volume. "Hermes' Heteronymous Appellations" was originally published in *Archai: Notes and Papers on Archaic Studies,* #2, Franconia, N.H., 1978. The present paper includes over sixty additions to the epithets of Hermes. "A Mythological Image of Girlhood: Artemis" in this English translation by Hildegard Nagel was first published in *Spring 1969.* This version has been slightly emended by Magda Kerényi. "The Amazon Problem" appeared in *Spring 1971* and bore the dedication "In Memoriam Franz Riklin." The translation is by Murray Stein. "Hephaistos: A Pattern of Introversion" was first printed in *Spring 1973.* It has been slightly emended for the present volume. The Postscript was written especially for *Facing the Gods.* "Red Riding Hood and Grand Mother Rhea: Some Images in a Psychology of Inflation" is the first publication of this article. "Hestia: A Background of Psychological Focusing" is being published here for the first time. "Ariadne, Mistress of the Labyrinth" has never before appeared in print. "Dionysos in Jung's Writings" was published originally in *Spring 1972.*

J.H.

INDEX

A

Achilles, 47, 48, 72, 73, 74
Adler, A., 87, 161
Adonis, 116
Adrasteia, 7
Aeschylus, 7, 8, 47, 52, 141
Agamemnon, 52
Aglaia, 73
Akmon, 60
Alcestis, 7–11, 19
alchemy, 2, 89, 95, 101, 116, 153, 160
altar, 9, 19, 24, 94
amazons, 47, 49–51, 53–55, 57–62, 64
Ananke, 1, 5–11, 13–19, 22, 26–27, 29
Anat, 51
Androgeos, 144
androgynous, androgyny, 50, 56, 59–60,
    140, 144, 145
Anesidor, 71
anima, 52–53, 55–60, 63, 78, 95, 140, 142,
    146–148
animus, 51, 55, 63, 70, 74–76
Answer to Job, 61
ants, 25–26, 117
anxiety, 6, 15, 88
ape(s), 71, 153, 157
Aphrodite, 29, 51, 57–58, 64, 69, 75, 79,
    94, 104, 107, 118, 141
    Areia, 51
    Harmonia, 54
Apollo, apollonian, apollonic, 8, 18–19,
    31, 43, 49, 103, 107, 115, 130, 142,
    151
Apollodoros, 54, 58, 92, 117, 131
Apollonius of Rhodes, 92
Ares, 29, 48–52, 54, 58, 60–61, 75–77, 79
    rampart of Olympus, 52
Ariadne, 58, 137–40, 142–43, 145–48
Aristophanes, 115
Aristotle, aristotelian, 11–12, 16, 24–25,
    27, 71
arm(s), 2, 32, 48, 67, 76–77
arrow(s), 42, 44, 50, 107, 119
art of memory, 2, 3, 28
Artemis, 27, 39–44, 48–50, 56–57, 59, 63–
    64, 94, 107, 141–142, 146
Asclepius, 7, 8, 47, 52, 141
Astarte, 51
Atalanta, 42, 49

Athene, 1, 18–20, 26–28, 31, 39–40, 44,
    52–53, 68, 75–76, 79–80, 94, 107,
    141–142
    Hygieia, 27
    Pallas, 39, 41, 52
    Polias, 26
Athnetos, 4
Atropos, 15

B

Bacchae, 8, 93
Bacchus, 49
Bachelard, G., 104–106
battle, battler, battling, 31, 47, 52, 54, 76–
    78, 141
bear, 42–44, 157
Bergson, 159
Bia, 7–8, 18, 21
Bible, 96
Birth of Tragedy, 151
blood, 10, 18
Boccaccio, 72
bond(s), 57, 85, 162
bow, 42, 44, 48, 50
breast, breasted, 7, 26, 55, 67
bride, 41, 143–144
Briseis, 52
Britomartis, 49
Brunnhilde, 155
Bruno, G., 28

C

Callimachus, 39–42, 44
Camilla, 49
cave, 19, 72, 94, 157
chain, 7, 76, 78
Chalybs, 60
Chaos, 14–16, 106–107
Charybdis, 88
Charis, 73
chastity, 58–59, 104
child, 2, 18, 23, 29, 39, 40–41, 44, 77, 80,
    93, 105, 146–148, 159, 161
Christ, 10, 25, 57
Chronos, 6
chthonic, Chthonios, 80, 92, 153
Cicero, 105
circle, 6, 74, 84, 101

Plutus, 115
pomegranate, 93
Poseidon, 29, 93, 96, 103
possession, 85–86
potnia, 9
Priapus, 118
Prometheus, promethean, 7, 18, 70, 93
Prometheus Bound, 8, 10–11
Psyche, 2, 117
psychopomp, 138
puer, 29, 105, 12
puer aeternus, 2, 31, 57–58, 64
pyromania, 78
Pythagorean, 6

Q

queen, (Amazon), 47, 54, 60–61

R

Rank, O., 91–92
Reich, W., 17
renaissance, 25, 47, 71
Rhea, 69, 92–93, 96–97, 103–104
rhetoric, 18, 20–21
Rivera, D., 67
Rohde, 151, 153, 159

S

sacrifice, 19, 48, 54, 59, 103
Sartre, J.-P., 137
Saturn, saturnian, 2, 29, 31, 93
Scylla, 88
self, 1, 12, 56–57, 59, 84, 88, 94–96, 101–102, 148, 158, 163
Semele, 143–144, 147
senex, 2
sexual intercourse, 48–49
shadow, shadowy, 4, 64, 74, 156
shield, 30, 32, 48–49, 72–74
sin(s), sinned, (original), 5, 15, 18–19
Sirens, 26
smiles, 4, 39, 56
smith, 41, 60, 69, 73, 76
snake, 8, 80, 92
Sophocles, 8, 21, 141
spear, 48, 56, 82
spirit, 1, 11, 20, 50, 53, 70–71, 78, 80, 116, 154–155, 159–160
   martial, 54
   patriarchal, 55, 63

Strabo, 48
Strauss, 139
suffer, suffering, 1, 2, 8, 17, 20, 26, 52, 71, 77–78, 85, 88–89, 93, 159
sun, 68, 73, 92
sword, 47, 52, 131
Symposium, 24–25

T

Tasso, T., 47
Telemachos, 119
temple, 21, 30, 49, 103–104
Thanatos, 4, 138
Theia, 92
Themis, 92
Theseus, 48, 54, 57–58, 80, 137–46
Thetis, 73, 92
Thoas, 145
Thomas Aquinas, 11
thread, 138, 145, 147
throne, 16, 77, 80
tie, 6–7, 10, 54, 59, 78–79
Timaeus, 13–14, 16–17, 25
time, 5–7
Titan(s), titanic, 70, 92, 94
Tocqueville, A., 105
Trojan War, 77
Typhon, 75, 78

U

Ulysses, 21, 25, 161
Underworld, 3, 9, 31, 41, 43, 67, 70, 92–93, 96–97, 111, 144, 157

V

vase, 47, 60, 139, 155
Vesta, vestal virgins, 103–104, 107
Vivo, G., 24–25
Virgil, 49, 157
virgin, virginal, virginity, 27, 41, 56, 58, 104, 107, 144
virtue, 30, 58, 85, 103
vision, 23, 26, 32, 83, 93, 111, 146, 157
voice, 31, 162–163
Vulcan, 71, 78 (see *supra, s.v.* Hephaistos)

W

Wagner, R., 154–155
walls, 52, 106, 130